Dimensions of Advertising Theory and Practice in Africa

DIMENSIONS OF ADVERTISING THEORY AND PRACTICE IN AFRICA

Edited by
Rotimi Williams Olatunji
& Beatrice A. Laninhun

Published by Amalion Publishing 2013

Amalion Publishing
BP 5637 Dakar-Fann
Dakar CP 00004
Senegal
http://www.amalion.net

Copyright © Rotimi Williams Olatunji and Beatrice A. Laninhun 2013

ISBN 978-2-35926-018-2 (paperback)
ISBN 978-2-35926-019-9 (ebook)

Cover designed by Will McCarty

Cover photograph by Baye Arona Ndiaye. Copyright © Amalion Publishing.

Printed in the United Kingdom by CPI Group (UK) Ltd., Croydon, CR0 4YY

All rights reserved. No part of this publication may be reproduced, transmitted, or stored in a retrieval system, in any form or by any means, without permission in writing from Amalion Publishing, nor be otherwise circulated in any form of binding, media or cover than that in which it is published.

CONTENTS

Tables viii
Figures... viii
Boxes ix
Contributors x
Introduction: An Overview of Advertising in Africa.................... xv
    Beatrice A. Laninhun & Rotimi Williams Olatunji

I: THEORETICAL AND ETHICAL ISSUES

Chapter 1
Indigenous Forms of Advertising Media in Africa: What Relevance in an Age of Globalisation? 2
    Rotimi Williams Olatunji & Assay Benjamin Enahoro

Chapter 2
Theoretical Approaches to Understanding Representation and the Language of Advertising 13
    Sydney Friendly Kankuzi

Chapter 3
Linguistic Approaches to Meaning-Making in Advertising............. 30
    Julius Abioye Adeyemo

Chapter 4
Advertising, Semiotics and Strategic Brand Management 36
    Nnamdi Tobechukwu Ekeanyanwu & Nelson Okorie

Chapter 5
Deception in Advertising: Ethical and Legal Imperatives 51
    Olayinka Egbokhare

Chapter 6
Social, Ethical and Regulatory Issues in Advertising:
The Case of Nigeria 68
Olujimi Kayode

Chapter 7
Public Relations and Propaganda: Relationships and Relevance 79
Sunday Adekunle Akinjogbin & Noeem Taiwo Thanny

II: THE POLITICS OF ADVERTISING IN AFRICA

Chapter 8
Advertising in a Globalising Culture: The Nigerian Experience 100
Rotimi Williams Olatunji

Chapter 9
Media Liberalisation in Kenya: Who Benefits? 111
Jacinta Mwende Maweu

Chapter 10
Revisiting the Woman Question in Advertising 123
Gilbert Motsaathebe

Chapter 11
Representations of Work in Television Advertising
in South Africa: The Employment Equity Act of 1998 141
Sydney Friendly Kankuzi

Chapter 12
The Rise of Political Advertising on Television in South Africa 159
Sibongile Sindane

Chapter 13
A Discourse-Analytical Investigation into the Nature of Afrikaans
and English Radio Advertisements in South Africa 182
Angelique van Niekerk & Mariska Bertram

III: INTEGRATED MARKETING COMMUNICATION

Chapter 14
Covert Advertising in Home Videos: Implications
for Brand Management 204
Olalekan Ganiyu Akashoro & Shaibu Husseini

Chapter 15
Cultural Paradoxes of Global Advertising in Satellite TV
Broadcasting 215
Chinenye Nwabueze

Chapter 16
Internet Usage and the Imperative of Online Advertising
in Africa 229
Oluseyi Soremekun

Index... 247

TABLES

Table 2.1: Moves and Strategies Used in a U-Fresh Laundry Soap Advertisement 16
Table 3.1: Lexical Items in Common Use in Four Semantic Fields .. 34
Table 5.1: Respondents' Views on Whether TVCs Brainwash Consumers 64
Table 8.1: Global Advertising Agencies 102
Table 10.1: Categories and Characteristics of Analysis 132
Table 10.2: Analysis of Magazine Advertisements 133
Table 16.1: World Internet Usage and Population Statistics 235
Table 16.2: Internet Usage Statistics for Africa 236
Table 16.3: The Top Fifteen African Countries in Internet Usage 239
Table 16.4: The Top Ten African Countries in Internet User Growth 240

FIGURES

Figure 4.1: Aspects of the Sign 43
Figure 16.1: The New Media Concept and the Society 233
Figure 16.2: Selected Online Advertisements 243

BOXES

Box 13.1: Pendoring Advertisement for a Radio Station
in Afrikaans 196
Box 13.2: Loose Translation of Pendoring Advertisement
in English.. 197
Box 13.3: Loerie Advertisement for a Soft Drink,
Lemon Twist 199

CONTRIBUTORS

Julius Abioye Adeyemo is a lecturer in the Department of Public Relations and Advertising at the Adebola Adegunwa School of Communication, Lagos State University, Nigeria. He is also a doctoral student in the University of Ibadan, Nigeria.

Ganiyu Olalekan Akashoro is a lecturer in the Department of Public Relations and Advertising at the Adebola Adegunwa School of Communication, Lagos State University, Nigeria. He has authored and co-authored several journal articles and has contributed to chapters in books in different spheres of communication. His areas of specialisation are marketing communication, communication theory and media audience studies. He is currently a doctoral candidate in the Department of Mass Communication, University of Lagos, Nigeria.

Sunday Adekunle Akinjogbin teaches in the Department of Public Relations and Advertising, School of Communication, Lagos State University and a doctoral candidate at the University of Lagos, Nigeria.

Mariska Bertram is at the University of the Free State (UFS) in Bloemfontein, South Africa.

Olayinka Egbokhare lectures in the Department of Communication and Language Arts at the University of Ibadan, Nigeria. Her PhD thesis examined the socio-cultural influences of television commercials on consumers in southwestern Nigeria. Her current research interests include media effect, advertising message development, consumer behavior and advertising research.

Nnamdi Tobechukwu Ekeanyanwu is Senior Lecturer, Department of Mass Communication, Covenant University, Ota, Nigeria. He holds a PhD in International Communication and teaches courses in print journalism, public relations and advertising. He was formerly Director, International Office and Linkages of Covenant University. Dr. Ekeanyanwu is a Susi Scholar and a recipient of the US State Department-sponsored Fellowship for Scholars of Journalism and Media in 2011.

Assay Benjamin Enahoro teaches mass communication at Delta State Polytechnic, Ogwashi-Uku, Nigeria. Currently, he is a doctoral student of mass communication at Benue State University, Makurdi, Nigeria. He has published articles in scholarly journals and contributed chapters in several books. His research interests are in information and communication technology, international communication and comparative media studies, media, democracy and good governance, population communication, and public relations and advertising.

Sydney Friendly Kankuzi is a Lecturer in Media, Communication and Cultural Studies and former Head of Language and Communication Department at Chancellor College, University of Malawi. He holds a B.Ed (Teaching of English) from the University of Malawi, a BA Honours in Cultural and Media Studies from the University of Natal, and an MA in Cultural and Media Studies from the University of KwaZulu Natal in South Africa. Currently, he is reading for a Ph.D in Journalism Studies at the School of Media, Film and Journalism at the University of Ulster in Northern Ireland.

Olujimi Kayode is the head of the Department of Journalism at Adebola Adegunwa School of Communication, Lagos State University, Nigeria. He is a former director of the Nigeria Institute of Journalism and had served in various panels on the development of journalism education in Nigeria. His research papers have appeared in several international journals and books, and he is also a doctoral candidate in Department of Mass Communication, University of Lagos, Nigeria.

Shaibu Husseini is a performing artist, journalist, film critic and public relations practitioner and a post-graduate student in the Department of Mass Communication, University of Lagos. He writes for one of Nigeria's flagship newspapers, *The Guardian,* and is an Associate Member of the Nigerian Institute of Public Relations (NIPR).

Beatrice Adeyinka Laninhun (PhD) is Senior Lecturer, and formerly, Acting Head, Department of Communication and Language Arts, University of Ibadan, Nigeria. Her research interests are in the areas of advertising, television broadcasting and development communication. She was also the National Treasurer, African Council for Communication Education, Nigeria Chapter and member, Advertising Practitioners' Council of Nigeria (APCON) as well as the Nigerian Institute of Public Relations (NIPR). She has published extensively in learned journals, locally and internationally.

Jacinta Mwende Maweu is a lecturer in the School of Journalism and Media Studies, University of Nairobi, Kenya. She has two separate masters degrees in Philosophy and Mass Communication respectively. Currently Maweu is a PhD student at Rhodes University in South Africa. Her areas of specialisation are the political economy of the media and philosophy of mass communication.

Gilbert Motsaathebe is a senior lecturer in the Department of Journalism, Faculty of Informatics and Design at Cape Peninsula University of Technology in Cape Town. He is an accredited mentor and assessor in the area of television journalism, with seventeen years of media industry and teaching experience. He has taught at a number of institutions in South Africa and Japan. Prior to his teaching career, Motsaathebe worked as a television news producer and output editor for Bop TV, SABC and ETV in South Africa. He has published in the area of media, gender and development and is the author of *The Ultimate You: How to be the best you can be in 30 days* (2006).

Angelique van Niekerk has a PhD in Linguistics and an MA in Marketing Communication. She lectures in both the Afrikaans and Dutch Department (Linguistics) as well as the Communication Sciences Department (copy-writing) at the University of the Free State in Bloemfontein, South Africa. Her field of expertise is applied linguistics within the field of advertising copy-writing and has published on discourse-analytical approaches to intertextual advertisements, graphology in print advertising, interactive print advertisements vs. interaction in print advertisement and the use of controversy as an approach in South African advertising.

Chinenye Nwabueze (PhD) is a lecturer in the Department of Mass Communication, Faculty of Social Sciences, Anambra State University, Nigeria. He is currently the Deputy National Coordinating Secretary, African Council for Communication Education (ACCE), Nigeria. His areas of interest are media use, journalism and traditional communication.

Nelson Okorie is a lecturer in the Department of Mass Communication, Covenant University, Ota, Nigeria where he obtained his BSc. (Public Relations and Advertising); MSc. (Mass Communication); and PhD (Health Communication). He has published a number of papers in the area of development communication.

Rotimi Williams Olatunji is an Associate Professor in the Department of Public Relations and Advertising, Adebola Adegunwa School of Communication, Lagos State University, Nigeria. He has a PhD in Advertising as Communication from the University of Ibadan, Nigeria. His research interests are in economic and social issues in advertising, advertising and culture, consumerism, political communication, marketing communication and tourism marketing. He has several publications in books, journals, and refereed conference proceedings.

Sibongile Sindane has an MA from Witwatersrand University, Johannesburg in South Africa and is currently a lecturer in the Department of Communication Science at the University of South Africa (UNISA). She is now reading for a PhD. Her research interests are research methodology, political communication, international communication, advertising, marketing, new media and ICT.

Oluseyi Soremekun has an MA in Communication Arts and an MA in Mass Communications. He has taught at the Department of Mass Communication, Moshood Abiola Polytechnic, Abeokuta, and at the Nigerian Institute of Journalism, Lagos, Nigeria. He has extensive professional experience in the advertising industry in Nigeria and is an Associate Registered Practitioner of Advertising and an Associate Member of the Nigerian Institute of Public Relations. He is currently the National Programme Officer, Communication and Information at the UNESCO office in Abuja, Nigeria.

Noeem Taiwo Thanny is at the Department of Public Relations and Advertising, School of Communication, Lagos State University, and a doctoral candidate in the Department of Mass Communication, University of Lagos, Nigeria.

INTRODUCTION: AN OVERVIEW OF ADVERTISING IN AFRICA

BEATRICE A. LANINHUN
& ROTIMI WILLIAMS OLATUNJI

In *Old Africa Rediscovered* (1970), Basil Davidson demonstrates clearly that Africa has not just birthed great ancient civilisations, such as the Egyptian and Great Meroe civilisations and other great empires and kingdoms, but has also kept pace with subsequent developments in other parts of the world, notwithstanding the infamy of centuries of slavery and colonisation. The present era of globalisation, which some scholars refer to as one of Western domination of the globe (Olurode 2003), demonstrates Africa's integration into, if not subjugation by, the advanced societies of the world. The interactions between Africa and the rest of the world have produced mixed blessings, and the advertising industry presents an especially fertile ground in which to explore the consequences of Africa's integration into the global economy. This book x-rays the theory and practice of advertising in Africa gleaned from the purview of the socio-cultural, economic and political dimensions of an institution which remains a formidable catalyst of development and an active promoter of commercial free speech.

Eurocentric scholarly traditions will always point to ancient European civilisations as the source of most innovations in the world. Afrocentrism will always maintain the opposite. The truth is that the different societies of the world have all contributed something to the development of global culture, although not in equal proportions. This is equally true of advertising. In the first chapter, "Indigenous Forms of Advertising Media in Africa: What Relevance in an Age of Globalisation?", Rotimi Williams Olatunji and Assay Benjamin Enahoro address the topic of Africa's contribution to advertising by asking three key questions: Can we say that traditional societies lacking in Westernised forms of media culture actually engage in advertising practices? To what extent is the use of indigenous forms of communication media in Africa relevant to the needs of such societies, both in the past and now? Is there any future for indigenous advertising media in Africa in a fast-paced, globalised environment?

They argue, through an extensive comparative analysis of the different indigenous advertising media in ancient European and African societies, that advertising is not alien to the African continent. They show that the most dominant indigenous advertising media in Africa were oral, as was also the case in ancient European societies, but they also find evidence of other indigenous African advertising media such as papyrus, wall paintings and the use of other arts in African societies prior to the arrival of print media. Olatunji and Enahoro point out that the modern "traditional" media (print, broadcast and outdoor) have overshadowed indigenous forms of media everywhere in the world, including in Africa, just as today's "new" media now seem to be doing with respect to the traditional media. However, they argue for the continued co-existence of the different media of advertising, with differing impacts and significances, and thus foresee the adaptation and integration of indigenous African advertising media within the framework of both the traditional media of advertising and the new media.

In every field of learning, theories are used both to clarify present phenomena and to predict future developments. This insight underpins the important contribution of Sydney Friendly Kankuzi in Chapter 2, "Theoretical Approaches to Understanding Representation and the Language of Advertising". Kankuzi approaches "representation" very broadly as the process through which members of a culture use language to produce meaning and theorises that pictures are a kind of writing in so far as they are meaningful. Thus, advertising is a language, and each advertisement uses specially produced signs to create meanings shared by members of a given culture. Chapter 2 closes with some recommendations on the importance of language and semiotic theory to advertising education and practice. In particular, Kankuzi recommends the integration of three main theoretical approaches, the intentional, reflective and constructionist, maintaining that such integration will empower practitioners with the knowledge and skills to develop culturally more sensitive advertisements.

In Chapter 3, "Linguistic Approaches to Meaning-Making in Advertising", Julius Abioye Adeyemo discusses linguistic strategies for meaning-making in advertising using selected print advertisements as case studies. Two levels of linguistic categories are examined, that of substance and that of situation. Adeyemo argues that advertising's power to shape human opinion is achieved largely by its linguistic strategies, which are carefully and creatively strung together to appeal to the psyche of the public. At the level of substance, advertisers make use of phonographological devices such as alliteration, assonance, puns, interrogation, apostrophe, abbreviation and defiant spellings in their ad payoffs. Adeyemo's analysis provides some clues to the realisation of meaning in ad payoffs, which are used to draw attention, persuade and ultimately secure patronage of goods and services. At the level of situation, Adeyemo examines the lexico-semantic devices such as repetition, acronyms and homographs, which are aimed at getting the attention of prospective buyers.

Chapter 4, "Advertising, Semiotics and Strategic Brand Management", by Nnamdi Tobechukwu Ekeanyanwu and Nelson Okorie, uses the concepts of "signifier" and "signified" to illustrate the dyadic nature of signs and to explore the idea that semiotics could partner with advertising to achieve a synergic approach to strategic brand management. Ekeanyanwu and Okorie argue that the use of semiotics in promoting advertised messages serves as an ideal tool for reaching large numbers of people economically. Semiotics, among other things, plays a major role in advertising by catching the attention of the intended audience through the placement of images, texts, colours and other signs as part of an overall advertising strategy. They add that, since advertising campaign strategies are constantly changing, the application of semiotics within cultural frameworks must be encouraged so as to achieve an all-round advertising goal in strategic brand management.

Chapter 5, "Deception in Advertising: Ethical and Legal Imperatives", by Olayinka Egbokhare, and Chapter 6, "Social, Ethical and Regulatory Issues in Advertising: The Case of Nigeria", by Olujimi Kayode, explore the ethical implications of advertising practice. In Chapter 5, Egbokhare reviews the twin concepts of puffery and deception in Nigerian advertising. Using a careful examination of the Code of Advertising Practice of the Advertising Practitioners Council of Nigeria (APCON), she discusses the legal prescriptions for maintaining ethical advertising standards and warns that responsible practice should never overlook the need for high ethical conformance.

Egbokhare's conclusions are largely in line with Kayode's in the following chapter, which examines the diversities of viewpoints as to the desirability, or otherwise, of advertising in society by examining the social, ethical and regulatory aspects of advertising. Kayode contends that advertising is both a mirror and a shaper of society. One of the areas in which advertising is influenced by and, at the same time, influences the society as a whole is the ethical aspect. Kayode argues that, although people may have been overloaded with information from advertising to the point of intrusiveness and clutter, the usefulness of advertising should not be lost sight of. Good advertising, he says, makes useful products and services known, contributes to fuller employment, educates the public and contributes to rising standards of living. Paraphrasing Day (2004), Kayode notes that the ethical imperatives for the advertising practitioner should respect the interests of others and uphold human dignity, truthfulness and integrity. To this list, he adds the need for good advertising to enhance fundamental human rights and commercial free speech. In the context of the diversity of regulatory frameworks within the Nigerian environment, Kayode argues that regulation is needed most in situations where consumers are likely to be deceived by false or limited information or when advertising may cause some harm to its audience through its contents and presentations. While noting the ongoing debates on the proper extent of regulations in advertising, the author concludes that the essence of regulation is to promote good and socially responsible advertising.

One of the most contentious issues in the communication discipline is how to distinguish public relations from propaganda. While some scholars and professionals hold the view that both are essentially the same, others see clear and crucial differences. Even though both are forms of persuasion and rely on the same media of communication, they serve different purposes and objectives, yet they interface in many ways. This is the context in which Sunday Adekunle Akinjogbin and Noeem Taiwo Thanny in Chapter 7, "Public Relations and Propaganda: Relationships and Relevance", examine the negative perceptions surrounding propaganda and the impact of these perceptions on our understanding of public relations. They discuss the different forms, strategies and techniques of propaganda and conclude that, whatever their differences, both propaganda and public relations will continue to serve as relevant marketing communication tools to lubricate modern advertising.

Marxism holds that the economy is the foundation or structure upon which "superstructures" such as politics, religion and culture are built. However, the superstructures arguably influence the economic base of society in turn. This interplay is explored by Rotimi Olatunji and Jacinta Maweu in Chapters 8 and 9 respectively. In Chapter 8, "Advertising in a Globalising Culture: The Nigerian Experience", Olatunji identifies four distinct phases in the historical development of advertising in Nigeria, the colonial era (1928–1971), the era of indigenisation policy (1972–1985), the era of structural adjustment (1986–1998) and the era of neoliberalism (1999 to the present). He identifies three distinct creative strategies which have been adopted by global advertising agencies. The first approach is the globalisation or standardisation approach. Here, the central office of the ad agency sends its subsidiaries a completed advertisement for wholesale use. The second approach, the "prototype" strategy, allows subsidiaries to adapt materials from the central office to local cultures. The third approach enables subsidiaries to create their own advertising campaigns using the central office's work plans as guides. The last two approaches can be referred to as "glocalisation" approaches. While acknowledging the benefits of advertising standardisation, Olatunji notes that glocalisation is a process that has a high regard for local content in advertising creation and production and thus allows for customised messages to be used to reach buyers in different markets by fitting the message for each particular market or country. Glocalisation accommodates differences in cultural, economic, legal, media and product features between countries and within each country. Olatunji concludes with a discussion of the influence of globalisation on advertising practice in developing African countries.

The era of political liberalisation in Kenya (1990 to the present) has witnessed a wind of democratic change and attendant calls for the liberalisation and privatisation of the economy, including the media. In Chapter 9, "Media Liberalisation in Kenya: Who Benefits?", Maweu recounts how, between 1990 and 2010, both print and electronic media outlets in Kenya increased greatly in number. She discusses the implications of this growth for the Kenyan advertising industry, noting that the media in Kenya depend fully on advertising revenues and argues that this, in effect, enables advertisers to influence media content, using several case studies to support this claim. Thus, Maweu observes that the pluralisation of the media in Kenya has not necessarily translated to a diversity of viewpoints; private media owners are increasingly pursuing profits and selling audiences to advertisers. The private media emphasise entertainment to the detriment of other components as the industry climate exerts pressure on the media to avoid stories that are detrimental to advertisers' interests. Although the media are expected to act as public watchdogs and facilitate informed dialogue on critical and topical issues in the society, the effect of liberalisation in Kenya, Maweu argues, has been to force the "independent" media to collude with elite economic and political interests at the expense of the citizenry.

In Chapter 10, "Revisiting the Woman Question in Advertising", Gilbert Motsaathebe observes that, for a long time, women have been denigrated, stereotyped and objectified in advertising messages. In this context, Motsaathebe notes that women are the biggest consumers of advertised products and that advertising engages more women than men in selling brands. He points out that it has been assumed that women are more likely to respond to ad messages than men but advertising has had a tradition of portraying women negatively, as mere objects to sell products, and, in the process, has exploited women's images, sex and other traits, thus entrenching gender stereotypes and the oppression of women in society. However, Motsaathebe argues, modern awareness campaigns and advocacy activities have brought about significant improvements in the depiction of women in advertisements, and the media are now inundated with images of modern, sophisticated women. To test this hypothesis Motsaathebe uses a content analysis of selected magazines to take a closer look at contemporary advertising's imagery of women, looking, in particular, at disjunctures and continuities. He discusses his findings from an African cultural perspective and concludes by proposing ways to contain some of the problems his analysis uncovers.

In his second contribution to this book, Sidney Friendly Kankuzi discusses how work is depicted in South African television advertising in Chapter 11, "Representations of Work in Television Advertising in South Africa: The 1998 Employment Equity Act". In an effort to address discriminatory employment arising from the history of apartheid, the South African parliament passed the Employment Equity Act in 1998 to regulate the practices of that country's labour market. Using the 1998 act as a case study, Kankuzi examines the challenges that would face advertising if its cultural content were to be regulated by the act. Against that backdrop, Kankuzi examines the possibility of using the act as an index for analysing television advertising's representations of work. He argues that, like any other media genre, advertising must conform to certain internal characteristics which, if ignored, cause unnecessary conflict between advertising as a business and as a culture. The chapter concludes that advertising content can best be regulated internally through self-censorship and market forces, while the state should play a peripheral role as civic educator and mediator, helping to create critical television viewers and addressing their complaints.

Chapter 12, "The Rise of Political Advertising on Television in South Africa", by Sibongile Sindane, situates the long-standing debate about whether political advertising on television is more about image than issues in a specifically South African context. She examines political advertising on South African television during the 2009 pre-election period using a qualitative thematic content analysis as a means of interpreting the data. Her findings show that the political advertisements on television during this period were generally informative and addressed important political issues more than just the images of parties and candidates.

In Chapter 13, "A Discourse-analytical Investigation into the Nature of Afrikaans and English Radio Advertisements in South Africa", Angelique van Niekerk and Mariska Bertram use the 2005–2006 Loerie and Pendoring advertising awards in South Africa to examine the language (e.g. dialogue and code-switching) and language-related strategies (e.g. humour and intertextuality) in the award-winning radio spots. In the process, they give an overview of the special linguistic nature of radio advertising against the background of the functions of radio as a medium and the creative principles of radio advertising. Their analysis of the data is consistent with a didactic-academic goal to provide practical guidelines for the writing of creative and believable radio advertisements that echo the strengths of word-of-mouth advertising.

In Chapter 14, "Covert Advertising in Home Videos: Implications for Brand Management", Ganiyu Olalekan Akashoro and Shaibu Husseini explore the effectiveness of covert advertising (product placement) in films and television programmes as a function of variables such as audience profile (religion, culture, age, sex, literacy level etc), context of the plot, match of the product with the programme type, story and characters, access to technology and the audience's feelings about the endorsers. They argue that covert advertising's ability to leverage the entertainment value of programming to create a strong psychological effect on viewers is the main reason this strategy is gaining ground in media, albeit belatedly in developing societies such as Nigeria.

Akashoro and Husseini submit that, in spite of many shortcomings, covert advertising has great potential for strengthening a brand (or enhancing its equity) and in sourcing additional funds for film productions, especially in the face of the inability of most film producers, especially in developing countries, to attract sufficient funding from traditional sources. Thus, covert advertising has proved resourceful in the arduous task of breaking up the clutter in the media and product market as well as in reaching consumers of promoted products or need-satisfiers. However, in spite of its numerous benefits, which include its clutter-free features and the advantage of bringing in additional sources of income for filmmakers, they point out that film practitioners in Nollywood (as the Nigerian home video industry is dubbed) have yet to fully exploit the technique.

Chinenye Nwabueze in Chapter 15, "Cultural Paradoxes of Global Advertising in Satellite Television Broadcasting", looks at the globalisation of the advertising industry and argues that advertising at any level cannot be separated from culture. Thus, advertising messages and productions are inevitably cultural packages and vehicles, and global advertising on satellite television sells foreign cultural practices and ideas as well as particular goods and services. He points out that audiences in Africa now watch more global satellite television than local television and argues that the cultural influences of satellite and internet broadcasting in Africa should be an issue for reflection. Adopting an analytical approach to discuss the link between satellite television content and global advertising, including the relationship between international advertising and global advertising, and the relationship between international advertising and cultural marketing, Nwabueze takes a position akin to the view which equates globalisation with the imposition of Western culture, since the global media are largely owned and dominated by European and American conglomerates. He concludes by recommending that advertising regulatory bodies in Africa should screen out harmful cultural contents of global advertisements and ensure that advertisers are more sensitive to the cherished ethos and values of African societies.

Owing to revolutionary breakthroughs in information communication technologies and in the telecommunications industry, new advertising media are daily emerging and arguably have the potential to supplant traditional advertising media. Against this background, Chapter 16, "Internet Usage and the Imperative of Online Advertising in Sub-Saharan Africa", by Oluseyi Soremekun, discusses the development of internet advertising and examines its special attractions (interactivity, low cost, real-time access etc.) for advertisers. In addition to a detailed discussion of the different types of internet advertising, the author examines the challenges of advertising through the internet to consumers who may be illiterate or poor.

Beginning from the days of oral-media-centered practice, the integration of the African continent into the global vortex (in politics, economy, culture and education) has impacted significantly on the development of advertising theory and practice. However, in spite of the rapid changes in the practice of advertising, word-of-mouth, person-to-person, personal selling, direct marketing and other such practices bear the mark of a uniquely African contribution to marketing promotion that can hardly be ignored, even in a globalised environment. Available research across the African continent points in the same direction, showing that advertising both influences and is influenced by society. Multi-disciplinary, multi-dimensional and integrative approaches undoubtedly present the most viable option for the study and practice of advertising in Africa, as in other parts of the world. This requires a shift from the traditional isolationist approach to one which explores marketing communication in a holistic manner. The new approach is popularly called integrated marketing communication, also referred to as the new advertising. The African continent is not insulated from the increasing use and relevance of internet advertising. What we may add, in closing, is that integrated marketing communication will continue to be relevant and attract increasing inputs from scholars and practitioners across other disciplines. That, in essence, is one of the lessons that globalisation has taught the world community.

References

Davidson, B. 1970. *Old Africa Rediscovered*. London: Longman.

Olurode, L. 2003. Gender, Globalization and Marginalization in Africa, *Africa Development* 38: 67–88.

I
THEORETICAL AND ETHICAL ISSUES

CHAPTER 1

INDIGENOUS FORMS OF ADVERTISING MEDIA IN AFRICA: WHAT RELEVANCE IN AN AGE OF GLOBALISATION?

ROTIMI WILLIAMS OLATUNJI & ASSAY BENJAMIN ENAHORO

Introduction

Advertising is rooted in culture. As Nwagbara (2010: 162) puts it:

> Cultural norms and values provide direction and guidance to all members of a society in all aspects of their lives, including their consumption patterns. No meaningful communication occurs outside a cultural setting. Advertising, as marketing communication, takes place within defined cultural borders. Professional calling, educational attainment, age grouping, religious affiliation, socio-economic status or other cultural indicators by which individuals are distinguished in the society operate within specific boundaries that dictate accepted lifestyles, values, and tastes of the environment.

Flowing from the above, it is imperative that advertisers take cognizance of the cultural element of the people. Arens (1999) avers that advertisers find it much easier to work with consumers' tastes than to change them. Therefore, any good advertiser should be concerned with what happens within the consumers' purchase environment. Lin (1993) contends that, of all business activities, marketing actions are most prone to cultural error. A solid understanding of the cultural composition of a people and of the factors that shape culture over time, such as race and nationality, language and cultural values, is key to achieving success at the global and national levels (Bovee et al. 1995: 196).

The notion that advertising messages are non-personalized and are channelled through the public or mass media limits our understanding to advertising as it exists in Western societies, where media culture is at an advanced stage. Can we say that traditional societies lacking in Westernized forms of media culture do not engage in advertising practices? To what extent is the use of indigenous forms of communication media in Africa relevant to the needs of such societies, both in the past and now? Is there any future for indigenous advertising media in Africa in a fast-paced globalized environment? These are the issues addressed in this chapter.

Advertising in Ancient European and African Societies

A comparative analysis of indigenous forms of advertising media in ancient European and in African societies will give us a better insight into the evolution of advertising media across societies as well as equip us with the knowledge to appreciate significant changes that have taken place over the years. The history of advertising is widely believed to be as old as the history of mankind, but the modern form of advertising is only a few hundred years old, dating back to the era of mercantilism and, later, capitalism in Europe. However, advertising had been in existence even before the age of printing. It first existed in oral forms and went though various evolutionary periods in different societies of the world.

Greco-Roman and, later, medieval Europe had different forms of advertising that can best be described as ancient (Dyer 1982). Baigi (1992: 4) reports that the Phoenicians, as far back as 1200 BC, painted messages on stones or near the paths where people often walked to announce the sale of their wares. The ancient Phoenicians practiced what was called "silent trade". Much later, when they engaged in long-distance trade, the Phoenicians' ships berthed in foreign ports and sent criers around town, often with signboards, to announce their arrival. Bhatia (2000: 68) observes:

> [I]n ancient times the most common form of advertising was by word of mouth; however, commercial messages and political campaign displays have been found in the ruins of Pompeii. Egyptians used papyrus to create sales messages and wall posters, while lost-and-found advertising on papyrus was common in Greece and Rome. Wall or rock painting for commercial advertising is another manifestation of an ancient media advertising form, which is present to this day in many parts of Asia, Africa and South America. The tradition of wall paintings can be traced back to Indian rock-art paintings that go back to 4000 BCE.

In most parts of ancient Europe, shopkeepers announced their goods through the oral medium. The services of street callers, called town criers, were utilised to make known or advertise goods. Fruits and vegetables were sold in the city square from the backs of carts and wagons, and their proprietors used town criers to announce their whereabouts for the convenience of the customers. The town criers also used media such as bells and horns to get buyers and sellers together in exchange relationships, sometimes called trade by barter. This took place in societies such as Greece, Babylon, Egypt, Rome and the like (Ehigie and Babalola 1995). When the towns and cities of the Middle Ages began to grow, but the general populace was still unable to read, pictures were used to indicate words. For instance, a cobbler was represented by a picture of a boot, a tailor by a suit of clothes, a blacksmith by a horseshoe and so on.

As early as 1100 AD, inn-keepers in France hired town criers to promote samples of their fine wines, and everyone has heard of "sweet Molly Malone," who cried "cockles and mussels, alive, alive-O" through the streets of Dublin. From these town criers was born the old adage that "the best form of advertising is word-of-mouth" (Rulli: 1999: 5). Sandage and Fryburger (1971: 18) note that governments gave town criers formal recognition to the extent that they were even chartered by medieval regimes. King Philip Augustus of France issued a Decree in 1258 "forcing a shopkeeper to employ a crier". Advertising continued essentially in this oral form until the introduction of printing technology (Sandage and Fryburger 1971: 18).

The evolution of advertising in Africa followed a similar pattern of development. In pre-colonial Africa, just as in pre-modern Europe, the use of town criers existed in several societies, and it has been amply demonstrated that oral communication and traditions remained important modes of social dialogue in African societies for a long time. Examples include oral narratives (epics, legends, and explanatory tales), poetry (praise poetry, chants, and songs) and epigrams (proverbs, riddles, puns, and tongue twisters). These oral genres were significant in helping to link the past and the present, construct collective worldviews and identity, educate the youth, express political views and provide entertainment and aesthetic pleasure. They were also very useful in the promotion of commerce in traditional African societies. The use of oral genres as custodians of collective tradition, sources of entertainment and means of trade promotion are well documented in many African societies.

As a medium, oral forms of communication have proved useful for the construction, dissemination and consumption of ideas through drama, music and dance in a number of African societies. African drama dates back to ancient times and includes pantomime, dance-drama, masque, shadow theatre, heroic recitation, praise-poetry and market comedy by itinerant troupes and uses, in various combinations and with different degrees of sophistication, role-playing, dialogue, mime, movement, dance, song, puppetry, costume and scenic spectacle. All of these have proved useful as media of advertising in African societies.

Traditional rulers disseminated information to their subjects mainly through the services of town criers. Town criers, it may be said, primarily evolved in Africa for political communication purposes. The use of criers to disseminate information about goods and services was a later development that came with increased sophistication of trade and commerce. Initially, goods were advertised mainly through the use of symbols (Akinawo 1979). It is noteworthy that this practice was similar to the Phoenician "silent trade" discussed earlier. Later, the use of town criers to announce the sale of cattle, slaves and other goods became common, with Molokwu (2000: 9) noting that the town crier was "most effective as an attention catcher".

For the scholar in the field of modern marketing communication, advertising practice is often traced back to Western civilisation. Since the modern media are most highly developed in Europe and the United States, little or no consideration is given to the contributions of Africa to the practice of advertising. However, it is on record that the very first form of printed advertisement originated with the ancient Egyptians, who used papyrus to make sales messages and wall posters. Wall or rock paintings for commercial advertising is another manifestation of an ancient advertising form, which is used to this day in many parts of Africa.

Distinctive Media of Advertising in Traditional African Societies

What then were the distinctive media of advertising in traditional African societies? Town criers carried advertising messages from place to place, as discussed above. The town crier was the village "broadcaster" of messages. He carried messages from the chiefs to the villagers, usually late at night or very early in the morning when everybody was still at home. The town crier beat his gong to attract the attention of villagers and compel them to listen to his message. The voice of the town crier rang out loud and clear, travelling to all parts of the village. Wilson (1987) highlighted the various roles of the town crier, which included news reporter, messenger, political spokesman, envoy, contact person, courier, postman, broadcaster and so on. The town crier reached his varied audiences through several media, including ideophones, which Wilson (1987) describes as self-sounding instruments that produce sound without the use of any intermediary medium. Town-criers also used membranophones, instruments on which sound is produced through the use of membranes. Talking drums are ready examples. The third category of media employed by town criers were aerophones, media that produce sound as a result of the vibration of a column of air. Instruments in this category include flutes, whistles, horns and trumpets.

Symbolography, a form of graphic representation, was also a common medium. Belonging to this category are the use of media such as palm fronds, decorated sticks and cryptic writing as found among the Igbo in southeast Nigeria, as well as the use of signals like fire, gunshots, cannon shots and so on. Colour schemes, music, symbolic displays and real objects are other devices employed by the traditional town crier to spread news about goods and services. In light of the above, Wilson (1987) listed the main advertising channels in traditional African societies as follows:

- Display of products on a stand, tree stump or flag pole
- Use of peripatetic hawkers and vendors
- Use of fragrances, odours and aromas
- Singing and drumming.

In addition to this, person-to-person modes of communication were employed to promote individuals or organisations through praise-singing. Entertainment and public announcements were also useful public relations devices in traditional African societies.

A supplement to the use of the town-crier is the popular art of hawking in most African societies. Town-crying and hawking were the earliest forms of advertising and have survived in many Nigerian villages up to now (Ezejideaku and Ugwu 2010: 2). In almost every rural setting in Nigeria, hawking is a common form of advertising. People who have things to sell engage in hawking to make potential buyers notice them. Hawking is done early in the morning and evening when everybody is at home. For instance, it is common to hear hawkers in Isoko dialect in the Niger Delta saying *wa te de emeri kpokpo* ('come and buy fresh fish'), *wa te de akamu* (come and buy pap) and so on. Indeed, hawking is not limited to rural settings nowadays but has also become an urban phenomenon, especially along the highways.

The talking drum was developed and used by several cultures in tropical Africa. It served as an early form of long-distance communication, often used for ceremonial and religious purposes. Ceremonial functions could include dance, rituals, story-telling and communication of points of order. There are many variations of talking drums in Africa. Among the Wolof of modern-day Senegal in West Africa, the drum is called *tam tam*. Among the Yoruba of southwest Nigeria, it is called *gan-gan, dun dun, emele* or Iya Ilu. It is known as *dondo* by the Ashanti of central Ghana, *lunna* by the Dagomba of northern Ghana and *kalangu* by the

Hausa of northern Nigeria. Talking drums are also used in eastern, central and southern Africa, and called by various names.

Wikipedia (2010) asserts that "under ideal conditions, the sound can be understood at 8 km (5 miles), but interesting messages usually get relayed on by the next village". The term 'talking drums' or 'jungle drums' is also a euphemism for gossip, rumours or the grapevine. It is not surprising, therefore, that in several African societies, pre-colonial people used drum telegraphy to communicate with each other for centuries and that European expeditions in colonial times were often surprised to find that news of their progress and rumours about their intentions had been carried through the woods in advance of their arrival through the use of the drums.

As conveyers of messages, including commercial messages, drums were limited and subject to misinterpretation, as they were not "languages in their own right":

> The sounds produced are conventionalized or idiomatic signals based on speech patterns. The messages are normally very stereotyped and context-dependent. They lack the ability to form new combinations and expressions (Wikipedia 2010).

Peddling, on the other hand, a clear, sonorous and rhythmic type of "yo-heave-ho", was a special way to attract customers or passengers by sellers who travelled about the streets to sell their goods in traditional African societies. The ringing or sounding of bells has also been a successful device to advertise or announce the arrival of goods in traditional African societies. Signboards, usually made of cloth, silk or boards, were another vivid way to attract attention to businesses. Mainly set up in front of shops and bars, they were also called bar signs or shop signs. Such signs have evolved from small, painted wooden signs hung over doorways to modern plastic signs, lighted signs, animated signs, billboards and even bumper stickers.

Traditional dance-drama groups have also played important roles in the dissemination of selling messages across communities. Dance, drama and praise songs are regular features of marriage ceremonies, circumcision feasts, naming ceremonies and other rites of passage, including chieftaincy ceremonies. In most traditional African societies, dance-drama groups were actively involved in the promotion of goods and services. This form of traditional advertising tells the villagers that there is a happy event taking place in the village. Singing is usually accompanied with talking drums, gunshots or trumpets. Once the villagers hear the commotion, they rush to the village square for further information.

There were other devices for disseminating commercial messages in traditional African societies, including the display of red flags on long bamboo poles to announce traditional medical facilities or shrines, employment of travelling theatre groups to broadcast the availability of goods for sale, the announcement of the sighting of a new moon with obvious implications for marketing, street-to-street or village-to-village hawking of goods and so on.

Relevance of Indigenous Advertising Media

The foundation for modern advertising was laid with the invention, first, of paper by the Chinese around 100 AD, its adoption in Europe around 1300 AD and the invention of the printing press in about 1448 by Johannes Gutenberg which revolutionized information retrieval, storage, processing and dissemination. The first printed advertisement in English followed soon after, when William Caxton printed a handbill in 1472 to advertise one of his prayer books. The handbill was pasted on church doors. The first newspaper advertisement in Britain consisted of the offer of a reward for the return of some stolen horses. The first newspaper advertisement in the United States appeared in the *Boston Newsletter*'s very first issue in 1704. That advertisement was designed to sell the newsletter in question.

The period of the industrial revolution in Europe witnessed a tremendous growth of the advertising industry. Capitalism led to mass production of goods, urbanisation and improvement of living standards. There was need for mass distribution of mass-produced goods and thus for a mass awareness of and demand for the goods. In response, newspapers readily served as vehicles through which industrial goods could be advertised. However, at this early stage of print media advertisements, advertising agencies were not yet in existence. Advertising agencies were established principally to help the media sell advertising space. The earliest forms of advertising agencies were essentially space-brokers or space-sellers. The practice was that advertising agencies bought space from publications, usually at wholesale rates, then resold the space (on a retail basis) to advertisers "at whatever markup they could demand" (Norris 1987: 10). This is similar to one of the functions of modern-day media independents.

Thus, the activities of the earliest forms of ad agencies in Europe and America were primarily directed at assisting the media, not the advertisers. Agencies sold space on behalf of newspapers The first ad agency in the US, called Volney B. Palmer, was established in Philadelphia in 1841 (Batra, Myers and Aaker 2006: 13). It serviced the media originally as a media brokerage firm. The fundamental shift from advertising brokerage to advertising agency occurred later, when agencies began to write copy and produce advertisements.

The modern Western form of advertising practice came to Nigeria with the British commercial *cum* colonial conquest. The Royal Niger Company (RNC), a British trading company which operated in the River Niger area before the amalgamation exercise of 1914, initially imported British manufactured goods and exported raw materials such as palm oil, cocoa, timber, ground nuts and other primary products to the United Kingdom. The company later became known as United African Company (UAC) and on 13 August 1928 incorporated in London an advertising company called West Africa Publicity Limited (WAP). This was the first advertising agency that in Nigeria. WAP later adopted LINTAS as its business name to coordinate its advertising activities in Nigeria (Molokwu 2000: 7). In other African nations, modern advertising practice was introduced in a similar way through formal contacts with colonialism or western commerce.

Since then, globalisation has brought standardised forms of advertising practice everywhere in the world. Advertising agencies have similar structures and functions, including message creation (copywriting), account management, media planning, buying and monitoring, research and development and so on. The mass print and electronic media provide the main channels through which ad messages are transmitted to the public. Interestingly, the advertising media that originally replaced indigenous forms of media are now referred to as "traditional" as opposed to the new media of the Internet and other Information Communication Technologies (ICTs). Advertising media are now truly globalised, unlike the forms of advertising media in traditional African or other ancient societies. How relevant, therefore, are the indigenous advertising media in this contemporary globalised environment?

Wilson (1987) identified several limitations of the use of indigenous advertising media. These include the absence of a standardised vocabulary for describing and analysing communication concepts, channels and processes. According to Wilson (1987: 98), there is a clear absence of "an appropriate language which can be universally applied". Similarly, Okigbo (1995: 216), notes that "indigenous advertisements involve minimal planning, modest creativity and have limited channels for their expression, unlike many of the contemporary or modern advertisements that we have in the mass media today". Moreover, the hegemonic influence of globalised media limits the usefulness, efficiency and effectiveness of indigenous advertising media. Oral media in particular are highly limited for reaching the diversified, heterogeneous audiences of today's globalised environment. Even where signs, symbols and drums are used as advertising channels, there are no universally agreed meanings for such symbols, sounds or signs. In sum, a reliance on indigenous advertising media will severely hamper an advertising message's reach, frequency and efficiency.

However, the foregoing does not in any way limit the usefulness of indigenous advertising media in contemporary African societies. It should be noted that advertising audiences today are more heterogeneous today than they were at the beginning of the 20th century. In fact media audiences are now greatly atomised and fractionalised (Olatunji 2003). Apart from the very high cost of mass media advertising channels, there are a multiplicity of media today, a situation which has further heightened the challenge of audience fragmentation. An absolute reliance on media advertising, therefore, defeats the goal of effective marketing management. In response to the above, a new concept called Integrated Marketing Communication (IMC) has evolved.

IMC is a management concept designed to make all aspects of marketing such as advertising, sales promotion, public relations, direct marketing and the like work together as a unified force. Essentially, IMC is a management approach that aligns and maximises the communications impact of various disciplines. Vargas (2005: 1) notes that IMC is "a way of looking at the whole marketing process from the viewpoint of the customer". The intention is to provide clear, unified, consistent and compelling customer-focused messages. The major tools employed in IMC advertising include word-of-mouth, outdoor media, personal selling, events marketing, publicity, sales promotion, public relations, telemarketing, Internet advertising and relationship marketing. It is observable that advertising media are now highly personalised. Word-of-mouth, direct selling, person-to-person marketing and relationship marketing are more widely used than ever, owing to cost and other marketing advantages. Moreover, a good number of television and radio commercials exploit the advantages offered by oral advertising media. Commercials are now laden with entertainment, drama and music rather than the purely informative or logical appeals of Western advertising traditions. For example, there have been numerous uses of entertainment and drama to launch or promote telecommunications brands in Nigeria, including the Etisalat and Airtel commercials. Even the famous "My Friend Udeme…" campaign launched by Guinness Nigeria relied on African traditional storytelling devices as epitomized by the griots of Senegal and other traditional storytellers in other parts of Africa.

Conclusion

Although indigenous advertising media may not be effective in reaching heterogeneous audiences simultaneously, they are nonetheless useful for reaching targeted individuals and groups in a relatively cheap and efficient manner. Cultural practices, including the use of advertising media, involve a deep appreciation of the dynamism, relativity and universalistic nature of developmental goals and aspirations. African societies can never remain relevant and active players in advertising practice if they totally rely on indigenous advertising media to disseminate selling messages. It is important to adapt or adopt recent trends and practices in global advertising media. At the same time, however, the integration of indigenous advertising media into modern advertising practice in Africa can greatly enhance its relevance to local cultures, mores, and sensibilities.

References

Akinawo, G. 1979. How to assess advertising proposals. Doghudje, C.A (Ed.) *How to Get the Best Results from an Advertising Agency.* Apapa, Lagos: Times Press Nigeria.

Arens, W.F. 1999. *Contemporary Advertising.* Seventh Edition. Boston: McGraw-Hill.

Batra, R. Myers, J. G and Aaker, D.A. 2006. *Advertising Management.* New Delhi: Prentice-Hall of India Private Ltd.

Bhatia, Tej K. 2000. *Advertising in Rural India: Language, Marketing Communication and Consumerism.* Tokyo: Tokyo University of Foreign Studies.

Biagi, S. 1992. *Media Impact: An Introduction to Mass Communication.* Belmont, California: Wadsworth Inc.

Bovee, C.L., John V. Thill and George P. Dovel. 1995. *Advertising Excellence.* New York: McGraw-Hill.

Dyer, G. 1982. *Advertising as Communication.* New York: Methuen & Co.

Ehigie, B.O. and Babalola, S.S. 1995. *Understanding Consumer Behaviour.* Ibadan: Newborne.

Ezejideaku, E. and E.N. Ugwu. 2010. The linguistics of newspaper advertising. *Language in India* 10 (3). www.languageinindia.com

Lin, C.A. 1993. Cultural differences in message strategies: A comparison between American and Japanese TV commercials. *Journal of Advertising Research* 33 (4) 1992: 40–48.

Molokwu, B. 2000. *Principles of Advertising.* Lagos: Advertising Practititioners Council of Nigeria (APCON).

Norris, J.S. 1984. *Advertising.* New Delhi: Prentice Hall of India Ltd.

Nwagbara, G. 2010. Culture, stereotypes, and advertising in Nigeria: Repositioning the female models. *Nigerian Journal of Communication* 8 (1).

Okigbo, C. 1995. Integrated marketing communication: The new advertising. *Advertising Annual Volume II,* 215–25.

Olatunji, R.W. (2003). The Impact of the Structural Adjustment Programme on the Advertising Industry in Nigeria (1986–1996). Unpublished PhD Thesis, University of Ibadan, Ibadan, Nigeria.

Sandage, C.H. and Fryburger, V. 1971. *Advertising Theory and Practice.* Illinois: Richard D Irwin Inc.

Vergas, R.D. 2005. Integrated Marketing Communications – An Effective, Comprehensive Approach, *Business Ventures, Fairfax County Economic Quarterly Newsletter for Small, Minority and Women Owned Business,* p.1.

Wikipedia. 2010. Drums in communication. http://en.wikipedia.org/wiki/Drums_in_communication (retrieved 24/12/2010)

Wilson, Desmond. 1987. Traditional systems of communication in modern African development: An analytical viewpoint. *African Media Review* 1 (2): 87–104.

CHAPTER 2

THEORETICAL APPROACHES TO UNDERSTANDING REPRESENTATION AND THE LANGUAGE OF ADVERTISING

SYDNEY FRIENDLY KANKUZI

Introduction

This chapter discusses three major theoretical approaches to understanding the concept of representation and their relevance to the language of advertising. It is divided into three major sections which highlight the basic concerns of each of these approaches and examine the extent to which they can explain the language of advertising. The chapter closes with some recommendations on the importance of these theoretical approaches to advertising training programmes.

Hall (1997a: 61) defines representation as "the process by which members of a culture use language (broadly defined as any system which deploys signs, any signifying system) to produce meaning". A sign is anything that stands for something else (Eco 1976: 16). Therefore, language may use all sorts of signs besides the written and spoken word (Hall 1997b: 4-5). Barthes (1972), for example, regards a photograph as as much a form of language as a newspaper article. He reasons that pictures are a kind of writing in so far as they are meaningful, tracing this understanding of language to the period before the invention of the alphabet when objects or drawings, as in pictographs, were accepted as speech (119). In this regard, advertising is a language, and each advertisement is a speech act that uses specially produced signs to produce meanings shared by members of a given culture. Thus "language provides one general model of how culture and representation work" (Hall 1997b: 6).

Theoretical Approaches to Representation

The intentional, reflective and constructionist approaches to explaining the process of representation in advertising are discussed in this section. Bearing in mind that "meanings can only be shared through [a] common access to language" (Hall 1997b: 1), each of these approaches is based on certain epistemological assumptions about how language functions.

Intentional Approach to Representation

The intentional approach to representation propounds the view that "it is the speaker, the author, who imposes his or her unique meaning on the world through language. Hall (1997a: 25) explains that "words mean what the author intends them to mean". Epistemologically, this position is informed by the intentional theory of language, which perceives language as an intentional activity: "a sentence has meaning because the utterer has certain intentions" (Platts 1979: 86). One school of thought within the intentional approach draws a distinction between sentence meaning (the grammatical meaning of an utterance) and utterer's meaning (the producer's intended meaning of an utterance). Thus, the meaning of a linguistic expression cannot be known unless its producer's intention is identified. Another school of thought within the intentional approach, which has exerted considerable influence on discourse analysis, also links meaning to producer's intention, but goes a step further to draw a distinction between intent (the 'purpose' the producer intended) and purpose (the 'purpose' the interpreter perceives). This school argues that an effective text is one that an interpreter perceives as achieving the purposes that its producer intended. Thus, the receiver ideally needs to personally consult the author for the meaning of a text, but, in practice, this is not necessarily the case because, in normal circumstances, the form and content of the text adequately reveal the producer's intended meaning (Chimombo and Roseberry 1998).

This second school of thought also sees a close link between purpose and intent, on the one hand, and the functions of language on the other. According to Chimombo and Roseberry (1998), the functions of language help classify a text by specifying its degree of factuality and the purpose which it reveals. Thus, in relation to factuality, a text may be based either on fact, speculation, imagination or any combination of these. In turn, the degree of factuality determines the purpose that a text may serve, whether selling, transferring information, entertaining, edifying or revealing the producer's self. Here again, this school of thought recognises various possible combinations and degrees of importance and dominance of purpose in texts. For example, a newspaper feature article about a worrisome issue such as climate change may incorporate some speculation about science's ability to address the problem in order to edify readers as they learn about the alarming reality. In this view, the producer of a text creates the intended meaning through tangible functional stages called "moves", which are accomplished through limited sets of strategies. Thus, the analysis of moves can reveal the strategies which a text uses to accomplish its intended purpose. Basically, moves are of five functional types: obligatory, optional, iterational, split and joined (Chimombo and Roseberry 1998).

Obligatory moves are those that are compulsory to a particular genre; they distinguish genres from each other. For example, a news story is expected to at least contain moves which identify its newsworthiness, its characters and its sources. Optional moves are those that supplement obligatory moves depending on need. In the case of a news story, these may include linking the story to similar previous ones to achieve thematic continuity. Iterational moves are made repeatedly in a text to generate a desired effect in the reader's mind. For example, a news story may repeatedly describe a football player as 'lethal'. Move-splitting occurs when one move is embedded within another and is common in situations where one move contains several strategies. Conversely, move-joining occurs when two moves appear to combine into one. When this happens, a single phrase or clause combines the functions of two separate moves.

Relevance of Intentional Approach to the Language of Advertising

The intentional approach raises substantial points relevant to the understanding of the language of advertising. The fact that the producer of an advertisement influences meaning, for example, is indisputable; it takes a producer's conscious effort to create an advertisement that can generate intended meaning in a reader's mind. It is also true that an advert may be based on fact, speculation, imagination or some combination of any of these. A "U-Fresh" laundry soap advertisement commonly featured on Malawi Television, for example, persuades consumers to buy the soap based on: (a) the provable fact that it removes dirt efficiently; (b) speculation that it is the best laundry soap on the market; and (c) the soap's imagined excellent quality capable of tempting consumers to use it as a bath soap and a toothpaste among other uses.

Similarly, factuality is not only a prevalent characteristic of advertising, but it also occurs in different degrees in advertisements depending on the producer's intention. An advertisement may have the dominant purpose of selling, but it may also make considerable efforts to entertain and inform as well as to reveal the manufacturer of the product in question. The U-Fresh advertisement described above makes deliberate effort to introduce the self (the manufacturer of U-Fresh) by displaying the name 'Candlex'. It informs targeted consumers that Candlex has improved the power of its already unique soap, persuades them to try the soap for themselves and entertains them through the use of amusing characters.

Table 2.1: Moves and Strategies Used in a U-Fresh Laundry Soap Advertisement

Moves	Strategy
Identifying the problem with other soaps	An unhappy car owner walks towards a young man who is washing the former's car using soap that does not produce much lather
Presenting the solution and identifying potential customers	The car owner drops a green tablet of soap into a bucket of water which the young man is using for washing the car.
	The boy rubs the green soap on a piece of cloth, producing much lather.
	The boy smiles with wonder as he enjoys washing the car using the green soap.
	A woman who is about to bathe asks the car owner to pass her the green soap tablet.
	The woman is amazed when she realises the man is about to use the green tablet as a toothpaste.
Persuading potential customers to buy the product	A male voice-over explains that U-Fresh is a powerful soap which makes laundry simple and can be used for bathing and other domestic purposes.
	The voice-over also explains that the power of U-Fresh has recently been improved.
Identifying product outlets	A male voice-over announces that U-Fresh is sold in all wholesale and retail shops across the country.

Just like other genres, advertising representations also use moves which are implemented through the use of strategies. Advertising can be likened to poetry in that both are faced with the challenge of using the least possible amount of signs to communicate complex messages attractively and within the shortest possible time and/or space. An advertising producer addresses this challenge by translating the moves into strategies which in turn create narratives that generate their intended meaning within the given time and/or space. Table 2.1 illustrates moves and their respective strategies used in the U-Fresh advertisement.

The moves of advertising also have various characteristics which reflect the producer's intended purpose. Product and service advertisements, for instance, are obliged to use moves that identify the product or service in question as well as moves that show its use(s). It is also not unusual for product and service advertisements to provide additional information, for example, concerning how or where the product or service can be obtained and whether any privileges such as discounts and warranties are offered. Similarly, iterational moves are a common feature of product and service advertising. Advertisers believe they can increase an advertisement's chances of interpellating target consumers by strategically repeating desirable qualities of the product or service in question. In TV and Internet advertising, such qualities may take the form of colourful flashes or blinks which the audience is very likely to notice.

Move-splitting and move-joining are equally important features of advertising representations. An imaginary bank advertisement slogan, "Why pay auto-teller charges when others are enjoying free services", for example, is first and foremost a move aimed at showing that there is a problem with banks that charge auto-teller transactions. However, within it is embedded a move for showing that the bank that produced the advertisement provides a solution to the problem at hand. Another imaginary bank advertisement could include the slogan "Your first bank", which combines the move for showing that the bank was the first to be established in the area and another one showing that it offers the best banking services in the area. This, in fact, occurs in an advertisement in Nigeria, where one of the commercial banks, Firstbank PLC, unarguably the first commercial bank in the country, adopts the pay-off "First bank … truly the first".

In advertising, move joining may be achieved in two ways, through the use of lexical ambiguity or through the use of lexical omission. An advertiser may omit some important words in an advertisement slogan in order to give a preferred message privileged visibility or audibility. The slogan "First bank… truly the first", for example, uses verbal ambiguity to join the moves that produced it; the lexical item 'first' is both historical and numerical. The slogan "studded for extra pleasure" of Manyuchi, one of Malawi's leading male condom brands, perfectly illustrates move-joining by omission. Although most Malawians associate condom use with birth control and prevention of sexually transmitted infections (STIs), the Manyuchi slogan associates condom use with sexual pleasure. The producer of the advertisement verbally omitted these two popular uses by embedding their moves into the one for sexual pleasure to give the latter a privileged visibility.

Although advertising is basically business-oriented, it is heavily influenced by culture, as evidenced through move-splitting and move-joining. The decision to join moves in the Manyuchi advertisement, for instance, was influenced by the cultural context of the English language, which permits explicit talk about sexuality in public. In contrast, the producer was culturally compelled to join together the move for sexual pleasure with that for STI prevention when creating the vernacular (Chichewa) version of the slogan, namely 'Tseketseke ukudziteteza' ('sweetness while you protect yourself'). In Chichewa, explicit public talk about sexuality is taboo. Semantically, 'Tseketseke ukudziteteza' implies that the sexual pleasure that may be enjoyed from condom use is of secondary importance to STI's prevention, hence the slogan's easier public acceptability.

However, despite its relevance to the language of advertising, the intentional approach has shortfalls which render it inadequate to explain the language of advertising. Firstly, the approach denies the social character of meaning by over-emphasising the role of the producer of the text in meaning creation. As Hall (1997a: 25) argues:

> [People's] private intended meanings, however personal to [them], have to enter into the rules, codes, and conventions of language to be shared and understood. Language is a social system through and through. This means that [people's] private thoughts have to negotiate with all the other meanings for words or images which have been stored in language which [their] use of the language system will inevitably trigger into action.

Although an advertiser or their agency may claim authorship of a text, they cannot justifiably claim sole authorship of the meaning that the text generates. Practically speaking, an advertising producer is required to ensure that whatever message they communicate conforms to the rules, codes and conventions of the language of the target audience. If they violate this requirement, they risk creating advertisements which either may not easily interpellate the target audience or may get rejected by the audience altogether. One example will suffice to elaborate this point. In Malawi, during the late 1990s, Population Services International (PSI) introduced a new condom brand named 'Chishango' (meaning 'Shield') and packaged it in a box bearing a picture of a shield and the slogan 'Chishango, Kupherera Basi' ('Shield, nothing but blocking the darts').

As part of its marketing strategy, PSI developed print-media advertisements, wall posters and billboards bearing the picture and the slogan. Although the condom was the first to be advertised publicly in Malawi, it was adopted with considerable ease by the general public partly because it used signs and linguistic rules which most Malawians easily identified with. In most Malawian tribal traditions, a shield symbolises protection from enemies, and during this time AIDS was viewed by many Malawians as one of the country's worst enemies.

In 2005, PSI re-branded the Chishango condom and packaged it in a box bearing a picture of a scantly-clad woman's torso, suggestively revealing one thigh and her navel. Advertisements for the re-branded condom attracted wide condemnation from religious groups, civil-society groups and the general public for being indecent, pornographic and degrading, regardless of the fact that the woman's torso was superimposed on a background of a shield and that condom use was no longer a new phenomenon to Malawians. The Malawi Censorship Board responded to the public outcry by banning the advertisement from public display. PSI was compelled to replace the half-naked woman's torso with a picture of a fully dressed, smiling, youthful couple. The picture was complemented by the slogan 'kunjoya utatchena' ('enjoying while you are properly dressed'), where the word 'dressed' refers to wearing a condom and not necessarily the couple's clothes. The slogan was created by skillfully embedding the move for sexual pleasure into that for STI prevention.

The second problem with the intentional approach is its denial of multiplicity of textual meaning. Although proponents of the approach argue that "intent and purpose can be specified by discovering and identifying all of the relevant elements of a text, including culture, they maintain that in practice a text cannot be effective unless the interpreter perceives it as achieving the producer's purpose(s)" (Chimombo and Roseberry 1998). What this means is that an advertisement can be said to be meaningful only if it fulfils the producer's intended purpose. In the case of the Chishango advertisement, PSI could easily have disassociated itself from all unintended meanings which Malawians had deciphered from the advertisement. On the contrary, advertisers understand that their texts may trigger unintended meanings in the minds of the audience and that they are answerable for these.

Reflective Approach to Representation

The reflective approach to representation maintains that meaning is intrinsic to things that are found in the real world (Hall 1997a). Therefore, language is simply a mirror of reality. Hall (1997a) observes that the approach is sometimes called mimetic, after the notion of mimesis, which fourth-century BC Greeks employed to explain how language and art mirror nature. Unlike symbolic signs, which do not resemble the things which they represent, mimetic signs communicate by resembling the things to which they refer. The reflective approach to representation was a dominant influence behind the worldview of medieval Europe. During that period, the world was viewed through the epistemological filter of Christianity, which regarded everything that existed in the world not only as having a divine purpose but also as reflecting the divine. Blackness, for example, was associated with evil because it was believed that the devil, the author of evil, was black. Similarly, goodness was associated with whiteness/lightness because it was believed that God, the source of goodness, was full of light. However, mimesis or resemblance is not limited to ancient Greece and medieval Europe. To date, mimesis is a common aspect of many cultural practices. When African children mould clay babies as their parents dance in masks resembling all kinds of living things, they use mimetic signs.

Relevance of the Reflective Theory

The reflective approach is informed epistemologically by the mapping view of language, which argues that "there is a common world out there and ... languages are analogous to maps of [that] world" (Grace 1987: 6). A critical look at the reflective approach, therefore, generates some practical insights into the language of advertising. Since advertising is a social activity, it makes sense to expect it to communicate through the process of reflection, at least in the simplest sense of the word. It is not unreasonable, for example, to expect advertising to reflect the beliefs and practices of the society in which it exists. Similarly, it is logical to expect an advertisement targeted at children to reflect certain attributes of children and the world in which they live. Otherwise it is likely to be culturally misappropriated.

Cultural misappropriation of meaning in advertising is exemplified by what happened in Malawi in the mid-1990s when cell phones were just being introduced in the country. Telekom Networks Malawi produced an advertisement which used the slogan, 'Telekom Eya!', an adaptation of a Vodacom slogan, 'Yebo, Yes!' in South Africa. However, although the word 'Eya' is a direct translation of the Zulu word *Yebo* (Yes), it is not used in Malawi for saying 'hello' when answering a phone call. Consequently, the advertisements did not make sense to most Malawians and, as a result, had to be abandoned. In contrast, the company around the same period developed advertisements which named cell phone packages after well-known local fish species. The business executive package was named 'Bombe', while the standard one was named 'Chambo'. Of all large fish species found in Lake Malawi, Bombe is the biggest and most scarce while Chambo is the commonest. Malawians easily adopted these names into their phone vocabulary because they were able to associate with them culturally.

However, despite its relevance to the language of advertising, the reflective approach may be criticised for presenting a tunnel view of meaning through its tendency to conceptualise language as a window through which people see the world. In other words, the approach assumes that the process of representation is independent of the extra-linguistic environment. To understand how a language represents a particular reality, one must "analyse the synchronic structures of [that] language without considering … anything beyond the kind of features which figure in linguistic descriptions" (Grace 1987: 8).

Thus, the meaning of an advertisement is expected to be found in the synchronic structures of the advertisement, which are a direct reflection of nothing but the reality which the symbols used in the advertisement reflect. This epistemological assumption triggers one fundamental question; why do different languages represent the same reality differently if meaning is intrinsic to things and the role of language is to reflect these things? The mapping view of language tries to rationalise this conceptual problem by arguing that the problem is not language *per se* but the fact that "[people's] access to knowledge of this world is imperfect; different peoples (speaking in different languages) have arrived at slightly different understandings of it" (Grace 1987: 6). Such rationalisation, however, contradicts the central idea of the reflective approach, namely that representations offer transparent windows on the world. As Fabian (1987) argues, representations can never truly depict reality because, from a philosophical point of view, the idea of representation itself presupposes a difference and distance between reality and whatever may be said to have been reproduced to represent it. It follows that it is impossible to reproduce reality accurately even if one earnestly desires to do so. What we call representations of reality (with assumptions of neutrality and completeness embedded within them) are simply fabricated representations that work for us, that is, they "[enable] us to work on the world together" (Fabian 1987: 754). Fabian rightly describes this fabricated reality as "privileged representations" because, although they do not accurately represent reality, they are privileged enough to represent our "subjective" view of reality, or what we think is close to reality.

Privileged representations are a typical feature of advertising in a world characterised by sophisticated computer-based technologies which tend to enhance the advertising producer's creative abilities to communicate abstract things. In 2010, for example, several advertisements on South Africa's SABC 1 television network were designed to communicate abstract qualities of human life. Soul Food, one of South Africa's most popular fast food restaurants, for example, produced an advertisement in which a person's craving for Soul Food chicken was represented by a monkey carried on a man's back whose size increases as the man's craving increases until the man has to leave his work place, go to a Soul Food restaurant, buy some chicken pieces and take a bite.

Although the advert successfully communicates the fact that Soul Food sells delicious fried chicken which people crave, the advertisement in no way reflects the reality of food cravings because there is no affinity between the monkey and the man's craving. Similarly, even if there were some resemblance between the appearance of the monkey and the craving, it would be unrealistic to claim that the rate at which the monkey's size increases is a true reflection of the rate at which the man's craving increases. As a matter of fact, viewers are not able to establish that the growing monkey represents the man's craving for soul food until the man bites a soul food chicken piece and the size of the monkey immediately dwindles drastically.

Constructionist Approach to Representation

The constructionist approach propounds the view that meaning is socially constructed because the material world in which things and people exist is separate from the symbolic systems that give it meaning (Hall 1997a: 25–26). As Potter (1996:98) explains:

> Reality enters into human practices by way of the categories and descriptions that are part of those practices. The world is not [already] categorised by God or nature in ways that [people] are forced to accept. It is constituted in one way or another as people talk about it, write about it, and argue about it.

Grace (1987) clarifies this point by observing that the construction of reality may be seen in both the way people select subject matter or objects and their characteristics that they want to talk about and how they talk about them. Therefore, unlike the reflective approach, the constructionist approach sees the effective environment as more cultural than natural. Consequently, it emphasises the role of cultural constructs in the way people understand and respond to the external world as opposed to the part played by the characteristics of that external world.

The fact that people select what they want to talk about and how they want to talk about it implies that they have imperfect access to knowledge of the real world. What they access is data about the world, which they theorise to create its models which language reflects in turn. The constructionist approach, however, recognises that there are limits to the social construction of meaning. The real world imposes some constraints on the process of representation, which consequently prevent people of different cultures from having completely random experiences (Grace 1987: 6). For example, although different cultures have different ways of understanding family relationships, their understanding of the roles of parents and children tend to have a lot in common. The constraints that the real world imposes on how language constructs reality suggest that the fundamental difference between the constructionist and reflective approaches is the way each interprets the extent to which language cannot construct that reality. The reflective approach is more rigid than the constructionist on this matter. This is a critical conceptual difference, according to Grace (1987: 6.):

> Differences of emphasis can be most important – fully as important as differences of empirical fact and even much more so. What is really important is what questions are effectively askable by those who take a particular view as their point of departure. The important differences between basic views of language (or of any other subject matter) are in what is regarded as problematic and what is taken for granted.

Relevance of the Constructionist Theory

The constructionist approach offers a dynamic explanation of the language of advertising because it problematises the process of representation in many ways that the reflective approach does not (Grace 1987: 10). For example, it assumes that there is no satisfactory way of separating what is said from how it is said. This is an important claim with regard to advertising representation because the true meaning of an advertisement lies in how the content is presented to the audience. This is why consumers sometimes accuse advertisers of misrepresenting certain social groups. The dynamism of the constructionist approach is also evident in its view that culture not only shapes language but also finds expression in it. As a result, language and culture are so inseparable from each other that it is impossible to say where one ends and where the other begins. In turn, this inseparability of language and culture implies that language-culture systems have individual ways of choosing what can be said and how to talk about it.

The constructionist approach, therefore, acknowledges the existence of language-culture systems which have significantly different views about the world, hence its relevance to the language of advertising. For instance, the language of advertising is different from that of journalism because of the linguistic choices that each genre has to make to generate meaning. The semiotic approach to advertising "suggests that the meaning of an [advertisement] does not float on the surface just waiting to be internalised by the viewer, but is built up out of the ways that different signs are organised and related to each other both within the [advertisement] and through external references to wider belief system" (Leiss et al. 1990: 201). An advertisement that promotes the rights of homosexuals in one country, for example, may not be easily transferable to another country with a different belief system.

Semiotics implies that advertising generates meaning first and foremost by transferring the meaning of one sign to another within the syntax of the given advertisement. This is also the case when any signs in a given advertisement are juxtaposed without necessarily being linked by a narrative. They are assumed to have the same meaning, even though the connection is random (Williamson 1978: 25). A popular South African "Surf Excel" television advertisement released in early 2000 juxtaposes the washing powder with a South African television celebrity named Chichi without necessarily linking the two by a narrative. The gorgeous Chichi catwalks down a street and comes to a building site where, to the astonishment of male bricklayers, she takes mortar and places it on a brick wall as if she is one of them. A voice-over then highlights Surf Excel's power to remove dirt and stains from clothes and to facilitate easy ironing.

Essentially, there is no link between Chichi and the washing powder except for the fact that what Chichi's gorgeous clothes mean to South Africans is what the washing powder is trying to mean to them too. Surf Excel earns the meaning that it shares with Chichi simply by association, although to the reader the relationship may seem a natural one. Williamson (1978: 25) sums up this thought when she notes that "the advertisement presents this transference of meaning to [the viewer] as a *fait accompli*, as though it were simply presenting two objects with the same meaning, but in fact it is only in the advertisement that this transference takes place".

Leiss et al. (1990) observe that the transfer of signs is incomplete within an advertisement, hence the need for the reader to complete it. For instance, the Surf Excel advertisement does not explicitly say that the clean wash and the easy ironing that one experiences with the washing powder are like the imagery the audience experiences through Chichi's gorgeous clothes. Williamson (1978) drives this point home when she points out that advertising leaves a gap, which the audience must fill so that they can become both listener and speaker, subject and object. The reader is given two signifiers and is required to make a signified by exchanging them. However, the linking work is not done in the advertisement but in its form, thereby drawing the reader into the transformational space between the units of the advertisement (25, 44). The transfer of meaning also cannot take place unless the first signifier already has significance to the audience (Leiss et al. 1990: 203). For example, the reader needs to know what Chichi already stands for within the world of television and glamour in the black community of South Africa; she is a symbol of gorgeousness. Advertising simply uses "an already existing mythological language or sign system and ... [appropriates] a relationship that exists in that system between signifier [Chichi] and signified [glamour, beauty] to speak of its product in terms of the same relationship" (Williamson 1978: 25). The transfer of meaning in advertisements also works through a process of differentiation. In reality, there is little difference between brands of the same category (Williamson 1978: 24). All Surf washing powders work more or less the same way. Chichi's image, together with the context in which it is portrayed, differentiates Surf Excel from all other brands within its range.

Williamson (1978: 25) uses the term "referent system" to refer to the sign system from which the product draws its image and argues that the sign is lifted out of it to be placed in the concerned advertisement so that it may be referred back to. In other words, referent systems are important because "they constitute the body of knowledge from which both advertisers and audiences draw their inspiration" (Leiss et al. 1990: 203). Writing from a pragmatics point of view, Tanaka (1998: 6) criticises semiotic's assumption about a pre-existing body of knowledge, arguing that it is misleading because it does not explain the criteria that members of the audience use to choose relevant information from a wide range of knowledge that they have at their disposal. However, a careful look at Tanaka's argument shows that it wrongly assumes that it is the job of the semiotician to predict exactly which personal experience a given reader will use to interpret a given message. On the contrary, from a semiotics point of view, it does not matter which experience or knowledge a reader uses to decode the meaning of a given advertisement as long as one keeps in mind that the reader's socio-cultural knowledge and experience play an important role in how they read media messages.

That advertising uses referent systems to create meaning implies that it generates meaning through both denotation and connotation (Leiss et al. 1990: 205). For example, denotatively, the Surf Excel advertisement tells the reader that Surf Excel is a powerful washing powder that leaves the washing looking gorgeous, like Chichi's clothes. However, at the connotative level, it tells the reader that Chichi is a symbol of gorgeousness. Furthermore, the fact that all the bricklayers appearing in this advertisement are not only male but are also perplexed when they see Chichi placing the mortar on the wall tells the reader that bricklaying is a man's job. All this information does not come from within the text. This is why Hall (1973: 176) observes that "connotative codes are the configuration of meaning which permits a sign to signify, in addition to its denotative reference, other, additional implied meanings .... Codes of connotation are more open ended".

Tanaka (1998) also contends that the distinction between denotation and connotation is so unclear that any attempt to separate the two is misleading. He particularly stresses that perception is not independent of cultural knowledge and adds that this is supported by cognitive psychology's view that perceptual systems transform information from sensory representations into conceptual representations:

> The central thought processes integrate information derived from the senses with information stored in memory, determining what is actually perceived. Thus even the processing of information derived from the senses is affected by cultural knowledge (Tanaka 1998: 2).

Tanaka's argument, however, has limited applicability. For example, a person may be able to know that a black image of a cell phone with a red diagonal line across it placed at the entrance of a banking hall means that cell phones are prohibited in the hall. However, due to cultural knowledge, the person may wrongly think that they are prohibited to control noise rather than crime.

The validity of the distinction between denotation and connotation in the language of advertising is supported by theories of market segmentation and resonance within advertising. The theory of market segmentation conceptualises audiences as being fragmented into small market segments that require specialised operative codes due to their cultural differences. As Leiss et al. (1990: 208) observe:

> Advertisers like working with narrowly defined groups rather than with diffuse, broadly based general audiences. The more narrowly one can define an audience and the more specialised the knowledge one can draw from, the more certain one can be of speaking to people in a language they will respond to.

Market segmentation is usually based on the target audience's income, geographical location, social-economic status, usage patterns, brand loyalty, and lifestyle (Jhally 1989). Advertisers use psychographic research to identify lifestyle patterns of the intended audience by combining their demographic data with various well-established psychological attributes. Psychographic research would, for example, be interested to establish how people spend their working time and leisure time, how they relate with their immediate environment and how they view important social issues (Plummer 1979: 125-6). For example, it may not be worthwhile to use images of rugby players in an advertisement targeted at African residents of KwaMashu, an area on the periphery of Durban, who spend their leisure time watching football rather than rugby.

The resonance theory of communication recognises the crucial role played by shared socio-cultural knowledge and experience in the creation of meaning.

It argues that advertisements are effective when they evoke the personal experiences of viewers. Therefore, the critical task of advertisers "is to design a package of stimuli so that it resonates with information already stored within an individual and thereby induce the desired learning or behavioural effect" (Jhally 1989: 121). There is no doubt that some of this knowledge is cultural. However, resonance is not synonymous with reflection. In essence "advertising draws its materials from the experiences of the audience, but it reformulates them in a unique way. It does not reflect meaning. [It] rather reconstitutes it" (Jhally 1989: 129). There is consensus among scholars that "the images in commercials are of idealised rather than typical people" (Furnham and Farragher 2000: 2). As Leiss et al. (1990: 200) observe:

> Advertising indeed draws deeply from the dispositions, hopes and concerns of its audiences, but it reformulates them to suit its own purposes, not reflecting meaning but rather reconstituting it. Looking at advertisements today is a bit like walking through a carnival hall of mirrors, where the elements of our ordinary lives are magnified and exaggerated but are still recognisable.

A television advertisement about Wimpy "Big Mouth Burger" shows a man opening his mouth wide with the help of his fingers in preparing to eat the burger. This is a typical exaggeration of how one prepares to eat a big burger, but the action is recognisable by the audience because it more or less taps into their personal knowledge and/or experience of burgers. In his classic discussion of how advertising represents gender roles, the American sociologist Erving Goffman (1979: vii) articulates a similar point:

> Advertisements depict for us not necessarily how we actually behave as men and women but how we think men and women behave. This depiction serves the social purpose of convincing us that this is how men and women are, or want to be, or should be, not only in relation to themselves but in relation to each other.

Moreover, the language of advertising constructs social reality through its effort to address large numbers of people within a short time. Ideally, advertisers are capable of designing advertisements that can interpellate each person individually. However, they cannot do this due to resource constraints. Their option, therefore, is to produce very short advertisements that draw from the dreams, desires and aspirations of thousands or millions of consumers. They do this by drawing from what they believe is knowledge that they share with the audience, which in turn helps them interpret the way the audience thinks (Leiss et al. 1990: 200). However, practically speaking, there is no way a thirty-second advertisement can mirror the shared experiences and dreams of so many people. Consequently, the images that are seen in advertisements are merely a reconstituted reality. As

Furnham and Farragher (2000: 2) point out, "due to time constraints imposed upon them, and the need for effective communication of the advertiser message … some degree of stereotyping is inevitable". Giaccardi (1995: 113) sums it up by pointing out that advertising has three fundamental aspects, namely a reality referred to, a new perspective and a communicative aim. These three aspects enable advertisers to look at reality and make deliberate decisions to present it in a particular way to meet their goal of persuading the audience to purchase a given product or service.

Conclusion

Advertising is often perceived as a business, thereby automatically divorcing it from critical cultural studies. This chapter has argued that advertising has rich cultural aspects which can enrich the study of the genre. The discussion has shown how the language of advertising constructs meaning. As Jhally (1987: 142) observes:

> advertising absorbs and fuses a variety of symbolic practices and discourses. The substance and images woven into advertising messages are appropriated and distilled from an unbounded range of cultural references [and recombined artfully] around the theme of consumption.

In this context, it is recommended that the three approaches to advertising representation discussed in this chapter should be included in advertising curricula to guide the theory and practice of advertising. In this way, practitioners can be empowered with the knowledge and skills for developing culturally sensitive advertisements. As already shown, culturally insensitive advertisements can cost advertisers time, money and hard-earned reputation.

The fact that this discussion has shown that the intentional and reflective approaches cannot fully explain advertising representations does not mean advertising should have nothing to do with them. On the contrary, the two approaches offer useful cultural insights which may form the theoretical basis of lower-level curriculum for professional advertising training, while the constructionist approach may inform the advanced level.

References

Barthes, R. 1972. The Imagination of the Sign. In R. Barthes. *Critical Essays*. Evanston IL: Northwestern University

Chimombo, P. F. and R.L. Roseberry. 1998. *The Power of Discourse: An Introduction to Discourse Analysis*. London: Lawrence Erlbaum.

Eco, U. 1976. *A Theory of Semiotics*. Indiana: Indiana University Press.

Fabian, J. 1987. Presence and Representation: The Other in Anthropological Writing. *Critical Inquiry* 16: 753–72.

Furnham, A. and E. Farragher. 2000. Cross-cultural Content Analysis of Sex-Role Stereotyping in Television Advertisements: A comparison between Great Britain and New Zealand. *Journal of Broadcasting and Electronic Media* 44 (3). http://web10.epnet.com (Retrieved 07/05/2012)

Giaccardi, C. 1995. Television Advertising and Representation of Social Reality. *Theory Culture and Society: Explorations in Critical Social Science* 12 (1): 109–131.

Goffman, E. 1979. *Gender Advertisements*. Cambridge, MA: Harvard University Press.

Grace, G. 1987. *The Linguistic Construction of Reality*. New York: Croom Helm.

Hall S. 1973. The Determinations of News Photographs. In Stanley Cohen and Jock Young, eds. *The Manufacture of News: Social Problems, Deviance and the Mass Media*. London: Constable.

Hall, S. 1997a. The Work of Representation. In S. Hall, ed. *Representation: Cultural Representation and Signifying Practices*. London: Sage and Open University Press.

Hall, S. 1997b. Introduction. In S. Hall, ed. *Representation: Cultural Representation and Signifying Practices*. London: Sage and Open University Press.

IRIN. 2002. Conservative Malawi Grapples with Sex Education. http://www.irinnews.org/Report/39867/MALAWI-Conservative-Malawi-grapples-with-sex-education (Retrieved 07/05/2012).

Jhally, S. 1987. *The Codes of Advertising: Fetishism and the Political Economy of Meaning in Consumer Society*. London: Pinter.

Leiss, W., S. Kline, and S. Jhally. 1990. *Social Communication in Advertising: Persons, Products and Images of Well Being*. Second Edition. New York: Routledge.

Platts, M. 1979. *Ways of Meaning: An Introduction to a Philosophy of Language*. London: Routledge and Kegan Paul.

Plummer, J. 1979. Lifestyle Patterns. In J. Wright, ed. *The Commercial Connection: Advertising and the American Mass Media*. New York: Dell.

Potter, J. 1996. *Representing Reality: Discourse, Rhetoric, and Social Construction*. London, Thousand Oaks, New Delhi: Sage Publications

Tanaka, K. 1998. *Advertising Language: A Pragmatic Approach to Advertisements in Britain and Japan*. London: Routledge.

Williamson, J. 1978. *Decoding Advertisements: Ideology and Meaning in Advertising*. London: Boyars.

CHAPTER 3

LINGUISTIC APPROACHES TO MEANING-MAKING IN ADVERTISING

JULIUS ABIOYE ADEYEMO

Introduction

This chapter explores the linguistic strategies of meaning-making in advertising using selected print advertisements as case studies. The various linguistic devices employed by copywriters to convey or project their thematic preoccupations (which may either be implicit or explicit to the audience) are discussed. Writing on the language of advertising, Katherina (1979: 24) observes that the language of advertising is not a careless exercise but a carefully planned attempt to influence a group of persons to behave in a definite way. To accomplish this goal, she observes, the language of advertising must be pictorial, emotional, suggestive, expressive, actual, common and credible. Obviously, advertisers are aware of the power of language. This chapter examines the substance and the situation levels of linguistic categories in some selected Nigerian print advertisements in order to appreciate the linguistic imports of those ad pay-offs.

Advertising, according to the Advertising Practitioners Council of Nigeria (APCON) (1988: 2) "is a form of communication through the media about products, services or ideas paid for by an identified sponsor". Similarly, John (cited in Adebayo 1996: 1) asserts that advertising is the art of disseminating marketing information through various media of communication at the expense of the company for the purpose of increasing (or maintaining) effective demand facilitating the sale of specific goods and services. We can therefore say that advertising is a form of communication intended to inform, influence and persuade consumers to take a desired action, that is to buy, accept or have a positive view of what is advertised. According to the APCON Code (1988: 1), the following are the key functions of advertising in Nigeria:

- Attracting attention to a product, service or idea, that is, making it known.
- Getting the target audience to accept the product, service or idea by developing interest in it.
- Sustaining these positive dispositions and attaining constant acquisition, that is, continued patronage.
- Evaluating and reviewing the above so as to maintain performance.

In a nutshell, when advertising is created, planned and executed, it not only creates awareness but leads to new and improved products or services. This brings about healthy competition, leading to mass production, high profits, industrial growth, and above all, more jobs for the masses.

Language and Advertising

The linguistic model used in this chapter is systemic functional grammar (SFG), a neo-Firthian school of thought developed by MAK Halliday in 1961. My choice of the Hallidayan model is predicated upon its explanatory and descriptive adequacy. More importantly, in SFG, language is seen as a resource for meaning-making. Meaning, to the systemists, is function in context. Language, as a form of behaviour, reveals what we do with a purpose as determined by the socio-cultural milieu of the speech community.

With language, human language can create or destroy, convince or confuse, persuade or dissuade, acclaim or defame, unite or disunite (Crystal 2004). Consequently, language can be manipulated to achieve either positive or negative ends. Firth (1935 cited Crystal 2004) argues that language is a way of behaving and making others behave, while Austin (1962) observes that language is never used in a vacuum; utterances always perform actions, which can be assertive, directive or informative, and, in turn, the listener will either be persuaded, encouraged, discouraged, warned or entertained.

Advertising is a field of discourse where language use is one of the principal tools for bringing goods or services to the knowledge of consumers in order to induce desirable actions. The language of advertising, therefore, must be persuasive and emphatic. Language, in this context, is the paramount factor in marketing success. Thus, Dyer (cited in Olapade 1995: 1) observes that the language of advertising has a "vast power" in shaping perceptions, pointing out that the language used in advertisements is often aimed at "sensationalism, propaganda, censorship, indoctrination, brain washing and perhaps hoodwinking". Do advertisers therefore use language to lie? To answer this simply, we can say that what advertisers aim at is to win the sympathy of their prospective buyers through the power of words and that language in advertising, as in every sphere of life, can be manipulated to the extent of deceiving others.

The language of advertising is often comparative in order to bring out the higher quality of a product, especially when a similar product or service is offered by a competing brand. Hillary (1998: 243) confirms that the language of advertising "must be impressive and simply irresistible using comparative and superlative adjectives" (so, for example, "MTN, Your better connection", "Michelin – tougher safer for longer", "New Blueband margarine – more nourishing – Tastes even better" etc.).

Brevity is another feature of advertising. Brevity helps to sustain the interest of the audience and to make a lasting impression. The following ad pay-offs illustrate the point: "Etisalat, now, you are talking", "Starcomms: We speak your language", "Honder E ½: durable and fuel efficient, less fuel, longer rides." From these three slogans, it can be seen that advertisers give brief information about the products or services being advertised.

In a nutshell, the language of advertising is always carefully chosen. It may be descriptive, assertive, convincing and appealing. Consequently, connotative, words, alliterative phrases, hyperbolic phrases and imperatives are common features of the language of advertising. The result, as Strouse (2000) concludes, "is that the language of advertisement has a powerful force ... [and] shapes consumer motivations, life style and product choice and makes a consumer give what it says a special prominence in his mind".

Phonographological Devices in Advertisements

Osoba (1999) argues that the use of sound effects (the phonic) is analogous to graphology in underscoring messages. In advertising, the use of certain phonological devices such as repetition of sounds (alliteration and assonance) are pertinent features used to create musical effects and aesthetic appeals as well as evoking certain ideas or emotions.

Alliteration is the repetition of the same consonant sound at the beginning or end of two or more words in succession. As a literary device, it is used to achieve acoustic and rhythmic effects. An advert payoff in *Tell* magazine (No 18, May 3, 1999) illustrates the device very clearly: "Top Tea, Top quality, Top Taste, Top Flavour, Top Aroma". Here, the repetition of the voiceless alveolar plosive /t/ seven times in word-initial position (with the voiceless bilabial plosive /p/ repeated five times in word-final position) creates a strong effect of alliteration denoting a sense of the "pleasantness" and pleasure to be derived from the brand of tea being advertised.

Assonance is the repetition of internal vowel sounds, which creates a musical or melodious effect. The *Tell* magazine slogan above also uses assonance through the repetition of the open lax back vowels /symbol/ five times, thereby creating a sort of melody. In the following example from the same magazine (No. 19, Nov 17, 1997) "St. Moritz – The cool, smooth choice", there is a repetition of the high back tense vowel /u:/ in "cool and smooth", which conveys the alleged cooling and stimulating effect of the tobacco product.

Another important phonographological device is the pun, a play on words which has the effect of inducing laughter. Thus, the slogans "Glo with pride" (*Tell*, No. 38, Sept. 22, 2003) and "Let Lipton provide that hospitali-tea (*Tell*, No. 45, Nov 5, 2001) use puns to create humour and also to make the slogans conversational.

Graphological Devices

The question mark (?) is employed in advertising to request the reader's choice. The semantic import of a question mark expresses not only the interrogative but also a degree of surprise, though the questions in advertisements are usually rhetorical, for example, "Wouldn't you rather bank with us?" (*Guardian*, December 21, 2003) and "Why compromise? You can now afford the whole picture" (*Guardian*, November 26, 2002) In the first of these examples, we see an expression of great surprise as financial firm asks a rhetorical question of a seemingly confused person who, perhaps, is in a dilemma about which bank to open an account with. The question comes at the right time and is meant to invite the confused would-be customer. In the second example, we see a thought-provoking question addressed to any office or business which has hitherto compromised quantity for quality when printing. The slogan is a clarion call to acquire a quality printer (i.e. the particular printer being advertised).

Apostrophes (') are a graphological device used to show omissions and contractions. They both enhance space management and make advert payoffs look conversational, for example, "Intercellular, let's get connected" (*Punch*, February 25, 2003), "My little girl's getting married" (*Vanguard*, January 15, 2003) and "Wouldn't you rather bank with us? (*Guardian*, December 21, 2003). Similarly, abbreviations are used frequently in advertisements not just to save space but also as memorable shorthand for a company's name or for a product or service, for example, "MTN, your best connection" (*Guardian*, November 26, 2002) and "Habib Nigeria Bank Ltd: HELP from Habib (*Punch*, April 1, 2003, where MTN stands for Mobile Telecommunication Network (the company name) and HELP stands for Habib Easy Leasing Partnership (the financial product being advertised).

Defiant spellings are used to foreground a message and get attention. Such stylistic deviations are meant to forcefully draw the attention of readers, for example, the APTECH "Xperience" (*Guardian,* November 26, 2003) and the Intercellular slogan "Let's get connected, you and 'i'" (*Punch*, February 25, 2003).

Lexico-Semantic Devices

Lexical items in advertisements are often carefully selected to give clues to the advertisers' intentions. More importantly, lexical items are selected, organised and deployed to get the reader's attention. Gregory and Caroll (1978) point out that variation in language use yields diatypic varieties. The dimensions of such variations are contextually categorised as field, tenor and mode of discourse.

In advertisements, the types of product or service being advertised determine the lexical choices. In our data, we have identified some semantic fields which include automobile products, telecommunication services, food and beverages and banking services. An assemblage of lexical items found in common use in the data in each field is shown in Table 3.1.

Table 3.1: Lexical Items in Common Use in Four Semantic Fields

A	B	C	D
Automobile products	Telecommunication services	Food and beverages	Banking services
Efficient	Talk	Aroma	Investment
Performance	Connection	Taste	Insurance
Comfort	Speak	Edible	Retirement
Elegance	Language	Nourishing	Pension
Safety	Powers	Delicious	Confidence

As Table 3.1 shows, the lexical sets in advertisements for automobile products are often chosen to reflect comfort, durability and utility, for example, "Don't just ask for a water tanker, ask for the efficient Mercedes-Benz" (*Punch* Tuesday, April 1, 2003), "Smooth, ultra-quiet performance of the Sephia" (*Punch,* December 12, 2002), "Toyota Corolla: See the difference, Feel the difference, Drive the difference" (*Guardian,* October 9, 2003). In advertisements for telecommunication services, on the other hand, the lexical choices are often made to suggest promise, reliance and prompt services, for example, "MTN your best connection"

(*Guardian*, November 26, 2003), "ECONET Wireless – inspired to change your world" (*Punch*, December 12, 2003), "Starcomms, we speak your language" (*Punch*, April, 2003), "Intercellular, the freedom to choose" (*Punch*, February 25, 2003) and "Globacom, people, power, possibilities" (*Guardian*, January 5, 2003) .

The lexical choices in food and beverage advertising are aimed at whetting the readers' appetites by making the products seem irresistible and creating pictures of delicious meals, for example, "Gulder, the ultimate beer" (*Vanguard*, October 23, 2003), "St. Moritz, enjoy smooth, fresh taste" (*Tell*, No. 17, December, 2000), "Maltina, catch the excitement" (*Punch*, December 12, 2002), "Soya oil, edible soya oil – a nourishing rich and free from cholesterol" (*Tell*, No. 18, May 1999).

Conclusion

The language of advertisements is strategically and creatively packaged in print media to persuade the publics to which it is targeted. The data in this chapter focused mainly on two levels of language, substance and situation, and showed that all phonographological details are devices of meaning-making in advertisement. Finally, at the situation level, lexical choices are targeted at certain semantic fields. This multidimensionality of meaning-making in advertisements is considered necessary for advertisements to successfully perform their perlocutionary acts of persuasion.

References

Adebayo, O.O. 1996. *Integrated Approach to Advertising*. Lagos: Right-Time Computers.
APCON. 1988. *The Code of Advertising Practice*. Lagos: Advertising Practitioner's Council of Nigeria.
Austin, J.L. 1962. *How to Do Things with Words,* New York: OUP.
Crystal, D. 1997. *The Cambridge Encyclopedia of Language*. Cambridge, CUP.
Gregory M. and S. Carroll. 1978. *Language and Situation: Language Varieties and their Social Situation*. London: Routledge and Kegan Paul.
Hillary, C.C. 1998. *Principle and Practice of Advertising,* Lagos: MELAG Ltd.
Katherina, O.N. 1979. *Language Use in Advertising.* India: Jhafa Publications.
Olapade, F. 1995. A Stylistic Analysis of Newspaper Advertisements. Unpublished BA Long Essay.
Osoba, G. 1999. *Linguistics and Literature,* Lagos: LASU.
Strouse, M.G. 2000. *Advertising: An introdiction*. London: New Print Books.

CHAPTER 4

ADVERTISING, SEMIOTICS AND STRATEGIC BRAND MANAGEMENT

NNAMDI TOBECHUKWU EKEANYANWU & NELSON OKORIE

Introduction

The phenomenal growth of advertising in the 21st century has helped to sustain a consumer culture and create new markets. Advertising has been regarded as a marketing communication catalyst that aids productivity, but, as White (2000) has noted, it is also an ideal tool to build strong brands and create unshakeable consumer loyalty. Generally speaking, the purpose of advertising is to inform customers about the existence of a brand or to help reinforce commitment to that brand. Advertising consists of a series of related, well-turned and carefully placed adverts that reinforce personal selling and sale promotion efforts. It may communicate information about a sale promotion or announce a public relations event. Ultimately, it helps to maintain loyalty to the brand, offer customer service and reinforce existing bonds, relationships and commitments between the customer and the advertiser. The task of *competitive* advertising is to seduce one brand's loyal users and persuade them to consume one's own brand.

The use of semiotics in promoting advertised messages is as an ideal tool for reaching large numbers of people economically. In the European market, there is an increasing awareness of the use of semiotics in advertising. This awareness is evident in the large number of articles in marketing and advertising journals which mention or discuss signs and semiotics as marketing communication tools. In 1989, the first Marketing and Semiotics Symposium was held in Copenhagen. This symposium was arranged by the Marketing Institute of the Copenhagen Business School and attended by various people from universities and business schools. The event demonstrated the new prominence of semiotics in the advertising industry, especially in advanced capitalist nations.

Since the inauguration of the modern advertising profession in Pennsylvania in 1841, when Volney B. Palmer opened his advertising agency, advertising methods have changed radically. Advertising no longer simply presents the benefits of a product, it creates an image for that product. In the 21st century, advertising is to strategic brand management what branding is to total product packaging and image. The main objective of this chapter is to examine the use of semiotics in advertising and brand management with particular reference to how semiotics affects strategic brand management. I discuss the various facets of brand management and the relationship of brand management to advertising and review the theory of semiotics as a backup link to its relationship to advertising. I begin with a general discussion of the nature of advertising and the advertising business before clarifying the relationship between advertising and brand management, then give an overview of the concept of semiotics, with an emphasis on the relationship between signs and meaning in theories of semiotics, particularly in Umberto Eco's work. This is followed by a discussion of the relationship between advertising, semiotics and strategic brand management. I conclude with some recommendations on the use of semiotics as a strategic brand management tool.

The Nature and Business of Advertising

Doghudje (1985) observes that advertising is a marketing communication tool whose aim is to build preference for advertised brands or services. Rossiter and Percy (1997:3) define advertising as a "relatively indirect form of persuasion ... designed to create favourable mental impressions that turn the mind towards purchase". The British Institute of Practitioners in Advertising (IPA) points out that the purpose of advertising is to create "the most persuasive possible selling message to the right prospect for the lowest possible cost" (cited in Rossiter and Percy 1997: 40). The American Marketing Association defines it as "any paid form of impersonal presentation and promotion of ideas, goods and services by an identified sponsor." Thus, advertising includes any form of paid strategic communication that is commercially oriented and aimed at informing, reminding and persuading the market of the existence and availability of a product, brand or service with the ultimate purpose of encouraging patronage and use.

White (2000) emphasises the complexity of advertising, noting how it interacts with numerous marketing concerns, including personal selling, product development, branding, merchandising and research. Cole (1979) categorises the numerous benefits of advertising to the advertiser as follows:

- announcing a product or service
- attracting buyers
- launching a brand
- promoting a public service course
- introducing new packages
- maintaining sales of certain packages
- increasing turnover and profits
- encouraging patronage and use of a particular product, brand or service.

The pivotal role of advertising, however, is to find new customers by generating sales leads, a concept used to refer to potential customers who have been identified as having a need for or interest in a product or service and the ability to purchase it.

In organisational management, determining the advertising objective is essential to the overall productivity and efficiency of products or services. Generally, the advertising objective should be realistic, precise, measureable and consistent with the firm's overall marketing and communication objectives. Setting objectives enhances the firm's ability to evaluate the effectiveness of its advertising.

Across the globe, companies use one or more of five promotional alternatives: advertising, personal selling, sale promotion, public relations and direct marketing. Three of these (advertising, sale promotion and public relations) are often used for mass selling because they are used with a group of prospective buyers (Berkowitz and Rudelius 2000). Furthermore, advertising supports other promotional efforts. It may communicate information about sale promotion or announce public relations events.

Importantly, advertising offers some significant advantages over other promotional techniques. The first is cost; advertising is relatively cheaper than other promotional alternatives. Advertising's second advantage is ease of repetition, which is often needed to get the message across effectively. Third, many consumers assign some level of prestige to advertising in the media. The simple fact is that when a product is advertised it has a better advantage in the marketplace (Jefkins 1998, Daramola 2003). However, scholars have also argued that advertising has several drawbacks within the context of the promotional mix. Belch and Belch (2003) list the most important of these as follows:

- Advertising cannot provide direct feedback, unlike personal selling and public relations
- Advertising is difficult to personalise

- Advertising cannot always motivate customers to action as effectively as personal selling will normally do.

Advertising and Brand Management

Advertising is a significant part of a range of marketing communication efforts that can support a brand (White 2000). A brand is any name, term, symbol, sign, design or underlying combination of these. Michael Jannini, Executive VP of Brand Management, Marriott International, defines a brand as follows:

> A brand is a promise. Your image, your message and your past performance should be clear and consistent indicators of the service you will deliver in the future, so people believe it is in their sincere best interest to come back to your brand time and time again (cited in White 2000: 121).

Brand management, according to Lindstrom (2005), is the art of creating and maintaining a brand. A brand must carry a "promise" that a product or service has a certain quality that makes it special or unique. It is this promise which appeals to the core desires of the consumer and releases a series of processes towards the eventual purchase of the product. The promise creates a bond that defines the relationship between the advertiser and the consumer. Brand management is also regarded as the application of marketing techniques to a specific product line or brand. It seeks to increase the product's perceived value to the customer and thereby increase brand franchise and equity. Marketers see a brand as an implied promise which may increase sales by making a favourable comparison with competing products. It may also enable the manufacturer to charge more for the product. The value of the brand is determined partly by the amount of profit it generates for the manufacturer and partly by the amount of money consumers are prepared to pay for any of the brand's manifestations. This value can result from any combination of increased sales and increased price, and/or reduced cost of goods sold and/or reduced or more efficient marketing investment. All of these may improve the profitability of a brand. In this regard, brand management is often viewed in organisations as a broader and more strategic role than marketing alone.

The annual list of the world's most valuable brands, published by *Interbrand* and *Business Week*, indicates that the market value of companies often consists largely of brand equity. Research in 2000 by McKinsey and Company, a global consulting firm, suggests that strong, well-leveraged brands produce higher returns to shareholders than weaker, narrower brands. Taken together, this means that brands seriously impact shareholder value, which ultimately makes branding a

Chief Executive Officer's key responsibility. A good brand name is particularly important and should be:

- Protected (or at least protectable) under the trademark law
- Easy to pronounce
- Easy to remember
- Easy to recognise
- Easy to translate into all languages in the markets where the brand will be used
- An attention-getter
- Suggestive of product benefits or usage
- Suggestive of the company or product image
- Able to distinguish the product's placing relative to the competition
- Attractive
- Able to stand out among a group of other brands.

Advertising is an important determinant for brand image, along with the physical characteristics of the brand, the price charged and the satisfaction that is derived from the brand. Consumers' knowledge about a brand is often quite high, particularly when the decision-making process involves a lot of fact-finding and comparisons between alternatives. As Jobber (2003: 15) points out:

> An analytic framework of a brand can be used to dissect the current position in the market place and form the basis of a new brand positioning strategy. The strength of the brand position in the market place is built on six elements i.e. brand domain, brand heritage, brand value, brand asset, brand personality and brand reflection.

Belch and Belch (2003) maintain that a brand must have a brand domain. This means that the brand must target a market where it competes with others in its area of offerings. Also, there must be a brand heritage, by which is meant the background of the brand and its culture, how it has achieved success over its lifetime. Brand asset makes the brand distinctive from competing brands through symbols, feature images and relationships, and brand value stands for the core values and characteristics of the brand in the market. Other important details are brand personality (the 'character' of the brand described in terms of other entities such as people, animal or objects) and brand reflection which refers to the ideas the brand wants to communicate to its consumers.

Understanding the need to develop the equity of a brand underlines the importance of brand management. Basically, brand equity refers to the value of an organisation's compared to competitor's brands. Hawkins et al (2003) note:

> Brand equity is the value consumers assign a brand above the functional characteristics of the product. Generally, brand equity is nearly synonymous with reputation of the brand. However, the term equity refers to economic value; thus, brands with good reputation have the potential for high level of brand equity, whereas unknown brands with weak or negative reputation have not.

Kerin and Berkowitz (2004) thus call brand equity the added value a given brand name gives to a product beyond the fundamental benefits provided. Brand equity, therefore, is essentially what drives buyers to purchase the brand as opposed to buying other brands.

In brand management, there are various types of brands which can be used in brand communication (Belch and Belch 2003, Jobber 2003). An 'economy brand' in brand communication refers to a brand targeted to a high-priced elasticity demand market segment. Another type of brand is the 'fighting brand', which is a brand created specifically to counter a competitive threat. For example, West African Milk Company (WAMCO) created Peak Choco to compete with Cowbell chocolate. A third type of brand is referred to as 'family branding'. This type of brand is usually used when there are several related products. This is the main reason why you can easily find this type of branding in multi-product companies. For example, LG is the name of a company that manufactures electronic products. It uses its name for all its products. However, we should note that there are also companies that prefer to give their products different brand names. This is referred to as 'individual branding'.

There are various kinds of strategies used to reach target markets (Bovee and Arens 1992, Belch and Belch 2003). These strategies are usually determined by the nature of the brand in its life cycle, that is, introduction, growth, maturity and decline stages (Bovee and Arens 1992, Jobber 2003, Jefkins 1998). One of the major brand strategies adopted by brand specialists and advertising experts is the generic strategy. The generic strategy is best employed when the brand is a leader in the category or when an increase in product category sales would benefit the brand. This approach forgoes claims of superiority or brand differences in favour of promoting the category.

On the other hand, co-branding is a common brand strategy in which two or more brands work together to market their products. For example, Unilevers' franchise, popularly known as Mr. Biggs, used co-branding with Coca-Cola in 2009.

Using 'brand characters' is another common brand strategy used in advertising and promotion. Brand characters refer to the use of characters or personalities to promote and reflect a particular brand. For example, Michael Power was a brand character for Guinness Nigeria between 1998 and 2002 in Nigeria. Fido Dido was a brand character for Seven-Up. Another important brand strategy is the resonance approach, which uses experiences with which consumers can identify on an emotional level and then places the product within the experiential context (Belch and Belch 2003).

The Concept of Semiotics

The term semiotics (also referred to as "semiology") derives from the Greek word semeion meaning "sign". It is also known as the "study of signs". Ferdinand de Saussure (1857–1913), a Swiss linguist, gave the subject its name when he first taught the course in general linguistics at Geneva University (Fiske 1990). Another key figure in the early development of semiotics was the American Charles Sanders Peirce (1839–1914). He constructed a triangular model to illustrate the relationship he termed "sign-object-interpretant". According to Peirce's model, a sign is anything from which meaning is generated. Saussure, however, proposed a different dyadic model. He saw the sign as a physical object with meaning which consists of a signifier and a signified. The signifier is the material vehicle for the sign, while the signified can be understood as the mental concept it represents, which is common to all members of the same culture who share the same language (Fiske 1990). In essence, semiotics is the study of sign action (semiosis). As such, it is a purely human phenomenon. All life forms engage in semiosis because they all use signs. However, only humans engage in inquiry into semiosis. Deely (1990: 5) thus observes that "[a]t the heart of semiotics is the realization that the whole of human experience, without exception, is an interpretive structure mediated and sustained by signs". Importantly, signs have three aspects: iconic, indexical, and symbolic (Eco 1979, Deely 2001). The interpretive aspect of a sign may emphasise any one aspect of the sign, so that a sign may be considered primarily an icon, primarily an index, or primarily a symbol. Thus, the association of the concept "deer" or "food" with tracks in the wood by some third party is symbolic, even though the relationship of the deer to the tracks is indexical and one may consider the indexical aspect of the sign the important relationship if one is tracking the animal. These aspects of the sign are further illustrated in Figure 4.1.

Semiotics is, therefore, a theoretical approach to communication which aims to establish widely applicable principals for the study of anything which stands for something else in some respect or capacity (Deely 2001). Signs can take the form of words, images, sounds or objects. Every medium used, whether television, radio or magazine advertisement, is constrained by the various channels that it

Figure 4.1: Aspects of the Sign

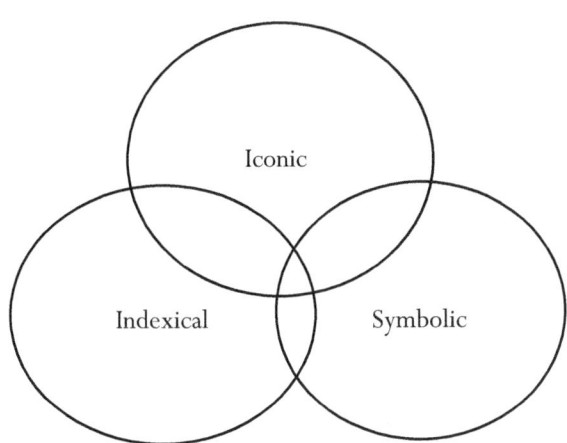

uses. For instance, even in the medium of language, words fail in attempting to represent certain experiences. Different media provide different frameworks for representing experience, but all media are semiotic systems (Eco 1976).

Sign and Meaning in Semiotics Theories

Umberto Eco's *A Theory of Semiotics* (1976) is regarded as one of the earliest seminal works which conceptualised semiotics into a theoretical model. Eco's approach regards the meaning of signals or signs as independent of the objects (i.e. things or events) to which they refer. He rejects the notion that iconic signs must be likenesses of their objects (Scott 2004). In his critique of Eco, A. Scott (2004: 1) explains:

> Eco's argument that the meaning of signals or signs is not necessarily determined by whether they refer to actual objects … [posits] that the existence of objects to which signals or signs may correspond is not a necessary condition for their signification.

As Scott observes (2004: 2):

> Eco criticizes the notion that a typology of signs may clarify the nature of sign function, arguing instead that any typology of signs may fail to explain how different kinds of signs may share the same modes of production. Eco thus argues that the correct approach to developing a unified semiotic theory should not be to propose a typology of signs but should be to provide a method of investigating

how sign-vehicles may function as signs and to provide a means of understanding how sign-vehicles may be produced and interpreted. According to Eco, a general semiotic theory should include not only a theory of how codes may establish rules for systems of signification but a theory of how signs may be produced and interpreted.

A theory of codes may, therefore, clarify aspects of signification, while a theory of sign-production may clarify aspects of communication. Eco defines "signification" as the semiotic event whereby a sign stands for something, while he defines "communication" as the transmission of information from a source to a destination. Communication is made possible by the existence of a code, or by a system of signification. Without a code or system of signification, there is no set of rules to determine how the expression of signs is to be correlated with their content. The use of a code or system of signification in order to correlate the expression and content of signs may be necessary in order to establish any form of communication (Scott 2004).

Scott (2004: 1) adds that, according to Eco, a complete theory of sign-production requires three elements:

> [A] theory of sign-production should include not only a theory of communication but a theory of "mentions" (i.e. referring acts) and a theory of communicational acts. A theory of communication may explain how information may be transmitted from a source (or content-continuum) through a channel (or expression-continuum) to a destination. A theory of "mentions" may explain how signs may be used for naming things and for making statements about actual situations. A theory of communicational acts may explain how a sender may transmit verbal or non-verbal messages to an addressee.

Eco insists that there is a "referential fallacy" in classical theories of semiotics. This is the false assumption that the meaning of a sign-vehicle is determined by its referent (i.e. by the object to which the sign-vehicle refers), as well as an "extensional fallacy", which is the false assumption that the meaning of a sign-vehicle is determined by its extension (i.e. by the class of objects to which the sign-vehicle refers). According to Eco, both the referential fallacy and the extensional fallacy may distort a theory of codes by promoting the false assumption that the object of a sign, or the class of objects to which the sign refers, is a necessary condition for the sign's meaning or signification (Scott 2004).

Eco also argues that the content and not the referent of a sign is the location of the sign's meaning. The meaning of a sign is a cultural unit, in that the meaning of every sign is culturally defined. A cultural unit may be defined as a semantic unit (i.e. a content unit or "sememe"), in that it may be analysed into its elementary semantic components (i.e. its "semes" or semantic markers). A cultural unit may also be defined as a syntactic unit (i.e. an expression unit or "lexeme"), in that it may be analysed into its elementary syntactic components (i.e. its syntactic markers) (Scott 2004).

A major semiotic theory that emphasises the importance of communication in promoting brands is Roland Barthes' theory of semiotics. This theory is rooted in the fact that every sign comes from a signifier and a signified and has a meaning; there is no such thing as an empty meaning (Barthes 1977). Barthes explains that signs are interpreted by individuals, each interpretation being influenced by that person's experiences and background. According to Barthes, messages, therefore, are constituted in two ways: through denotation (the literal meaning and reference of the sign) and connotation (the meanings suggested or implied by the sign). Krawsczyn (2010) notes that this theory requires communicators to delve beneath the surface of superficial communications to locate the true meaning of a message. Thus, semiotics helps one to acquire a better understanding of both people and communication processes. With regard to brand management, semiotics enables individuals, groups and organisations to reflect their identity as well as their values to the world. It helps companies to promote their equity base and project an image to a target audience in the manner they wish it to be perceived and remembered.

Advertising, Semiotics and Strategic Brand Management

Semiotics is now regarded as the cornerstone of brand equity management. This is because symbolic communication is tied to all forms of brand communication i.e. advertising, packaging and brand logo (Oswald 2007). Semiotics, among other things, plays a major role in catching the attention of the intended target market. The placement of certain images, text, colours, and other signs are key to the overall success of any advert.

Strategic brand management is premeditated, deliberate and tactical brand management using sophisticated and sometimes complicated, but classy and mature, methods to create a lasting and positive image of a product in the minds of the major markets. Strategic brand management is a complicated kind of product packaging which basically aims to create a superior product placement and, thus, carve a niche for the brand in the market. It is a holistic kind of brand management, hence our argument that semiotics could play a major role in particular advertisements that help build and manage brands.

The use of semiotics varies with the kind of product being advertised, but, among similar products, the overall theme of the adverts seems to stay the same with few exceptions. For example, many automobile adverts stress a feeling of freedom or excitement by using images that present the vehicle as more rugged or versatile than other vehicles. Alcohol adverts insinuate that you will be more popular on the party scene and will have more fun if you drink a certain brand.

Many brand strategy researchers have come to recognise the importance of brand communication in building and sustaining brand equity (Aaker 1991, Rice and Trout 2001, Oswald 2007). Brand communication can be achieved through a complex matrix of signifying elements, including material, structural, conventional, contextual and performance dimensions (Oswald 2007). The logo of "Mr. Biggs" is a good example. It strategically contains the following:

- Material – It is a visual icon.
- Structural – The golden arches and colour scheme, with the brand name superimposed on the arches in white.
- Conventional – The golden arches, the colour scheme and the brand name consistently signify the brand.

The matrix of these signifying elements suggests that communication serves to create, maintain and transform meaning (Bantz 1993, Sri Ranjan 2010). Advertising can serve in this context to facilitate the communication of signs and symbols to create and transform meaning. In addition, the effectiveness of advertised messages in developing a brand in the mind of a consumer depend on the symbolic interpretation of the advertised message. The sign, object and interpretant (or interpretation) must be manipulated in such a way that the receiver immediately recognises a product or brand and receives a specific meaning and, thus, a message. This is especially applicable to products aimed at a young market (Chandler 1997).

Sri Ranjan (2010) notes the power of verbal, audio and visual signs and observes that advertising, therefore, can serve as a powerful tool for building awareness, positive associations and long-term customer loyalty. McCracken (1996) states that consumers interpret advertised messages as a way of understanding their environment and themselves. This helps them to become the arbitrators of advertising meaning. He explains that advertised messages can be seen as a symbolic resource which brings new ideas and better versions of old ideas in order to advance marketing projects as well as to coordinate and manipulate individuals and society. In other words, signs, advertising and communication are three inseparable concepts for understanding consumer behaviour. Advertised messages construct, form and manipulate the perceptions and behaviours of consumers and the larger society. Thus, advertising experts usually do the following:

- Read the text.

- Read the culture, i.e. what is relevant to the product.
- Make connections between the two.

There is a cultural system – a common set of assumptions, beliefs and symbols called codes – which marks all the products of the culture: fashion, food, music, advertising, movies, television shows, and so on. The codes are taken for granted and embedded, largely unconsciously, in people's behaviour. Advertising experts drag the unconscious messages being transmitted into consciousness by isolating and identifying the signs to constitute the message (Sri Ranjan 2010).

In Africa, many companies have used semiotics in developing brands that reflect the socio-cultural environment in order to promote consumption. For example, Lovelife, an South African NGO concerned with adolescent reproductive health, made effective use of semiotics in billboards to reduce the rate of HIV infection among adolescents. It promoted sexual health and a healthy lifestyle (Delates 2001). Lovelife currently spends R13 million per annum (close to two million USD) on its billboards and R5 million on mobile outdoor media. The messages of Lovelife billboards have generated considerable discussion within the media and amongst communication experts in South Africa (Delates 2001, Lovelife 2001).

In another study, Lunga (2005) examined the use of semiotics in Stanbic Bank's pan-African brand campaign. The study revealed that the bank relied on African symbols, images and visuals to reflect the socio-cultural environments of African countries. The campaign succeeded in reproducing and maintaining power relations between South Africa and other African nations.

Conclusion

The business of advertising and brand management is changing rapidly, and so are the methods used to develop and target new markets. The application of semiotics in strategic brand management is an important brand communication tool used to achieve the goal of effective brand management. The use of semiotics in advertising leads to symbiotic exchanges of cultural codes that are both needed by the advertiser and contextualised by the consumers to create meaning. For consumers, these signs are used to create identities and differentiate one market from the other while simultaneously associating consumers with others through their consumption choices and patterns.

Our analysis of the relationship between advertising, semiotics and strategic brand management leads to the following recommendations, which are basically aimed at making the relationship a solid one and therefore increasing patronage of standard products which adopt its use. The recommendations are as follows:

- The use of semiotics in advertising should be carried out with creativity and dexterity. Companies are advised to consult with advertising experts and semiotics professionals in the placement of images, text, colours, and other signs which are key parts of the overall success of an advert, commercial or campaign.
- The use of semiotics in brand communication and advertising will be insignificant unless the strategy reflects the socio-cultural environment of the country. Advertising experts must take into cognisance the importance of culture in developing a brand as well as in the use of semiotics in advertising.
- The use of verbal, audio and visual signs in brand communication can powerfully capture the hearts and minds of consumers. When this is done with creativity, the output is usually productive.
- Manufacturers should further explore the use of semiotics in advertising and strategic brand management because of its capacity to serve as a means of identification to simplify handling or tracing, legally protect unique product features, signal quality level to satisfied customers, endow products with unique associations, produce competitive advantage and increase financial returns.
- Companies should re-strategize by reducing the number of brands they market. This process is known as brand rationalisation. Some companies tend to create more brands and product variations within a brand than economies of scale would support. Sometimes, they will create a specific service or product brand for each market that they target. In the case of product branding, this may be to gain retail shelf space (and reduce the amount of shelf space allocated to competing brands). A company may decide to rationalise their portfolio of brands from time to time to gain production and marketing efficiency or as part of corporate restructuring. Brand rationalisation reduces identification and recognition problems in the market and enhances competitive advantages. Semiotics is highly relevant in this regard.

Globalisation has thrown up the challenge of universal communication media. In spite of this, signs acquire appropriate meanings only within specific cultural conrext. Advertising strategists may adopt similar themes for advertising campaigns worldwide, but the goal of a globally understood and acceptable sign may be a mirage. Rather than standardise advertising messages or signs, advertising adaptation (or "glocalisation") may be a better alternative in situations where advertising localisation is impossible. This will incorporate cultural sensitivity into the use of semiotics in advertising.

References

Aaker, D. 1991. *Managing Brand Equity*. New York: Free Press.
Barthes, R. 1977. The photographic message. Trans. Barthes). In S. Heath, ed., *Image, Music, Text*. New York: Hill and Wang, 15–31.
Bantz, C. R. 1993. Cultural diversity and group dynamics: Managing differences in cross-cultural team research. *Journal of Applied Communication Research*, 21, 1–20.
Belch, G. and M. Belch. 2003. *Advertising and Promotion: An Integrated Marketing Communications Perspective*. New York: McGraw-Hill.
Berkowitz, N. and W. Rudelius. 2003. *Marketing*. New York, USA: McGraw-Hill.
Bovee, L. and W. Arens. 1992. *Contemporary Advertising*. Chicago: Irwin.
Chandler, D. 1997. Semiotics for beginners. http://www.aber.ac.uk/media/Documents/S4B/semiotic.html (Accessed on 17 February 2010).
Cole, H. 1979. *Advertising Practice*. Chicago: Pearson.
Daramola, I. 2003. *Introduction to Mass Communication*. Lagos: Rotham Press.
Deely, J. 1990. *Basics of Semiotics*. Bloomington, IN: Indiana University Press.
Deely, J. 2001. *Four Ages of Understanding*. Toronto: University of Toronto Press.
Delates, R. 2001. The struggle for meaning: A semiotic analysis of interpretation of Lovelife his and her campaign. *Cadre.org.za*. http://www.cadre.org.za/files/LL_billboard_eval.pdf (retrieved 11/05/2010)
Doghudje, M. 1985. *Advertising*. New York: Sage.
Eco, U. 1976. *A Theory of Semiotics*. Bloomington, IN: Indiana University Press.
Fiske, J. 1990. *Introduction to Communication Studies* (2nd Edition). NY: Routledge.
Hawkins, D. Best, J. and A. Coney. 2003.*Consumer Behavior: Building Marketing Strategy*. New York: McGraw-Hill.
Jefkins, F. 1998. *Advertising*. New York: McGraw-Hill.
Jobber, D. 2003. *Marketing*. New York: McGraw-Hill.
Krawsczyn, E. 2010. A Critique of Roland's Barthes's theory. http://oak.cats.ohiou.edu/~ek370397/semek.htm (retrieved 11/05/2010)
Kerin, R. and E. Berkowitz. 2004. *Marketing*. New York. McGraw-Hill.
Lindstrom, M. 2005. *Brand Sense: Build Powerful Brands through Touch, Taste, Smell, Sight, and Sound*. New York: Free Press.
Lovelife (2001). *Lovelife Franchise: A Manual for Franchise Holders*. New Jersey: Prentice Hall.
Lunga, V. 2005. Unpacking Stanbic bank African brand campaign using critical discourse analysis. *Lex et Scientia* 14 (1): 102–118.
McCracken, G. 1996. *Culture and Consumption: New Approaches to the Symbiolic Character of Consumer Goods and Activities*. Bloomington, IN: Indiana University Press.
Oswald, L. 2007. Semiotics and Strategic Brand Management. http://www.media.illinois.edu/advertising/semiotics_oswald.pdf (retrieved 18/03/2010)
Rice, A. and J. Trout. 2000. *Positioning: The Battle of Your Mind*. New York: McGraw-Hill.
Rossiter, J.R and L. Percy. 1997. *Advertising Communications and Promotions*. New York: McGraw-Hill.

Scott, A. 2004. Umberto Eco's A Theory of Semiotics. http://www.angelfire.com/md2/timewarp/eco.html (retrieved 18/05/2010)

Sri Ranjan, G. 2010. Science of semiotics usage in advertisement and consumer perception. *Journal of American Science* 6 (2): 6–11.

White, R. 2000. *Advertising*. Cambridge, UK: Pearson.

CHAPTER 5

DECEPTION IN ADVERTISING: ETHICAL AND LEGAL IMPERATIVES

OLAYINKA EGBOKHARE

Introduction

The interface between advertising and culture is so strong that, over time, scholars have made many submissions on how one affects or is affected by the other. As Marshall McLuhan, a media visionary, postulated, "historians and archaeologists will discover that the advertisements of our times are the richest and most faithful daily reflections that any society ever made of its entire range of activities" (1964: 232). This view, expressed so many years ago, is of great relevance to my discussion here. My paper examines the interaction between advertising, culture and society with special attention to issues of puffery and deception. The questions to be answered include: what relationship exists between advertising and culture? Is advertising a shaper or a mirror of society? To what extent is the content of Nigerian advertising likely to have a negative impact on consumers? What constitutes puffery? Is puffery the same as deception? Why do advertising creatives employ puffery in developing their messages? What measures are put in place by regulatory bodies to combat puffery? Who and what are the regulatory mechanisms used to militate against deception and puffery?

Before we go further, however, we need to define culture. In the official *Nigerian Cultural Policy* (1997: 5), culture is defined as:

> the totality of a way of life evolved by a people in their attempt to meet the challenges of living in their environment, which gives order and meets their social, political, economic, aesthetic and religious norms and modes of organization, thus distinguishing people from their neighbours.

Thus, culture is an evolving experience amassed through an individual's quest to cope with environmental challenges, and it exists within a societal frame. Prosser (1978) presents culture as "the passing on of attitude, belief, thought and customs". Culture, therefore, serves as a form of control for members within a societal group or those who are brought up within it. For Hall (1973: 25–26), culture is a form of language, which though silent, speaks louder than words. He adds that it is a people's way of life, the sum total of their learned behaviour patterns, attitudes and material things.

A close look at the content of most advertisements suggests that what advertising does is to scrutinise a society and speak to it using selected symbols with which people can identify, language which they can understand and values which they can emulate. Ayeni (1999) emphasises that advertising which ignores the taste and culture of its target audience is sure to fail. The importance of culture to advertising is brought to the fore in the Nigerian code of advertising practice. The first article (2.3.1) of the code states that "all advertisement in Nigeria shall be legal, decent, honest, truthful and respectful and mindful of Nigeria's culture".

The effect of advertising on people's cultural value systems is an on-going controversy. Kleppner (1983) observes that one of the oldest and most prevalent criticisms of advertising concerns its effect on people's social values and general lifestyles. An irate analyst, cited by Kleppner (1983: 571), argues that:

> The possible outcome of TV advertisement is the encouragement of unsafe behaviour, confused assessment of products, promotion of parent-child conflict [and] modeling of hazardous behaviours (drug abuse and reinforcement of selfishness).

This argument almost succeeds in passing off advertising as an all-evil phenomenon which sets out to ruin the consumer. However, the analyst then admits that advertising "also encourages consumers' skills." Similarly, Alan During (cited in *Awake!* August 1998: 8) condemns advertisements as "hedonistic images ...[which] idealize consumption as the route to personal fulfillment and affirm technological progress as the motivating force of destiny" but admits that these traits are simply representative of the present age. In other words, advertising is a picture of society. Douglas, cited in Wilson (1995: 257), takes the debate a step further by declaring that "you can tell the ideas of a nation by its advertisements". Wilson, nevertheless, sees advertising as capable of shaping as well as simply reflecting people's values and lifestyles (1995: 270):

> Advertising is an important element of our culture because it [both] reflects and attempts to change our lifestyle. New cultural trends and fashion are first transmitted to the mass culture through advertising .... Advertising helps us to determine our social identity, it defines our sex roles and it shapes our attitudes

on health, success and lifestyle ... We are taught not so much by logic and dialogue as we are by advertising images.

There is an emphasis here on what advertising accomplishes in the consumer by way of creating new cultures. Cross (1996: 2) also believes that "the discourse of advertising has in effect re-created culture".

Looking at some of the specific effects of advertising, Fowles (1996), citing Hoggart (1968), asserts that advertising exploits people's weaknesses through language. He argues that advertising makes consumer craves things they neither need nor can afford. Stuart (cited in Danna, 1992), one of the most vocal critics of advertising during the great depression of the 1930s, traced the ill effects of advertising to the technological innovations which made possible the production of goods at a rate faster than people's purchasing power could match. For Stuart, this situation led directly to the commercialisation and trivialisation of human emotions and frailties in advertising. In other words, advertising exploits applied psychology and promotes envy, vanity and sexuality in order to sell industrial technologies and superfluity of goods. Stuart further accused advertising of robbing people of their appreciation of non-material, aesthetic, intellectual and moral things. In place of this, advertising has stimulated a relentless hunger for material possessions. In a collection of articles edited by Danna (1992:25); Stuart's influential critique is summarised as follows:

> Advertising creates a dream world: smiling faces, shining teeth, school girl complexions, cornless feet, perfect fitting union suits... odourless breath, regularised bowels, punctureless tyres, perfect busts.

In the view of such critics, the effect of advertising is a generally destructive force in the lives of consumers, especially low-income earners. It is inevitable, therefore, that advertising messages are shrouded in language that hides the truth from consumers.

Taking a more neutral stance, Bovee and Arens (1995: 9–10) argue that advertising has five main functions:

- To identify products and differentiate them from others.
- To communicate and inform people about new products.
- To induce consumers to try new products and to suggest re-use.
- To stimulate the distribution of a new product.
- To build brand loyalty.

Thus, what advertising does is to set an agenda and to battle for the mind of the consumer. Dominick (1990) notes that that this agenda-setting is influenced by factors such as "a person's interest in the information, his age, as well as his educational and political involvement". In the same vein, Grossberg (1998: 348) argues that factors such as individual differences, media differences, issues differences and salience constrain the media's power to set the agenda. Watson and Hill (1993:110) go further to observe that, through the agenda-setting models, advertising enables audiences to "not only learn about public issues and other matters … [but] also learn how much importance to attach to an issue or not from the emphasis the mass media place upon it". McCombs and Shaw (1997) cited in Griffin (2003) argue "the media may not only tell us what to think about, they also may tell us how and what to think about it, and perhaps even what to do about it. This portends that the media "has great potential to colour [or] distort an entire cultural worldview by presenting images of the world suited to the agenda of the media". This chapter is concerned with the extent to which advertising is capable of setting the cultural agenda in a society.

Cultural Norms Theory

Closely related to the agenda-setting theory is the cultural norms theory, which argues that "human behaviour is in large part governed by cultural norms with respect to given topics or situations" (Burgoon and Ruffner 1978: 342). These cultural norms are established and influenced by a range of factors, and the media are just one of these factors. Thus, McQuail (1987: 34) asks, "are the media changing something, preventing something or reinforcing and reaffirming something?" In other words do the media, including the advertising industry create cultural norms or merely reinforce existing norms? Similarly, Burgoon and Ruffner (1978: 336) ask: "Do these mass media serve to educate us about reality, or do they serve as substitutes for reality and for utilizing our own cognitive and interpretive abilities?"

Such questions become relevant when one reviews the numerous conflicting claims about the influence of the media. As MacNamara (1996: 20) observes:

> The media are … blamed for almost every social ill known in our society. The media have been said to cause crime, violence, teenage delinquency, promiscuity, and racial strife and drug taking. But in fact, little proof or evidence is available to substantiate these claims.

While discussing media and behaviour, Grossberg, Wartella and Whitney (1998) reiterated the views expressed in a landmark study on the media by Joseph Klapper, *The Effect of Mass Communication* (1960), which destroyed many of the myths concerning the power of the media and shattered many widely-held assumptions. From extensive research, Klapper concluded that "[m]ass communication was more likely to reinforce existing opinions than to change them, and more likely to produce modifications than conversions" (1960).

Not everyone agrees with Klapper, but his findings point out the danger of generalising about the media's power to change opinions or create new opinions. Modern mass communication studies as well as research findings in psychology reveal that "consumers draw their opinions from a range of sources, and media are but one influence" (MacNamara 1996: 20). Nevertheless, many analysts share McQuail's view (1987) that the mass media, through selective presentations and the emphasis of certain themes, create impressions among their audiences which structure or define common cultural norms concerning the emphasised topics in specific ways. (Burgoon and Ruffner 1978, Folarin 2005). In other words, the mass media have the potential to influence behaviour not only by reinforcing cultural patterns and norms but also by modifying existing norms or even creating new ones. As Burgoon and Ruffner (1978: 342) argue, the mass media breeds "cultural-level expectations that form the basis of cultural predictions", and Anderson (1997: 26–7) asserts that "there is a good deal of evidence to suggest that media contribute in various ways to shaping [a] particular cultural climate". In a more specific analysis, Trenholm (1994: 275) notes that, when one observes what characters do in TV dramas, one internalises behavioural norms:

> By viewing films, we learn about our culture's history and by reading magazines, newspapers and books, we confront questions of value. Media personalities act as role models for us.

Cultural norms theory, therefore, emphasises that the consumer's mind is not an uncultivated ground in which advertising can plant whatever it wishes. Advertising messages are built around ideas, ideals and beliefs that already exist in the consumer's mind. Dominick (1990: 519) sums up this view as follows:

> The media play a significant role in socialization. Sometimes this role is easy to detect; sometimes it is indirect and harder to see; at still other times, it is apparently slight. The mass media more or less mirror the society. In so doing, the media reflect the norms and values that society considers valuable and worthy of promulgation. In the normal course of disseminating information, the media transmit cues that reinforce values and behaviours considered acceptable by society.

Hence, the advertiser needs to work with ideas and concepts with which the consumer is already familiar. In other words, the advertiser needs to identify the existing patterns in a culture and then create adverts that are in consonance with consumers' beliefs and convictions.

For those who believe that the media shape society, the main concern is what view of life the media projects. One can then ask, if the advertising messages are full of puffery and deception, what interpretation will the consumers give these messages? What effect will these messages have on the consumer? Next, I review the topic of deception and puffery in advertising. First, we look at what constitutes deception and then examine the nature of puffery with a view to establishing how these two practices operate in advertising.

Deceptive Advertising

Before we assume that deception is a problem associated with advertising alone, Ford (1996) reminds us that "deception is present in many areas of human endeavour". As Nyberg (1993) observes, deception is essential to the normal operations of business, law, government and entertainment. While this is in no way a justification for deception, it suggests that the desire to deceive is born out of practical needs.

In advertising, deception involves the following elements as detailed by Wright (2000: 189–91):

- A representation, omission or practice likely to cause a substantial segment of potential customers to have a false belief about the advertiser's or a competitor's product.
- The deception is material – it is likely to influence the purchasing decision such that consumers are likely to have chosen differently if there had not been the deception.
- Someone has been or is likely to be injured as a result of the deception. The party harmed is usually a business that has lost sales to the advertiser or by a lessening of the goodwill associated with its products.

Aaker (1982: 40) lists the types of advertising deception as follows:

- False or misleading statements or exaggerations visual or verbal.
- Testimonials which do not reflect the real choice of a competent witness.
- Price claims which are misleading.
- Comparisons which unfairly disparage competitive product or service statements.
- Suggestions or pictures offensive to public decency.
- Claims insufficiently supported or which distort the true meaning or practicable application of statements made by professional or scientific authority.

To further clarify what is termed as deception in advertising, the US Federal Trade Commission (FTC) in 1984 (Mowen 1995: 825–8) held that an advertisement may be deemed deceptive if it has the capacity to deceive a measurable segment of the public and if consumers stand to lose a large amount of money or could incur physical injury as a result of the deception. Where an advertiser maintains that information in an advert constitutes an objective claim and is not deceptive, the FTC requires that "a standard of comparison exists against which the claim may be compared to determine if it is deceptive or not". Take, for example, the claim in a Polygrip commercial that denture wearers who did not use the product could not eat corn on the cob or apples without fear of their dentures loosening. It is easy to detect if this message is deceptive or not because the product can be tested and the claim verified before the commercial is aired. The same goes for all the adverts on detergents that claim to remove stains. One wash will prove or disprove the claims.

Deception, in general, means making a false statement which one believes is false to another person whom one has reason to think will believe the statement to be true (Bok 1988: 53 cited in Ayantayo 2005: 5). Thus, if an advertising message contains an innocent lie, half-truth and outright lie, deception has occurred. However, deception is often related to intent. We may want to ask whether the advertiser intentionally or deliberately deceived, but the FTC states that "whether or not the advertiser actually intended to deceive consumers is considered irrelevant". In other words, the advertising agency cannot escape sanctions for airing a deceptive message by simply saying they had no intention to deceive.

Advertising shapes consumers wants in such a way that consumers prefer products that are advertised. To many, the fact that an item appeared in an advert lends credibility or prestige to that product. This effect is enhanced if celebrity endorsers are used. Hence, advertisers manage consumer preferences through the medium of advertising. In several cases, consumers are buying advertising claims, not products.

Puffery in Advertising

It has been observed that some forms of deception are acceptable in advertising, while others are illegal. The challenge is to identify the complex boundary between legal and illegal deception. However, if some forms of deception are illegal in advertising, there are no laws against puffery. A closer look at what puffery will throw more light on why this is an acceptable practice in advertising.

Advertisers have a desire to make their products appear as the best possible option. Therefore, it is not unexpected that most advertising agencies employ puffery to showcase the merits of their product. Puffing and 'weasel words' are generally not considered deceptive in the eyes of the law. It is assumed that most reasonable consumers know a seller will exaggerate (Wright 2000: 188). Puffery refers to advertising statements which are not illegal but cannot be proven to be true. Puffery can also involve saying something that is technically true but misleading by virtue of what is omitted or left out.

By legal definition, puffery is advertising or other sales representation which praises the item to be sold with subjective opinions, superlatives or exaggerations, vaguely and generally, stating no specific facts. Thus, puffery can be termed falsity without deception, including advertising messages that avoid the facts. Hoffman (2006: 206)) states that "puffery as a legal term refers to promotional statements and claims that express subjective rather than objective views such that no reasonable person would take literally." Thus, puffery is generally not considered deceptive advertising because "it is so exaggerated that no reasonable consumer would take the claims literally". The term "reasonable consumer" is repeated so often in definitions of puffery that one may be tempted to think it cannot be misunderstood. For instance, what demographic and psychographic variables qualify one as reasonable? How reasonable are the following: an impressionistic child? A non-critical adult? An individual whose knowledge of figurative language is minimal?

While it is not uncommon for an advertisement to exaggerate product features in order to elicit consumer attention, how can we be certain the consumer will not take this as a fact? As Hoffman (2006) points out, the consumer has to be "reasonable" to know the message is just puffery, but what happens to the consumer who is unreasonable enough to believe anything is possible, especially in this age of advanced technology when we are repeatedly told that nothing is impossible? For example, can a consumer be blamed for believing the TV commercials from Bank PHB that state, "One day cars will run on water", where the car drives its owner to work and carries on a conversation with him. A consumer may well believe it is possible to use computer engineering to manipulate a car. What is indisputable is that, ultimately, puffery, as well as outright deception, affects trust in advertising.

Looking at the language of advertising, Wilmhurst and Mackay (1999: 233) observe that "[a]dvertising language is a manipulative, distorted and loaded language. Its primary aims are to attract our attention, catch our imagination and then dispose us favourably towards the product or service on offer. Thus, advertising routinely uses superlatives (best, most, greatest etc.) without substantiation. While citing Herschel and Nelson (1998: 36), Hoffman (2006) adds that puffery should only be about "maximising" an image; it should not expand into lying. Most adverts can be said to include puffery; advertisers usually try to portray their products as "best", "ideal", "of greatest value to the consumer", "best value for money", "no other like it", "the No. 1 choice" and so on. This is why puffery is not prosecutable; it is deemed to be harmless exaggeration or colourful hype. It entails bluffing, puffing, exaggeration, humour and overstatement. Thus, even though the claims are unsubstantiated, they are thought to be harmless banter or sales gimmicks. However, the concerns that arise are about the possible harmful effects of puffery on children or other vulnerable people who may not detect the humour, the pun or the exaggeration and may want to try out what they see in commercials. So if an ad is manipulative but not entirely untruthful, is it ethical?

There is a critical principle that marketers should never lie to consumers, because deception subverts trust (Mowen 1995: 361). Good advertising, therefore, is truthful, not misleading or deceptive, and is in good taste.

Wright (2000: 189) observes that "sixty per cent of newspaper space may be filled with advertising but that advertising does not command sixty per cent of the reader's attention". However, this works in two ways. Consumers may ignore advertising messages because they know that they come with barrages of puffery and even deception at times. On the other hand, could ad agencies be going overboard to employ puffery and sometimes outright deception, all in a bid to catch consumers' attention? Mowen (1995: 361) points out the truth effect which states that, if something is repeated often enough, people will begin to believe it. Considering the fact that advertising messages are often repeated, especially TV commercials, which have the most impact, is it not possible that even "reasonable people" may start to believe weasel words, puffery and deceptive advertising messages if they hear them often enough?

Nevertheless, findings from studies suggest that consumers do not always react positively to persuasion tactics that have nothing to do with the product. As Walter and Ellis (1996, cited in Cross 1996: 91) point out, "[i]n the scripted and manipulated commercial, however fanciful, the scene must strike a responsive chord and play to the audience's system of needs and values, or it will not sell products". The advertising message needs to resonate with the consumer's needs. Thus, exaggeration, puffery and outright deception may not work on consumers unless the messages reflect their real needs or values. For instance, consumers may be told that a particular brand of toothpaste will make them "successful and important" or that a certain beverage is the "food drink of future champions". Now these claims are drawn from expressed human needs as postulated by Maslow in his hierarchy of needs (Bovee and Arens 1982). That puffery and deception rely on established human needs, therefore, is a further reason why regulatory bodies need to pay more attention to such elements in advertising messages.

In "Reading Television Texts: The Postmodern Language of Advertising", Cross (1996: 2) observes:

> Peeling verbal signs off their traditional associations in attention-getting wordplay and fragmented syntax, advertising employs a kind of linguistic vandalism to create its spurious surface of language games appropriating words for use in a realm somewhere between truth and falsehood and motivating the signifiers to serve its own purposes- motivating the customer.

Here again, we are reminded that the aim of advertising is to motivate the consumer and that what we term deception or puffery arises out of the struggle for the mind of the consumer. Deception here is seen as a cross between truth and falsehood, but the art is so subtle it is often difficult to decipher which is which. As Cross points out, advertising plays word games, and these are often so clever that the advertiser may get away with anything; the message will be so well-scripted that the deception is hard to notice. Cross (1996) notes that advertising always disrupts language use:

> Language is coded and recoded in advertising to speak in its own marketplace tongues. Advertising has always played language games; its own special game is connotation, raising the stakes on words to enlarge their suggestiveness by shifting contexts (puns) or making new equations (metaphors) or changing their spelling (neologisms).

She further asserts that advertising moves language from the rational to the non-propositional level of the figural or the visual. Hence, we need to put rationality aside and just try to decode the message from the point of view of figurative usage.

Addressing Deceptive Advertising

To address the issue of deceptive advertising, we first need to ask who is liable for deceptive advertising. Many would be quick to say the advertiser, in other words, the company whose product is being advertised. But how culpable is the agency that produced the advert? The agency will be held liable if it willingly participated in the deception and knew (or reasonably should have known) that the advertising was deceptive. It is the responsibility of the ad agency to substantiate the claims that a company makes and not rely on the advertiser's brief alone. The agency is expected to conduct its own research and verify the claims made by the manufacturer.

Thus, advertising agencies have a major role to play in the campaign against deceptive advertising. Since the agency is liable for any accusation of deception in advertising, they must have a standard of what is right or wrong. An ethical advertising agency will guarantee that their advertisements will be honest and truthful as opposed to unscrupulous and misleading. They will ensure that they do not exploit the weak and the vulnerable. They will never lie to consumers. Some agencies now take a publicised ethical approach (mission statement), but, when agencies refuse to take the initiative to sanitise their business, punitive measures are put in place to check the activities of offenders. The penalties for engaging in deceptive advertising can take several forms:

- Cease and desist orders – the company might be asked to pull an ad and pay a fine if they violate the law again.
- Civil penalties – consumer redress which may take the form of refunds to customers who purchased the product.
- Corrective advertising – disclosures and other informational remedies which may involve purchasing additional airtime to correct the misinformation
- Bans and bonds – in severe cases of deception, a company may be required to leave the industry or post a bond before re-entering the industry.

The Advertising Standards Panel (ASP) of APCON (Advertising Practitioners Council of Nigeria) has the task of "protecting the public from deceitful and morally wrong advertisement". The panel is also charged with "ensuring that all advertisements conform to the prevailing laws of the Federation as well as the code of advertising ethics". Among other things, the panel ensures that adverts are decent, honest, and truthful and executed with a high sense of responsibility, as the basic principle of advertising demands. The panel's reach extends to all forms of advertising: print, broadcast, cinema, outdoor, labeling, packaging and internet advertising.

Regulations and negative incentives are the primary tools used to discourage deceptive ads. Whatever the description of the form of deception, whether misleading, falsifying or misrepresenting facts, deceptive advertising is dishonest and hurts both consumers and businesses. In fact, people sometimes wonder why firms would engage in false advertising. One suggestion is that "profit-maximizing firms may be willing to incur fines when the fine is less than the profit gained from false advertising".

Most purchasers and potential consumers learn about existing and new products and services from advertisements or from some other kind of commercial message. Therefore, advertising is one of the most closely scrutinised forms of public communication. It relies for its interpretation not only on the author but on the recipient. Therefore, the medium, the audience, the nature of the product, the context and the message must all be given equal evaluation when APCON makes a judgement about an ad's acceptability. As the apex advertising regulatory body in Nigeria, APCON has put in place a number of procedures and mechanism to ensure that Nigerian adverts are truthful, in good taste and respectful of Nigerian culture. Part 2, sub-section 3 of the code (2005: 6) states that all advertisements in Nigeria shall:

- be legal, decent, honest, truthful and respectful and mindful of Nigeria's culture.
- be prepared with a high sense of social responsibility and avoid misinformation or disinformation.
- always be in the interest of the consumer and the wider Nigerian society.
- conform to the principles of fair competition generally accepted in business and of fair comment expected in free human communication.
- enhance public confidence in advertising.

The other sections of the code, especially section 4, spell out in clear terms what the regulatory body expects in relations to claims, use of evidence or testimonials, wrong use of specialised terms, scientific terms, guarantee, warranty, hidden extras and other related issues. APCON places messages in the major media asking consumers to report any commercial they deem to be in bad taste. Before any advertising message from a producer goes on air, APCON's Advertising Standards Panel must have vetted the message and given it approval to run. ASP consists of the following organisations:

- Advertising Practitioners Council of Nigeria (APCON)
- Association of Advertising Agencies of Nigeria (AAAN)
- Newspaper Proprietors Association of Nigeria (NPAN)
- Consumer Protection Council (CPC)
- Outdoor Advertising Association of Nigeria (OAAN)
- National Agency for Foods, Drugs Administration and Control (NAFDAC)
- Advertisers Association of Nigeria (ADVAN)
- National Council of Women Societies (NCWS)
- Broadcasting Organisations of Nigeria (BON)
- Central Bank of Nigeria (CBN).

The organisations represented on this panel are expected to fully represent the interest of the different sectors of society. However, in instances where advertising messages escape the sledge-hammer of this panel, APCON still encourages consumers to report such adverts. One of APCON's fliers reads:

> Have you seen, read or heard an advertisement you consider inaccurate, makes false claims, exploits human misery, promotes unsafe practices, engages in unfair comparisons or is in bad taste? Take this step today: write to The Chairman, Advertising Standards Panel.

Other messages display phone numbers that can be called to report cases of false claims and related matters. A regulatory body's accessibility to consumers, speed of action, flexibility, degree of independence and scope have a great role to play in the campaign against deceptive advertising.

The Need for Media Literacy

Deceptive ads work best when consumers are uninformed. Some consumers interviewed during course of the research claim they do not watch or read advertisements at all, and if they do, the ads rarely 'penetrate' or connect with their consciousness, let alone transform their identity. However, the truth is we are all sometimes persuaded and seduced by advertising. Since this kind of persuasion is endemic to social life, the consumer needs to be schooled to filter deceptive messages out and fend off puffery. The consumer needs to know that some advertisers set out to defraud, offend or mislead the public.

Historian David Potter (cited by Fowles 1996) argues that the modern advertising industry is comparable to such long-standing institutions as the school and the church in the magnitude of its social influence. As a result of this influence, consumers must be constantly on guard and have a healthy skepticism for what is claimed by sellers. Since the aim of advertising is to influence choice, advertisers cannot be blamed for painting beautiful pictures of their products; the game is all about getting consumers' attention using the most captivating sales messages. Although it is not acceptable for advertisers to take advantage of the vulnerabilities of an uneducated or uninformed public, consumers have a responsibility to know the difference between reality and exaggeration.

Many consumers see control over the truthfulness of advertising as necessary, especially since children and other vulnerable people need special protection from the highly persuasive claims made by advertising. However, with advances in technology and the ever-increasing use of the Internet, all consumers remain prime targets for deceptive advertising practices. Consumers are also at risk of deceptive packaging, bait-and-switch sales promotion techniques and many misleading or fraudulent marketing practices. If we think the hullabaloo about deceptive advertising is uncalled-for, the findings from an earlier study conducted by this researcher disprove that view. In the study, selected consumers (450 respondents from Lagos and Ibadan) in southwestern Nigeria expressed their views on how advertising affects them. First, respondents were asked their view on whether television commercials brainwash people. Table 5.1 below presents their responses.

Table 5.1: Respondents' Views on Whether TVCs Brainwash Consumers

Response	Frequency	%	df	X^2	Sig
SA + A	237	57.4			
SD + D	176	42.5	1	9.01*	<.05
Total	413	100.0			

Key: SA - Strongly agree; A – Agree; SD – Strongly disagree; D – Disagree.

Two hundred and thirty-seven respondents (57.4 percent) believed TV commercials brainwash people. However, when asked whether TV commercials contribute good ideas to society, 94 percent respondents said yes. Next, the respondents were asked if watching TV commercials could affect their lifestyle and values as consumers. Over 78 percent said yes, 15.2 percent said yes, but only to a little extent, and a mere 6.4 percent did not believe that TV commercials influence consumers' lifestyle or values at all.

The next two questions asked to what extent TV commercials show real-life situations. About half the respondents (50.5 percent) agreed that TV commercials, to some extent, reflect the daily lives of Nigerians, while 31.3 percent said they reflected reality only a little. A mere 4.6 percent maintained that commercials do not reflect consumers' daily lives at all. As a follow-up to this question, consumers were asked if the situations depicted in commercials are true to life. Two questions were asked to confirm the reaction of the respondents and to detect cheaters. The first question was: "To what extent are TV commercials reflections of society?" Just over half (50.5 percent) of the sample said TV commercials to some extent reflect what happens in daily life. Almost a third (31.3 percent) said commercials are "to a great extent" a reflection of society. Just under 14 percent said they reflected society to a small extent, while less than 5 percent said commercials are to no extent a true reflection of society.

More than half of the sample (50.5 percent) felt that advertising is a reflection of the society to some extent but not to a great extent (31.3 percent). Only 13.6 percent felt advertising has little extent and 4.6 percent no extent. If TV commercials are truly reflections of society, one would think that they should not make use of situations that are not true-to-life. Yet 45.6 percent of respondents said commercials are "to a little extent" guilty of not making use of true-to-life situations, while 27.9 percent see some extent and over a quarter 26.4 percent see little or no extent.

The study also tried to find out the extent to which consumers compare the situations depicted in TV commercials with real-life situations. Almost half (48 percent) of respondents said they do this to some extent, while 29 percent individuals said they did this only to a little extent. One can conclude from this that a lot of the scenes depicted in TV commercials strike consumers as aspirational and do not always reflect situations that are true-to-life.

Having established the views of respondents on the relationship between TV commercials and real-life situations, the researcher enquired about the influence of commercials on consumers and the nature of the influence. First, the question was asked: do TV commercials influence you? An overwhelming majority (81.4 percent) said commercials sometimes influence them, and only 12 percent claimed they were not influenced. On the nature of influence, 45 percent said commercials influenced them positively. More than a quarter said the influence was both positive and negative, and only 8.4 percent said the influence was purely negative.

Conclusion

Advertising not only replicates the social fabric of our society but also has, in a large measure, assisted in its creation. The aim of advertising is to influence choices. In a bid to get the attention of the consumer, advertising uses puffery and deception. While puffery is usually treated as harmless exaggeration, deception is a prosecutable offence. A lot of the information learned by children is learned from TV with advertising as one of the major instructors. As one of the key institutions in the transmission of values to the larger society, advertising clearly plays a critical role in both reflecting and shaping culture.

Advertisers are very adept at addressing every group's insecurities and survival and self-esteem needs. Consumers pay attention to advertising messages, and regulatory bodies are concerned about ensuring that consumers are exposed to messages that are wholesome and devoid of unsupported claims and manipulated testimonials. Advertising can represent the best and worst of our culture. Advertising should not only be criticised for some of its deceptive content. It should be exploited as a medium of information dissemination because it can be used to teach and provide useful information, and it can actually enhance consumers' lives.

References

Aaker, D.A. 1982. Deceptive advertising. In Aaker, D.A. and Day, G.S., ed. *Consumerism: Search for the Consumer's Interest*. London: The Free Press.

Anderson, A. 1997. *Media, Culture and the Environment*. New Jersey: Rutgers University Press.

APCON. 1988. *The Code of Advertising Practice*. Lagos: Advertising Practitioner's Council of Nigeria.

APCON. 2010. *Vetting Guidelines*. Lagos: Advertising Practitioner's Council of Nigeria.

Awake! August 1998, p.8.

Ayantayo, J.K. 2005. Truthfulness as a factor in the language of advertising. In *International Journal of African & African American Studies*. Vol. IV, No.1.

Ayeni, F. 1999. Vote for Global Advertising, *Media Review*, pp. 22–5.

Bovee, C. L. and W. E. Arens. 1982. *Contemporary Advertising*. Illinois: Richard D Irwin Inc.

Burgoon, M. and M. Ruffner. 1978. *Human Communication*. New York: Holt, Rinehart and Winston.

Cross, M., ed. 1996. *Advertising and Culture: Theoretical Perspectives*. London: Praeger.

Danna, S.R., ed. 1992. *Advertising and Popular Culture: Studies in Variety and Versatility*. Bowling Green, OH: Popular Press.

Dominick, J.R. 1990. *The Dynamics of Mass Communication*. New York: McGraw Hill.

Federal Trade Commission. Retrieved from www.ftc.gov/bcp/scoff/documents.

Folarin, B. 2005. *Theories of Mass Communication. An Introductory Text*. Ibadan: Bakinfol Publications.

Ford, C.V. 1996. *Lies! Lies!! Lies !!! The Psychology of Deceit*. Washington, DC: American Psychiatric Press.

Fowles J. 1996. *Advertising and Popular Culture*. Thousand Oaks: Sage Publications.

Grossberg, L., E. Watella and D.C. Whitney. 1998. *Media Making: Mass Media in a Popular Culture*. Thousand Oaks: Sage Publications.

Hall, S. 1973. Cultural Studies: Two Paradigms. In *Media, Culture and Society*, Vol. 2, 57–72.

Hoffman, David. A. 2006. The best puffery article ever. *Iowa Law Review* 91: 206.

Klapper, J.T. 1960. *The Effect of Mass Communication*. New York: Free Press.

MacLuhan, M. 1964. *Understanding Media: The Extension of Man*. Cambridge: The M.I.T. Press.

Macnamara, J. 1996. *How to handle the Media*. Sydney: Prentice Hall.

McQuail, D. 1987. *Mass Communication Theory: An Introduction*. London: Sage.

Mowen, J.C. 1995. *Consumer Behaviour*. 4th ed. Eaglewood Cliffs, NJ: Prentice Hall.

Nyberg, D. 1993. *The Vanished Truth: Truth Telling and Deceiving in Ordinary Life*. Chicago: University of Chicago Press.

Russell, J.T and Lane, R.W. 1993. *Kleppner's Advertising Procedure*. Eaglewood Cliffs. N.J.: Prentice Hall.

Prosser, M.H. 1978. *The Cultural Dialogue: An Introduction to Intercultural Communication*. Boston: Houghton Mifflin.

Stuart, W. Elnora, S. Terence and W. E. Randal. 1987. Classical conditioning of consumers attitudes: Four experiments in an advertising context. *Journal of Consumer Research* Vol. 14 pp. 334–49.

Trenholm S. 1994. *Thinking through Communication. An Introduction to the Study of Human Communication*. Boston: Allyn and Bacon.

Walter, J. and G. Ellis. 1996. The selling of gender identity. In Mary Cross, ed. *Advertising and Culture: Theoretical Perspectives*. London: Praeger.

Watson, James and Anne Hill. 1993. *A Dictionary of Communication and Media*. London: Edward Arnold.

Wilson, J. 1995. *Mass Media, Mass Culture: An Introduction*. New York: McGraw-Hill.

Wright, R. 2000. Advertising. Harlow, UK: Pearson.

CHAPTER 6

SOCIAL, ETHICAL AND REGULATORY ISSUES IN ADVERTISING: THE CASE OF NIGERIA

OLUJIMI KAYODE

Introduction

Advertising, much like the mass media which it often supports, is everywhere and all around us in this country. Most people would readily agree that advertising is pervasive in its presence and influence across society. This seemingly overwhelming presence may not be unconnected with the fact that advertising takes place in the public sphere, where the media and socio-political stakeholders are major actors in conjunction with business interests, consumer needs and wants, creativity and regulatory institutions, both governmental and non-governmental.

In the advertising public sphere, the major stakeholders are advertisers, advertising agencies, mass media, consumers, government and regulators – both governmental and professional. Generally, advertisers and advertising agencies are closer, as they often operate in a consultant-client relationship, and both work closely with the mass media, which provide the channel through which advertising messages are disseminated to the public. The public, for its part, consists of consumers, customers, regulatory agencies and non-governmental activists.

Historically, advertising has contributed strongly to the modernization of society, both economically and socially. However, it has also been involved in diverse controversies, social, ethical and legal. Many of the controversies have stemmed from the economic roles advertising plays in society. Generally speaking, the controversies have concerned the ways in which advertising creates demand, especially through persuasive messages aimed at making people want a particular product, service or accept a certain idea or behavioural change. Advertisers defend themselves by arguing that creating demand contributes to the self-interest of both consumers and advertisers by adding value to products and services, especially in a free-market capitalist system. They also claim that advertising encourages competition and thereby increases choice, which is in the interest of consumers.

How does advertising add value to products and services? In the mid-1960s, a famous American psychologist named Ernest Dichter (cited in Kazmi and Batra 2004) asserted that a product's image, created in part by advertising and promotion, is an inherent feature of the product itself. Other studies had found that the positive image conveyed by advertising could make the product more desirable to the consumer. This is why, for instance, most people prefer Coca-Cola to other brands of cola drink. By making products better known, advertising makes them more desirable, and the image created by advertising is likely be perceived part of the inherent quality of the product. Advertising also adds value by informing consumers about new uses for a product and enabling consumers to choose the values they want in the products they buy, whether cheap and affordable or expensive and unique (Kazmi and Batra 2004). Arens (2006) sums up the defence of advertising's economic roles by asserting that advertising epitomises the "abundance principle", which states that, in an economy which produces more goods and services than can be consumed, advertising serves two vital functions: it keeps consumers informed about alternatives (complete information), and it allows companies to compete effectively for consumers' purchasing power (self-interest). Arens (2006) further argues that advertising stimulates a healthy economy and helps create financially healthy consumers who are informed, better educated and more demanding. This results in growing consumer advocacy and an unprecedented level of social criticism and regulation in modern societies.

Criticisms of advertising make it the whipping boy or scapegoat of society and reinforce misunderstandings of the nature of advertising, encouraging hostility to its practices and, by extension, to capitalism in general. Such criticisms have also created a platform for continuing calls for legislation and other restraints on what are perceived by critics to be the abuses of advertising and of big business and capitalism generally. Russell and Lane (1993) identify three key questions that need to be answered in order to evaluate objectively the economic roles of advertising:

- Is advertising more efficient than other forms of product information distribution?

- Does advertising contribute to corporate profits and consumer lifestyles?
- Does advertising contribute to the overall welfare of society?

While it is difficult to deal in generalities when examining the economic value of advertising, and equally difficult to isolate the economic value of advertising from its social consequences, the economic value can be situated within four dimensions: counterproductive, unproductive, somewhat productive and most productive, depending on the particular issue at stake and the side of the controversy to which one belongs (Arens 2006, Russell and Lane 1993).

Social Aspects of Advertising

The social aspects of advertising are often volatile and generate heated debates. Because it is so visible and pervasive, advertising is often criticised both for what it is and what it does. Many of the criticisms often fail to consider the complex social and legal environments in which contemporary advertising operates. However, many of the criticisms are based on real concerns of consumers about abuses of advertising practices, even if such criticisms are sometimes based on intuition and emotions. In and of itself, advertising is not evil, but for those who feel that it is intrusive and manipulative, the social aspects usually cause the most concern, while there are also ethical dilemmas surrounding the practices of advertising in modern society (Arens 2006).

Several broad areas could be examined in the context of the social impact of advertising. On the positive side, there are issues of advertising's effect on consumer's knowledge, standards of living and feelings of happiness and well-being, as well as the revenue support advertising provides for the mass media. On the negative side, there are several criticisms of advertising's social roles, such as the charge that it wastes resources and promotes materialism and that it perpetuates gender and other stereotypes. In addition, there are the issues of the alleged offensiveness of some of its messages, its clutter and the possible negative effects on children, the aged or the illiterate (Shimp 2000, Arens 2006). It is also pertinent to examine the notion of advertising as a social institution. Advertising as a tool of mass communication shares some of the traits of journalism, education and entertainment, but it is not any one of these three. Rather it is an institution much like family, school, media or religion. One purpose of an institution is to provide information on how to behave appropriately, structure social life productively and embody ideas about society. Each kind of institution may be influential on society in different ways. For instance, the purpose of a school is to teach, whereas the purpose of advertising is to inform and persuade. Another purpose of an institution is to help order human relationships into roles. For example, marriage as an institution puts people into familial roles, while the church or mosque creates religious roles for people. For its part, advertising establishes the role of the consumer and helps consumers make choices and judgements about which goods or services to purchase or use.

Advertising did not become an institution until late in the nineteenth century when manufacturers began to utilise advertising for product differentiation and branding. Branding gave power and influence to advertisers. Consumers started asking for and buying products by brand names, and, as a result, society became pervaded by advertising. Advertising thus became essential not only for commercial corporations but even for non-profit organisations and for social mobilisation and advocacy. The influence of advertising as a social institution had resulted in much debate over its benefits (or otherwise) to society, with some arguing that advertising simply mirrors society and others maintaining that it actually shapes society (Vanden Bergh and Katz 1999). Regardless of one's position in this debate, it is clear that advertising plays an important role in determining social issues and that it will continue to face opposition and be defended and adapted to accommodate the pressure of moral panics, consumerism and social activism.

Advertising as a Mirror of Society

Proponents of advertising argue that it merely reflects the tastes and values of society rather than shaping them (Arens 2006). Such arguments defend advertising by asserting that it reflects popular culture, builds the value of brands, creates a sense of belonging and supports society's values. Advertising's role as a reflection of popular culture is often presented through the use of cultural themes, concepts, metaphors and other such ideas as well as popular or familiar characters or celebrities and popular music. Advertising can express the value of a brand by creating such value in the perception of consumers. For instance, an advertiser may spend a lot on advertising the value that is placed on customer goodwill and building value in the product or service so intensely promoted. When advertising is used to depict familiar events, activities or scenes, it helps consumers to have a sense of belongingness to a particular social group such as housewives or mothers. Advertising reflects society's values where themes are based on prevailing cultural values, such as is prominent in the developed countries of the West, where individualism rather than communalism is often emphasised. The opposite is the case in some African countries, where communalism resonates with the people.

Advertising as a Shaper of Society

Advertising may be criticised for the ways in which it is able to impact and mould society. While they do not claim that advertising is necessarily the sole harmful influence on consumers and the general public, critics argue that the impact is powerful enough to be a cause for concern and one among several harmful shapers of societal values. In this context, advertising is said to shape society in the following ways. It promotes materialism and is harmful to children. It reinforces stereotypes and helps sell bad products. It dictates media choices, increases the cost of goods and services and is simply too intrusive and pervasive.

One of the most vocal complaints against advertising is that it makes people buy things they do not need, which reinforces materialism and further widens the gap between the 'haves' and the 'have-nots'. In a survey on consumer attitudes to advertising carried out by this author, most of the respondents agreed that advertising persuades people to buy what they do not need (Kayode 1985). The key question here is whether advertising can manipulate people, and the answer from the point of view of consumers seems to be that they believe it can and does. In general, critics of advertising tend to believe that it has powers to shape social trends and the way people think and act. Some argue that advertising can even dictate how people behave. They believe that even if an individual advert cannot control people's behaviour, the cumulative effects of advertising campaigns can be overwhelming (Vanden Bergh and Katz 1999).

Defenders of advertising are quick to reply that this is just 'salesmanship' and does not have any power to force people to buy anything they do not want. They argue that persuasion cannot be equated with coercion. People have free will and freedom to choose what they buy or even not to buy at all. In this view, advertising only educates and equips consumers to make informed purchase decisions. Kirkpatrick (2007) points out that it is difficult to separate the informative role of advertising from the persuasive, and that equating persuasiveness with coercion contradicts the volitional consciousness of people and denies their capacity to reason and to act according to their free will. It follows that, if advertising cannot coerce people to buy things they do not need or want, then the charge of encouraging materialism falls flat.

Another major issue is whether advertising is harmful to children. The underlying criticism against advertising to children stems from the fact that children are being targeted more and more, especially by television commercials, while it is believed that children are generally gullible and too young to make informed purchase decisions or understand the difference between real life and the images depicted in commercials. In addition, advertisements that are not necessarily targeted at children may still be seen by them, and some of these adverts concern products that are inimical to their health or well-being, such as alcohol and cigarettes.

In spite of the defense by the proponents of advertising that targeting children in adverts for children's products or services is merely targeting the appropriate audience for the products, not encouraging irresponsible behaviour, the enormous number of commercials in this category still causes serious concern in most countries. The result is that most countries, including Nigeria, now regulate advertising targeted at children. For instance, the Nigerian Code of Advertising Practice has a special section on advertising to children which deals extensively with issues such as inducements, appeals, exaggeration, safety, medicaments, child models, exploitation of innocence and children's exposure to "values that are not approved by society" (APCON 1988).

There is also the issue of whether advertising can mould society's beliefs by the way it uses stereotypes, which reduce people or objects into classes based on inferences that are made from an individual or social context. Many of such stereotypes concern race, ethnic group, age, gender and socio-economic status. For instance, advertising often presents women as weaker, home-based and domestic, while the aged have been presented as forgetful and certain ethnic groups as rural, rustic or semi-literate and so on. Advertisers, in their defense, claim they are merely reflecting society's attitudes towards such groups or the actual lifestyles of those people.

There are many other issues concerning advertising's alleged power to shape society. One is the vexed question of whether advertising uses subliminal power, working at the subconscious level of people's minds, to persuade them to buy what otherwise they would not. However, the controversy around subliminal advertising is not conclusive, and there seems to be no solid scientific evidence that advertising works on people's subconscious minds. Other claims are that advertising increases the cost of goods and services, that it helps sell bad products, that it is intrusive and pervasive and that it dictates media choices. While there are instances where advertising increases the cost of products, this is not always so. Indeed, advertising more often results in lower prices due to the economics of scale it supports. Concerning the issue of advertising being used to sell bad products, the point is that while there may be such cases, they seldom lasts for long, as consumers quickly reject a product that does not live up to expectations. Many products fail in the marketplace due to their inability to align with consumer expectations after their market entry, even when they are heavily advertised. A case in point is "Green Sands Shandy", a product that was introduced into the

Nigerian market by Nigeria Breweries but which was later withdrawn because it was neither a beer nor a cross between a beer and something else.

That advertising is pervasive is a fact of modern society. There is no doubt that advertising is part of our culture and influences it in some ways. However, it cannot be said to have the power to dominate the forces of religion, family, literature and so on, which contribute more strongly to the values of society. While the clutter issue is irksome to many people, most believe this should be tolerated as the price to pay for free TV, freedom of the press and a high standard of living. However, with the proliferation of new media, the pervasiveness of advertising is likely to intensify. Virtually every popular website is cluttered with advertising banners, and our e-mail boxes are flooded with advertising messages on a daily basis (Arens 2006). Besides, proponents of advertising have argued that it informs, improves standards of living and positively affects people's happiness and general well-being. This may not be totally incorrect.

Advertising is also accused of corrupting the mass media, for example, by influencing editorial decisions that favour the advertisers rather than the public interest. The media deny this and pride themselves on their role as public watchdog. It may be argued that advertisers' influence on the media cannot be denied, but it is a fact that the media resists this as an institution, even if there may be individual cases of succumbing to advertiser pressure.

The debate as to whether advertising mirrors or shapes society continues. However, the fact remains that advertising and society's values are probably interactive. The answer may simply be that advertising both mirrors and shapes society (Vanden Bergh and Katz 1999, Wells et al. 2007).

Socially Responsible Advertising

Whether advertising is a mirror or a shaper of society, it is no doubt an influential force. Because of this, it is used quite extensively, both by government and by business, to promote socially desirable activities. These may include campaigns on HIV and AIDs, family planning, environmental issues and so on.

There are two key social aspects of advertising that ought to be mentioned. These are the use of sex and nudity in advertising and the use of negative appeals such as fear. These issues dominate the call for less offensive advertising and for images and themes that are considered in good taste. Overall, there is a great deal of popular concern about the role of advertising in national development.

A study by Alozie (2005) concluded that it is difficult to ascertain the role of advertising on Nigeria's social, economic and national development and modernisation. The study found that most adverts were product-related and that less than a third were related to services, one indication of the relatively underdeveloped nature of the economy. It was also found that most adverts promoted non-essential products and services and were sponsored by national and multinational corporations rather than by government agencies. Advertising in Nigeria mostly promotes goods of foreign origin and are targeted mostly at elites rather than the masses.

In summary, we can conclude that while advertising may legitimately be criticised for offering incomplete information and, in some instances, for creating unwanted externalities, it should also be applauded when it contributes to the validity of the principles of free-enterprise economics. In most cases, by being a rich information source (albeit not a complete one), advertising contributes to the well-being of many buyers and sellers and, therefore, to the self-interest of both consumers and marketers.

Advertising Ethics

People may feel overloaded due to information from advertising and the consequent pervasiveness, intrusiveness and clutter. However, this has not detracted from the usefulness of good advertising. Good advertising makes useful products and services known. It contributes to fuller employment and educates the public in numerous ways. Overall it contributes to raising standards of living. However, there is also much bad and obnoxious advertising, although it should be mentioned that advertising in itself may not be good or bad but may be put to either end. For instance, if utterly useless goods or services are advertised or consumers are deceived by advertising claims, if less than admirable human tendencies are exploited, then such practices become harmful to society.

According to the Pontifical Council for Social Communications (2010), there is nothing intrinsically good or intrinsically evil about advertising. It can be used well, and it can be used badly. It can have beneficial results, and it can also have harmful impacts on individuals and society. It can be tasteful and in conformity with high moral standards, and it can be morally uplifting, but it can also be vulgar and morally degrading.

In the current complex corporate environment, advertisers, their agencies and the media constantly wrestle with ethical problems of content, presentation and the acceptability of a diverse number of claims and advertising practices. Russell and Lane (1993) have narrowed down the ethical dimensions of advertising into issues concerning advertising content and presentation and their nature or impact on society. They also argue that these issues do not have ready-made solutions but have to be tackled on a case-by-case basis.

Ethical philosophies have been debated for centuries and cannot be treated adequately in this chapter, but, for practical purposes, three levels of ethical responsibility can be applied to advertising. On one level, ethics comprise two interrelated components: traditional actions taken by people in a society or community and the philosophical rules that society establishes to justify past actions and determine future actions. These elements set the basis for the primary rules of ethics in a society. The standards thus created can be used to assess how far a practitioner or an advertiser has gone against ethical norms at the community level. In such a situation, the individual practitioner is subject to societal standards or norms, as is customary for the community or group.

Secondly, the attitudes and beliefs which comprise an individual's value system and which have been internalised based on socialisation through the family, school, peer group and religion add up to personal ethics. Ethical dilemmas often occur when personal ethics conflict with societal ethics. The third level of ethics concerns singular ethical concepts such as good, bad, right, wrong, duty, integrity and truth. Whether these concepts are considered absolute, universal and binding or relative and dependent on situations and consequences depends on each individual's ethical standards as influenced by religion, society and personal ethics. Thus, personal ethics and societal ethical norms both contribute to an individual's ethical and moral development in a combination that social psychologists do not as yet comprehend (Arens 2006). Thus, there are social ethics, professional ethics and personal ethics, and all three combine to provide ethical moorings for the individual, including the advertiser, which can withstand the test of time. The ethical imperatives can be summed up as respecting the interests of others, upholding human dignity and truthfulness and integrity (Day 2004).

Regulation of Advertising

Advertisers, agencies and practitioners are faced with a variety of regulations and restrictions that influence their decision-making. The situation in Nigeria in the past few decades has shown that regulation is necessary to protect consumers and competitors from the fraudulent, deceptive and unfair practices that some businesses choose to perpetrate (Olatunji 2003). While there are debates as to how thoroughly advertising should be regulated, one thing is sure. Regulation is needed most when consumers are likely to be deceived by false or limited information or when advertising may cause some harm to its audience through its content and presentation (Shimp 2000).

Advertising regulation in Nigeria occurs at both the governmental and professional levels. At the governmental level, the federal, state and, sometimes, local governments regulate according to edicts and legalism. There is also self-regulation at the professional level through organisations such as the Advertising Practitioners Council of Nigeria (APCON), the Advertisers' Association of Nigeria (ADVAN), the Association of Advertising Agencies of Nigeria (AAAN), the Outdoor Advertising Association of Nigeria (OAAN), all of which subscribe to the Nigerian Advertising Code of Ethics. In addition, other ancillary organisations such as the Broadcasting Organisation of Nigeria (BON), the Newspapers Proprietors Association of Nigeria (NPAN), the Nigeria Broadcasting Commission (NBC), the National Agency for Food and Drug Administration and Control (NAFDAC), the Nigeria Standards Organisation (NSO) and so on have established standards of practice, some of which are relevant to the practice of advertising directly or indirectly. There is also the legal environment of advertising, in which laws concerning trademark, copyright, deception, consumer protection, libel, defamation, and so on have regulatory import for advertising practice.

Advertising practitioners in Nigeria argue that government regulations are confusing because so many agencies of the state lay claim to the right to regulate the advertising industry. Although Act 55 of 1988 establishing APCON vested it with powers to regulate and control advertising in all its ramifications, other bodies such as the Central Bank of Nigeria, NAFDAC, the Consumer Protection Council and so on also have authority to control the industry in one way or another. Even the Federal Ministry of Works through the Federal Road Maintenance Agency (FERMA), along with some state-government agencies such as the Lagos State Signage and Advertisements Agency (LASAA), exert various degrees of control over outdoor advertising.

Conclusion

In order to have a good understanding of advertising and how it works, it is important to examine the social, ethical and regulatory aspects of advertising, especially as these are contextualised in the debate about whether advertising is a mirror of society reflecting people's tastes or a shaper of society influencing what people think, say or do. The contention of this chapter is that advertising is both a mirror and a shaper of society. While advertising often portrays popular culture, it is also a force that shapes and impacts society. It promotes materialism, targets children and reinforces gender, age-related, ethnic and other stereotypes. Advertising is, no doubt, an important cultural, social and economic institution and, as such, has been criticised and maligned by those who resent its influence and, at the same time, touted by those who ascribe some benefits to its activities. The debates and controversies have resulted in ethical imperatives as well as regulations that have been accepted throughout the world. In Nigeria the situation is not much different, and the various aspects of this pervasive industry will continue to be controversial. This chapter should be seen as an attempt to situate the broader debates within the Nigerian context.

References

Alozie, C.E. 2005. Cultural reflections and the role of advertising in the socio-economic and national development of Nigeria. In *Studies in African Economic and Social Development* 26. Miami: Edwin Mellen Press.

APCON. 1988. *The Code of Advertising Practice*. Lagos: Advertising Practitioner's Council of Nigeria.

Arens, F.W. 2006. *Contemporary Advertising*. Tenth Edition. Boston: McGraw-Hill.

Day, L.A. 2004. *Ethics in Media Communications: Cases and Controversies*. California: Wadsworth.

Kayode, O.O. 1985. Advertising in adversity: Opinions on marketing communications in a recession. Unpublished MSc Thesis, University of Lagos, Lagos, Nigeria.

Kazmi, H.H.S. and K.S. Batra. 2004. *Advertising and Sales Promotion*. Second Ed. New Delhi: Excel Books.

Kirkpatrick, J. 2007. *In Defense of Advertising: Arguments from Reason, Ethical Egoism, and Laissez-Faire Capitalism*. Claremont CA: TLJ Books.

Olatunji, R.W. 2003. The impact of the structural adjustment programme on the advertising industry in Nigeria (1986–1996). Unpublished PhD Thesis, University of Ibadan, Ibadan, Nigeria.

Pontifical Council for Social Communications. 2010. Ethics in advertising. http://www.vatican.va/roman_curia/pontifical_councils/pccs/documents/rc_pc_pccs_doc_22021997_ethics-in-ad_en.html (retrieved 08/05/2012)

Russell, T.J. and R.W. Lane. 1993. *Kleppner's Advertising Procedure*. Twelfth Ed. New Jersey: Prentice Hall.

Shimp, A.T. 2000. *Advertising Promotion: Supplemental Aspects of Integrated Marketing Communications*. Fort Worth, TX: The Dryden Press.

Vanden Bergh, G.B. and H. Katz. 1999. *Advertising Principles, Choice, Challenge, Change*. Lincolnwood, IL: NTC Business Books.

Wells, W., Moriarty, S. and J. Burnett. 2007. *Advertising Principles and Practice*. Seventh Edition. New Delhi: Prentice-Hall.

CHAPTER 7

PUBLIC RELATIONS AND PROPAGANDA: RELATIONSHIPS AND RELEVANCE

SUNDAY ADEKUNLE AKINJOGBIN & NOEEM TAIWO THANNY

Introduction

One of the most contentious issues in the communication disciplines is distinguishing public relations from propaganda. While some scholars and professionals hold the view that both are essentially the same, others argue the contrary. Even though both public relations and propaganda are forms of persuasion and rely on the same media of communication, they serve different purposes and objectives, yet they interface in many ways.

Historically speaking, 'white' propaganda, a type of propaganda which uses benign techniques to fight 'bad' propaganda and promote objectives that elites consider good (Baran and Davis 2006: 74), provided a basis for the development of promotional communication methods which are widely used today in advertising and public relations. Of course, both public relations and propaganda rely on public opinion to function effectively. The concern of this chapter is to show the relationships between these concepts, their relevance to society and how they interface. To have a better understanding of the relationships that exist between the two concepts, it is necessary first to clarify these concepts.

Clarification of Concepts: Public Relations vs Propaganda

Just like public opinion, public relations (PR) does not have a universally accepted standard definition. However, everybody has an opinion about what PR is, and virtually everyone uses its principles and methods every now and then. This cacophony of opinions has led to a lot of misconceptions equating PR with protocol, courtesy, goodwill, friendship, free gifts, annual parties, cash bonuses and so on (Daramola 2003). The lack of a universally accepted definition led American historian Robert Heilbroner (cited in Sietel 1989: 8) to describe the field as "a brotherhood of some 100,000 whose common bond is its profession and whose common woe is that no two of them can ever quite agree on what the profession is". However, both practitioners and communication theorists have made important efforts at arriving at a generally acceptable standard definition, and substantial headway toward a clearer understanding of the field has been made in recent years.

One of the most ambitious attempts to agree on a universal definition was initiated in 1975 by the Foundation for Public Relations Research and Education. Sixty-five PR leaders participated in the study, which synthesised 472 different definitions into the following (Seitel 1989: 9):

> Public relations is a distinctive management function which helps establish and maintain mutual lines of communication, understanding, acceptance and cooperation between an organization and its publics, involves the management of problems or issues, helps the management to keep informed on and responsible to public opinion; defines and emphasizes the responsibility of management to serve the public interest, helps management keep abreast of and effectively utilize change, serving as an early warning system to help anticipate trends, and uses research and sound and ethical communication techniques as its principal tools.

Edward Bernays, widely regarded as the father of the profession, sees PR (1952: 3) as a means of providing information to the public, a means of persuasion directed at the public to modify attitudes and actions and a means of integrating the attitudes and actions of an institution with its publics and the attitudes and actions of its publics with those of that institution. Another definition emerged from an assembly of Public Relations Associations in Mexico in 1978, where PR experts from thirty-eight countries developed "The Mexican Statement". This defines public relations as the art and social science of analysing trends, predicting their consequences, counselling organisation leaders and implementing planned programs of actions which will serve both the organisation's and the public's interest (Daramola 2003: 12). From the above definitions offered by various scholars and practitioners, it is clear that public relations has to do with relationship management between an individual, corporate organisation or government and its publics through communication. Moreover, it is a two-way process that is planned and supervised by the management to protect the mutual interests of an organisation and its publics.

Propaganda, on the other hand, is mostly understood today in a pejorative sense, as a deliberate effort to convey falsehood and untruthfulness. It is seen as an attempt to hoodwink the receiver into believing the story of the communicator and to swallow, as it were, the untruthful story hook, line and sinker. At best, it is seen as a process of communication craftily deployed by the propagandist to convey and promote believability over understanding and conviction (Aledeh 2010). However, propaganda has not always been seen as a strategy to promote falsehood and deceit. Originally, it was conceived as a communication strategy to positively project an otherwise just cause, to promote, propagate and spread the Christian faith. What then is propaganda?

Scholars have looked at the term from positive, neutral and negative perspectives, and various definitions have been offered. *The Chambers Compact Dictionary* (2009) defines propaganda as "the organized circulation by a political group, etc, of doctrine, information, misinformation, rumour, or opinion intended to influence public feeling, raise public awareness, bring about reform, etc." It further states that propaganda "originally refers to the administrative board of a Roman Catholic Church responsible for foreign missions and training of missionaries" and has its roots in the expression "to propagate", which simply means to spread or popularise ideas, etc. The Sacred Congregation for the Propagation of the Faith (*Sacra Congregatio de Propaganda Fide*) was established by Pope Gregory XV in the 17th century, as a congregation of the Roman curia having jurisdiction over missionary territories and related institutions.

However, Webster's also defines propaganda as "the spreading of ideas, information or rumours for the purpose of helping or injuring an institution, a cause, or a person" and as "ideas, facts, or allegations spread deliberately to further one's cause or to damage an opposing cause… [or] a public action having such an effect". In plain language, therefore, propaganda is a form of communication which can be deployed either for hurtful or helpful purposes. Nevertheless, according to Watson (2003: 92), the term 'propaganda' is generally associated with brazen strategies of persuasion and with information that is distorted, partisan or untrue. Thus, the noun ('propaganda') has acquired a bad name, but the verb ('to propagate') is something no society can do without. The spread of opinions, attitudes and beliefs, and the advocacy of change or reform, have been key elements of communication throughout history.

O'Donnell (2005, cited in Akinsiku 2011: 8), defines propaganda as the deliberate and systematic attempt to shape perceptions, manipulate cognitions and direct behaviour to achieve a response which promotes the desired intent of the propagandist. Nelson (1996) more comprehensively describes propaganda as a systematic form of purposeful persuasion which attempts to influence the emotions, attitudes, opinions and actions of specified target audiences for ideological, political or commercial purposes through the controlled transmission of one-sided messages via mass and direct media channels. Looking closely at these two definitions, the focus is on the communicative processes which allow propaganda to be considered objectively and then interpreted as negative or positive depending on the perspective of the viewer or listener. For Daramola (1994: 18), propaganda denotes an effort to influence people's actions, attitudes, beliefs or opinions through words, pictures, symbols, music and so forth. He argues that one of the most objective definitions of propaganda sees it as "a presentation of carefully selected facts and ideas arguing in favour of one viewpoint while obscuring the others".

Types of Public Relations and Propaganda

Although nearly every public has a special branch of PR devoted and dedicated to it, the most popular specialisation areas in the profession are employee relations, industrial relations, financial relations, community relations, customer relations, government relations, press relations and international public relations.

Public Relations

Employee Relations

This branch of public relations specialises in building better relationships between employees and management. One of the greatest challenges of employee relations is to encourage management to listen more and talk less, according to Lindheim (cited in Daramola 2003). This challenge increases as the work force of a company expands and the lines of communication between management and workers become more complex and stressful. Due to poor communication, misunderstandings arise, or workers feel they do not have adequate opportunity to express their views. To improve employee relations, management should be advised to provide better working conditions and listen more to workers' complaints and concerns as expressed by labour unions.

Industrial Relations

This area of PR deals with establishing and improving mutually beneficial relations between a company, other businesses and organisations within the same industry and related ones, especially in relation to the following categories: suppliers, distributors, competitors and labour unions. While a manufacturer depends on suppliers for raw materials, semi-finished goods, product components and other inputs, the company equally relies on distributors such as wholesalers to move the outputs of its factories and plants to the ultimate consumers or end users.

Financial Relations

This branch of public relations is dedicated to improving understanding through better communication with the financial publics of a company such as shareholders, stock brokers, pension fund managers, investors, stock exchange markets, banks and insurance agencies. The mission of financial relations is to provide a good understanding of the current financial position and the future prospects of a company, including its sales, prices, profits, earnings, taxes and so on.

Community Relations

This area of public relations is devoted to creating a relationship of good neighbourliness between an organization and other companies as well as groups within the community in which it is physically located.

Customer Relations

Customers are among the most valuable assets of any company. They are sources of repeat purchases, testimonials, references and new customers. Consumer relations specialists are experts in fostering better relationships with consumers through effective communication. Developing better relations with the consuming public is a monumental task even for large companies. A partial solution is to communicate with consumers through their sub-groups such as youths, men, women, mothers, fathers, parents, senior citizens, professionalsethnic and religious groups.

Government Relations

Government sets and enforces the rules by which all businesses must operate. Government relations specialists are engaged by business to assist in writing the rules and regulations as well as making a contribution in setting the political climate. An effective government relations representative must have a voice in ant relevant legislation or law enacted and play a role in determining government policies, especially taxation.

Press Relations

Although public relations and press relations share the same initials (PR), the two are not the same. Press relations is only a branch of public relations. It is also known as media relations. The objective of press relations is to maximise free publicity for a corporate event so as to create public knowledge and understanding.

International Public Relations

International public relations deals with fostering better relations with foreign publics through information adapted to the special circumstances of each national public. Although the global village has emerged due to technological advancement in the electronic media of mass communication, the task of communicating even the same message to different national publics is daunting due to variations in culture, languages, customs, traditions, biases, prejudices and preferences.

Propaganda

In contrast to public relations, the various types propaganda are classified according to the source and nature of the message. Modern practitioners of propaganda utilise various schemas to classify different types of propaganda activities. One such categorisation classifies propaganda as white, gray, or black according to the degree to which the sponsor conceals or acknowledges its involvement.

White Propaganda

This type of propaganda comes from an openly identified source and generally is characterised by gentler methods of persuasion. In other words, white propaganda is correctly attributed to the sponsor, and the source is truthfully identified.

Gray Propaganda

Gray propaganda, on the other hand, is not attributed to the sponsor and conceals the real source of the propaganda. The objective of gray propaganda is to advance viewpoints which are in the interest of the originator but which would be less acceptable to target audiences if the propaganda seemed to be "official". The reasoning is that avowedly propagandistic materials from a foreign government or identified propaganda agency might convince few, but the same ideas presented by seemingly neutral outlets would be more persuasive. An example of gray propaganda would be an article in a newspaper written by a disguised source. Other gray propaganda tactics involve wide dissemination of ideas put forth by others by foreign governments, by national and international media outlets or by private groups, individuals and institutions. Gray propaganda also includes material assistance provided to groups that put forth views deemed useful to the propagandist.

Black Propaganda

Black propaganda also camouflages the sponsor's participation, but, while gray propaganda is unattributed, black propaganda is falsely attributed. Black propaganda is rebellious and provocative; it is usually designed to appear to have originated from a hostile source in order to cause that source embarrassment, to damage its prestige, to undermine its credibility or to get it to take actions it would not otherwise take. Black propaganda is usually prepared by secret agents or an intelligence service, because it would be damaging to the originating government if it were discovered. It routinely employs underground newspapers, forged materials and planted gossip or rumours.

An additional category of propaganda might be termed "propaganda of the deed". This involves actions taken for the psychological effects they will have on various publics. Propaganda of the deed can also include such disparate actions as educational or cultural exchanges, economic aid, disaster relief, disarmament initiatives, international agreements, the appointment of investigating commissions, legislation and other policy initiatives when employed primarily for the effects they will have on public opinion.

Usefulness of Public Relations and Propaganda

Public relations is used by individuals, groups and corporate organisations to meet a variety of needs (Bernays 1952: 8). For example, public relations is an implementing factor in the many and varied competitive battles for public support in any country. Political parties use it when they compete for the public's vote, and so do labour unions when they compete for membership and jurisdiction. Management competes with management, industry with industry, company with company, product with product. Farmers compete with land markets, government support systems and the consumer's dollar; farm product competes with farm product. Social, educational, sport, entertainment, and church groups compete with one another for public favour and support.

In all these environments, public relations enables groups or individuals to cope more effectively with the accelerated modern transportation and communication networks which have increased the complexity of our lives. People are now more interdependent because the world is smaller. Our daily lives are affected by what people think of us, both near and far away. Public relations evaluates the potential impacts of public opinion and acts to meet the given situation. Through public relations, an individual or group can ensure that public decisions are based on knowledge and understanding. The public makes vital decisions both at the ballot box and the counter. People get their information in great part from the mass media, which also serve as sources of attitudes and actions. Such knowledge is a prerequisite to sound decisions. Public relations, therefore, enables individuals and groups on a broad basis to apply the findings of the social sciences to achieve better understanding and integration with their publics. Application of this knowledge is important to the preservation and development of our society. The public relations practitioner, as a specialist, attempts to apply the findings of social science as an engineer applies the laws of physics or a doctor the findings of medical research.

Public relations facilitates adjustment and accommodation to the times. People and institutions often lag behind contemporary public opinion, and the objective-minded public relations practitioner helps his or her client adjust to the contemporary situation, or helps the public adjust to it. Public relations brings to human maladjustments the skill and point of view of a technician with expert knowledge of how human relationships function. Maladjustments in many fields – commerce, industry, religion, and government – are based on misunderstandings of realities and/or ineffective communications processes. Conflict based on differing values is part of our competitive system, but conflict based on misunderstanding, ignorance and apathy is unnecessary and wasteful.

Public relations also provides a potent tool in the promotion of a better understanding of democracy. For one thing, it counteracts the tyranny of the majority and helps maintain respect for pluralism. It also provides knowledge and techniques to enable leaders to be more effective. In a democracy, leadership is dependent on understanding the public and knowing how to reach it. To citizens in general, public relations is important because it helps them to understand the society of which they are a part, to know and evaluate the viewpoints of others, to exert leadership, to evaluate the leadership efforts being of others and to persuade or suggest better courses of action.

To the businessperson, public relations is also vital. People in business deal with many publics – purveyors, workers, customers, governments, communities, retailers, wholesalers, stockholders, sources of credit and so on. Each of these publics plays its part in the life of an individual business. Insensitivity to any of these publics may affect the total relationships; relationships with the public do not depend only on what is actually done, they also depend on what members of any of these publics think has been done or not done.

Approaches to Propaganda

The main approaches to propaganda are discussed below.

Emotional Approach

Most propaganda is primarily emotional rather than rational in content. For Hitler, persuasion was only about generating collective emotion. The masses, he is reported to have said, are "like a woman, whose psychic state has been determined less by abstract reason than by an emotional longing for a strong force which will complete her nature. Likewise, the masses love a commander, and despise a petitioner" (Blain 1988 cited in Aledeh 2011: 10). In this view, the rational model of decision-making ignores the power of emotional prejudice to outweigh factual truth. Known facts cannot bleach out negative associations and the powerful emotions they inspire. The power of emotional appeals also arises partly out of our difficulty in resolving uncertainty, where there is no logical path but only multiple risk. Take the case of genetically modified foods. The concerned citizen remains mystified. One set of partisans point to the potential of GM crops to liberate the Third World from hunger, arguing that fewer pesticides are required and less land needs to be cultivated. Their opponents respond with the rhetoric of "Frankenstein foods". As O'Shaughnessy and O'Shaughnessy (2003) cited by Aledeh (2010) point out, people do not react in proportion to the probability of some particular outcome: epistemic emotions exist independently logical probability. Even when there is a recognition that some outcome is highly unlikely, there is always wishful thinking, while insecurity and uncertainty create a vigorous market for dogmatic reassurance. Thus, the appeal of propaganda is, in general, to emotion and not reason, and proceeds by dogmatic assertion, as if there could be no debate on the propositions advanced. In Le Bon's words "an orator wishing to move a crowd must make an abusive use of violent affirmation" (cited in Herzstein 1978 cited by Yusuf 2011: 18). Dogmatic assertion elevates mere value judgement to the status of truth or law and, contrary to Petty and Cacioppo (1981), people are persuaded when they are content to delegate their thinking to others, be it pundit, priest or politician. Constant assertion can stun consciousness, naturalising the perverse as normal and interrupting internal dialogue to prevent counter-argument.

Propaganda, therefore, is not a nuanced production. Its assertions have little qualification, and the arguments of opponents are parodied rather than rebutted. There is frequent recourse to ad hominem arguments, with opponents presented as either bigoted or self-interested. Repetitions, simplifications and black-white polarisations abound. President Ronald Reagan, for example, used anecdote and metaphor rather than argument, introducing citizens who had performed some selfless act, promulgating a never-never land of trickle-down effects and Laffer curves. In this mode, evidence is not assessed or explained but manipulated or invented. Propaganda texts contain scant recognition or capacity for intellectual abstraction. They are actively antagonistic to abstract thought, eschewing the tentative, the complex line of argument, the weighing and debating of evidence. The concern of the propagandist is not with how we think but how we feel.

Utopian Approach

Much propaganda relies on images of utopia – either a hoped-for utopia or one buried in the past. Many political extremists are disappointed utopians, and the vision of a perfect world is the implicit presence behind propaganda. This accounts for the extremism of propaganda and its rejection of compromise. It is impatience with the messiness, fluidity and compromise of the real world that identifies propaganda.

Persuasion

Most human beings are always, at least potentially, open to persuasion and, therefore, to that variant of persuasion known as propaganda. We may sometimes disobey our most dearly held principles or ideals, since principles are never specific commands but general rules, thus raising the possibility of deviance in any particular instance. We may be environmentally conscious shoppers but lapse on occasion. As Levitin and Miller (1979) show, the relationship between general ideology and specific choice is not strong. Our choices are not linear projections from our principles; if they were, our beliefs would be extraordinarily tenacious and saturate every action we undertook. Many decisions are complex and ultimately incoherent, drawing upon myriad beliefs and values, some contradictory, some changing in intensity according to context. If our principles do represent imprecise general rules rather than specific commands, the possibility of persuasion must exist in perpetuity, since there is always a potential openness in the application of the general rule to the specific case, a flexibility propaganda can always exploit. Thus, propaganda does not try to change values; it attempts to conscript them. Every advocate knows that values are almost impossible to alter overnight. They move slowly over time as a result of exposure to rival arguments and mature reflection. This is because values are difficult to change, since they are not open to factual correction. Values can be neither proved nor disproved. They are also part of a structure, and to alter one is to alter the relationship of all the variables in the system, a potentially life-changing event. Propaganda seeks only to interpret those values to yield different value judgments.

Default Belief Approach

Propaganda can be irrational but effective because it mobilises an individual's system of default beliefs. Discarded thoughts and the fragments of defunct ideologies may still survive like shadows that flit about in the recesses of our minds. They may come back if, for example, conditions change, challenging more recent structures of belief. Thus, the impact of propaganda can be very long-term indeed, encouraging adherence to a cause long after defeat has become inevitable or has even already occurred. Hopeless causes still have life left in them, testament to the enduring power of propaganda. There are many reasons for this. For example, we may have aspirations to bring about something but recognise that our goals will never be realized, yet we continue to pursue hopeless causes because it makes us feel we are doing something to bring about our vision. Lost causes litter the landscape of history and pass on from one generation to another. In addition, whereas beliefs may be changed by new information, emotions do not necessarily cohere with them, at least not straight away. They may continue to carry the charge created by past propaganda.

The Self-Deception Approach

A further explanation for the persistence of propaganda is its role in self-persuasion. The propagandist, whether party activist or religious missionary, internalises adherence by the activity of propagandising. In other words, the function of propaganda can degenerate into servicing the psychological needs of those who produced it. Herzstein (1978) points out that, by 1944, German imminent defeat in the Second World War was obvious, yet Goebbels continued to propagandise for victory, because "he was making propaganda as much for himself and the leadership as for the masses". Herzstein (1978 cited in Yusuf 2011: 18) argues that the later products of Nazi cinema and the slogan "Victory in death" represented "visions of salvation". For the Nazi elite, the aim was to transcend the doom-laden present via belief in an immortality conferred by the approving judgments of history and future generations of Germans.

The Fantasy Approach

Hyperbole does not make the mistake of asking for belief. It is a fantasy which we are invited to share, explicit and paranoid, but the fantasy does nevertheless affect perceptions of reality. One form of hyperbole is classic atrocity propaganda, for example, the British claim in the First World War that the Germans melted bodies for fat. Such fiction work not because people necessarily believe them but because they are willing co-partners in a process of self-deceit of which they may be fully conscious. They want to see their own darkest fears and angry broodings made visible and luminous. Propaganda does that for them. In other words, there is a political truth that exists independent of the objective factors in a given situation. Propaganda is hyperbole-fantasy whose aim is to trigger self-persuasion by getting people to imagine some event, encounter or person. They then talk themselves into believing or desiring something via this process of self-imagining. Much consumer advertising is also an invitation to share a fantasy, with the hope that imagining using the product will create an inner dialogue.

Techniques of Propaganda

As a very organised form of persuasion, propaganda involves the dissemination of biased ideas and opinions, often through the use of lies, deceptions, distortions, exaggerations and censorship. It is the communication of a point of view, moral, amoral or immoral, with the ultimate goal to persuade the recipient to accept the propagandist's view. However, when words are used as weapons, the truth is usually the first victim. Small wonder that the word "propaganda" has developed a negative connotation. The oldest trick of the propagandist is to demonise and dehumanise the hated other and make the enemy a faceless object. This makes it easier to hurt the opponent. In recent wars, propagandists have tried to mobilise hatred against the enemy, preserve the friendship of allies and enlist the cooperation of neutrals. A major goal is always to demoralise the enemy. The principle of any-means-to-an-end results in the spread of false rumours, the creation of gross exaggerations and the telling of outright lies. In addition, the propagandist has often imposed censorship to increase the effectiveness of propaganda. The Roman Catholic Church had its index of forbidden literature and Hitler's Germany its book-burning sessions. America at one time prohibited the printing of comic strips in which the term 'atomic bomb' appeared. An extreme form of propaganda which goes beyond just the use of words is brainwashing. Brainwashing is a method of influencing people to change their beliefs and accept as true what they previously had considered false, or to consider false what they previously had thought was true. Isolation, sleep and food deprivation and other terrible practices are considered appropriate if they work to further the goal of mind control.

According to Sourcewatch (2009 cited in Yusuf 2011: 22) information dissemination strategies only become propaganda strategies when coupled with propagandistic messages. The typical techniques of propaganda generation include:

- Appeal to fear: This seeks to build support by instilling fear in the public. For example, during the Second World War, Joseph Goebbels exploited Theodore Kaufman's *Germany Must Perish!* to claim that the Allies sought the extermination of the German people. This strategy was also adopted during the Nigerian Civil War by Odumegwu Ojukwu to boost the morale of his ill-equipped soldiers and to garner support within Biafran territory as well as securing the recognition of his republic by countries such as France and Tanzania.
- Appeals to authority: Appeals to authority cite prominent figures to support a position, idea, argument or course of action. The present ill-timed rebranding of Nigeria is a classic example of appeals to authority. Many prominent figures – religious leaders and traditional rulers – are being cited as supporting the rebranding process.
- Bandwagon: Bandwagon and inevitable-victory appeals attempt to persuade the target audience to take the course of action "everyone else" is taking. This technique reinforces people's natural desire to be on the wining side. It is used to convince the audience that something is an expression of an irresistible mass movement and that it is in their interest to join. "Inevitable victory" invites those not already on the bandwagon to join those already on the road to certain victory. Those already on the bandwagon are reassured that staying aboard is the best course of action. This technique was used by the Abacha/Diya junta to bring on board "progressives".
- Obtain disapproval: This technique is used to get the audience to disapprove of an action or idea by suggesting the idea is popular with groups hated, feared or held in contempt by the target audience. Thus, if a group which supports a policy is led to believe that undesirable, subversive or contemptible people also support it, the members of the group might decide to change their position. This was the case with the Abacha-foisted Constituent Assembly.
- Glittering generalities: Glittering generalities are intensely emotionally appealing words so closely associated with highly valued concepts and beliefs that they carry conviction without supporting information or reasons. They appeal to such emotions as love of country or home and desire for peace, freedom, glory, honour and so on. Though the words and phrases are vague and suggest different things to different people, their connotation is always favourable.
- Rationalisation: Individuals or groups may use favourable generalities to rationalise questionable acts or beliefs. Vague and pleasant phrases are often used to justify such actions or beliefs.

- Intentional vagueness: Generalities are deliberately vague so that the audience may supply its own interpretations. The intention is to move the audience by the use of undefined phrases, without analysing their validity or attempting to determine their reasonableness or application.
- Transfer: This is a technique of projecting the positive or negative qualities (phrase or blame) of one person, entity, object or value (an individual, group, organisation, nation etc.) onto another in order to make the second more acceptable or to discredit it. This technique is often used to transfer blame from one member of a conflict to another. It evokes an emotional response which stimulates the target to identify with recognised authorities.
- Oversimplification: Favourable generalities are used to provide simple answers to complex social, political, economic or military problems. Common man: The common or plain folks approach attempts to convince the audience that the propagandist's positions reflect the common sense of the people. It is designed to win confidence by communicating in the common manner and style of the audience. Propagandists use ordinary language and mannerisms (and clothes in face-to-face and audiovisual communications) in attempting to identify their point of view with that of the average person.
- Testimonial: Testimonials are quotations, in or out of context, cited to support or reject a given policy, action, programme or personality. The reputation or the role (expert, respected public figure etc.) of the individual giving the statement is exploited. The testimonial places the official sanction of a respected person or authority on a propaganda message. This is done in an effort to cause the target audience to identify itself with the authority or to accept the authority's opinions and beliefs as its own.
- Stereotyping or labelling: This technique attempts to arouse prejudices in an audience by labeling the object of the propaganda campaign as something the target audience fears, hates, loathes or finds undesirable.
- Scapegoating: This involves assigning blame to an individual or group not really responsible, thus alleviating the feelings of guilt of responsible parties and/or distracting attention from the need to fix the problem for which blame is being assigned.
- Virtue words: These are words in the value system of the target audience which tend to produce a positive image when attached to a person or issue. Peace, happiness, security, wise leadership and freedom are common examples of virtue words.
- Slogans: A slogan is a brief, striking phrase which may include labelling and stereotyping. Good slogans are self-perpetuating memes.

Techniques of Propaganda Transmission

The media of mass communication are the vehicles for transmitting propaganda messages. In the First and Second World Wars, posters, pamphlets, fine arts, music, theatre, literature and radio were widely used. The Nazis believed in propaganda as a vital tool in achieving their goals. During the Cold War, both the United States and the Soviet Union used propaganda extensively. They used film, television and radio programming to influence their own citizens, each other and other nations. The media became the vehicles to convey their white, black or gray propaganda.

In all these media, propagandists use a variety of techniques, but most techniques rely on some element of censorship or manipulation, either omitting significant information or distorting it. Hundreds of specific methods are used to propagate ideas and control minds, but, ultimately, all of them can be classified into a few overlapping categories, overlapping because, in practice, more than one category tends to be used at the same time.

Assertion

An assertion is an enthusiastic or energetic statement presented as a fact, although it is not necessarily true. Assertions often imply that the statement requires no explanation or substantiation but should merely be accepted without question. Examples of assertion, although somewhat scarce in wartime propaganda, can often be found in modern advertising propaganda. Any time an advertiser states that a product is the best, without providing evidence for this, an assertion is being made. The audience, ideally, should simply agree to the statement without reasoning or searching for additional information. Assertions, although usually simple to spot, are often dangerous forms of propaganda because they often include falsehoods or lies.

Bandwagon

Bandwagon is one of the most common techniques in both wartime and peacetime propaganda and plays an important part in modern advertising. It is a very powerful technique for exerting pressure on people by appealing to 'everyone else' who is enthusiastic about it. People have a tendency to follow what everyone else is doing. This tendency is reinforced by the inherent insecurity that almost everyone has. This insecurity makes them afraid to be different from others. The bandwagon technique is used to induce people into buying things they do not need, talking about things that are not appropriate and doing things that are questionable. Essentially, bandwagon propaganda tries to convince the subject that one side is the winning side because more people have joined it. The subject is meant to believe that, since so many people have joined, victory is inevitable and defeat impossible. Since the average person always wants to be on the winning side, he or she is compelled to join in. A modern twist involves convincing the subject that, since everyone else is doing it, he or she will be 'left out' by not joining in. This is, effectively, the opposite of the other type of bandwagon, but usually produces the same results. When confronted with bandwagon propaganda, we should weigh the pros and cons of joining in independently from the number of people who have already (supposedly) joined, and, as with most types of propaganda, we should seek more information.

Card-stacking

Card-stacking is a well-known art for cheating the ignorant or deceiving a gullible opponent. Card-stacking, or 'selective omission', is such a powerful method for propagating error that even a person familiar with the methods of propaganda can often be tricked. It is one of the seven fundamental techniques identified by the Institute of Propaganda Analysis. Card-stacking involves only presenting information that is positive to an idea or proposal and omitting information contrary to it. It is used in almost all forms of propaganda and is extremely effective. Although the information presented by the card-stacking approach may true, the technique is dangerous because it omits important counter-information. The best way to deal with card-stacking is to get more information.

Glittering Generalities

Glittering generalities are words that have inherently positive and are linked to highly valued concepts. When these words are used, they demand approval without thinking, simply because such an important concept is involved. For example, if a person is asked to do something in 'defense of democracy', they are more likely to agree, because the concept of democracy has an invariably positive connotation. Words often used as glittering generalities include 'honour', 'glory', 'love of country' and 'freedom'. When encountering glittering generalities, we should especially consider the merits of the idea itself when separated from the specific words.

Lesser of Two Evils

This technique presents an idea or proposal as the less offensive option. It is often used during wartime to convince people of the need for sacrifices or to justify difficult decisions and is often accompanied by blaming an enemy country or political group. When confronted with this technique, the subject should consider the value of any proposal independently of those it is being compared with.

Name-calling

Name-calling occurs often in politics and wartime scenarios but very seldom in advertising. It is the use of derogatory language or words that carry a negative connotation when describing an enemy. The propaganda attempts to arouse prejudice by labelling the target as something the public dislikes. Name-calling is often employed using sarcasm and ridicule and shows up often in political cartoons or writings. When examining name-calling propaganda, we should attempt to separate our feelings about the name from our feelings about the actual idea or proposal.

Plain Folks

This is an attempt by the propagandist to convince the public that his or her views reflect those of the common person and that they are for the benefit of the common person. The propagandist will often attempt to use the accent of a specific audience, as well as using culturally specific idioms or jokes. Especially during speeches, the propagandist may even attempt to intensify the illusion through imperfect pronunciation, stuttering and a more limited vocabulary. Errors such as these help add to the impression of sincerity and spontaneity. This technique is usually most effective when used with glittering generalities in an attempt to convince the public that the propagandist's views about highly valued ideas are similar to their own and therefore unarguable. When confronted by this type of propaganda, the subject should consider the proposals and ideas separately from the personality of the presenter.

Testimonials

Testimonials are quotations or endorsements, in or out of context, which attempt to connect a famous or respectable person with a product or item. Testimonials are very closely connected to the transfer technique, in that an attempt is made to connect an agreeable person to another item. Testimonials are often used in advertising and political campaigns. When coming across testimonials, the subject should consider the merits of the item or proposal independently of the person of organisation giving the testimonial.

Transfer

In this technique, the propagandist induces people to transfer their respect, admiration, reverence or faith from some well-known person to something (claimed to be) related to that person. For example, it is common to see sports and cinema stars endorsing a particular commercial product. The masses who hold these persons in respect transfer the same respect to the product. People who spread dubious doctrines and viewpoints often appeal to the opinion of some scholar or other. People who motivate others to indulge in questionable activities often point to well-respected persons who are already acting that way, and this breaks down resistance.

Transfer is often used in politics and during wartime. It is an attempt to make the subject view a certain item in the same way as they view another item, to link the two in the subject's mind. Although this technique is often used to transfer negative feelings, it can also be used in positive ways. By linking an item to something the subject respects or enjoys, positive feelings can be generated for it. However, in politics, transfer is most often used to transfer blame or bad feelings from one politician to another of his friends or party members, or even to the party itself. When confronted with propaganda using the transfer technique, we should question the merits or demerits of the proposal or idea independently of our convictions about other objects or proposals.

The Relationship Between Public Relations and Propaganda

Public relations is an offshoot of white propaganda, which provided the basis for the development of the promotional methods widely used today in advertising and public relations. The resurgence of interest in propaganda theory, according to Latinen and Rakos (1997, cited in Baran and Davis 2006: 78) is due to these techniques, which seem to be more effective in the contemporary world of corporate media ownership. Daramola (1994) notes that public relations and propaganda interface in many other ways. For example, they are both forms of communication or persuasion, involving elaborate and skillful planning and the implementation of carefully considered strategies and tactics. Furthermore, both public relations and propaganda contain essentially three elements, information, persuasion and integration. In other words, they both inform people, persuade people and integrate people with people. In addition, they use the same channels of communication, the mass media, to achieve their goals.

Public relations is used mainly by corporate organisations for marketing purposes, while propaganda is used mainly by governments, political groups and, sometimes, religious organisations. In other words, public relations (and advertising), otherwise called commercial propaganda, are more about marketing and corporate governance, while propaganda is more about power and politics. Also, while propaganda is used to manipulate the public to advance the interests of the propagandists, public relations is used to mould public opinion to advance corporate interests. Even though both public relations and propaganda use similar techniques to accomplish their goals, it is assumed that propaganda involves a greater degree of deception and disinformation.

Similarly, both public relations and propaganda rely heavily on the concept of public opinion and its power. Indeed, meaningful public relations and propaganda can be undertaken only after the bases for and nuances of public opinion are understood. Both work to influence public opinion, the attitudes that support it and the actions taken on its behalf. Influencing public opinion remains at the heart of public relations and propaganda. Also, public relations and propaganda serve as platforms for the development and understanding of democracy, particularly in a developed democracy like the United States where the opinion of the public is greatly respected when formulating policy decisions.

The evolution of public relations and propaganda can also be traced to the same reason – the increasing complexity of life – and to the pressure of multiple information sources, the judgments they demand and the consequent need to digest information quickly and rapidly. Public relations practitioners are basically interpreters. They interpret public issues for management while, at the same time, interpreting the philosophies, goals and objectives of management for the various publics. On the other hand, propagandists are basically alarmists who use various kinds of strategies such as media hype, spin, sensationalism and others to colour issues and blow them out of proportion so as to cause unnecessary fear and anxiety among the contending opponents. However, because of the way some practitioners of public relations operate, they have been called 'hired guns' or mouthpieces, and many people to see them as propagandists.

Conclusion

In this chapter, we have attempted to give an overview of public relations and propaganda and discuss their similarities and differences. It is clear from this discussion that there is a thin line between propaganda and public relations, particularly in the context of galvanising public opinion on behalf of an organisation, government or issue. As society advances in technology and grows in complexity, the main tool that will be used to integrate society is public relations, while propaganda will continue to be the lubricant of democracy.

References

Akinsiku, I. 2011. Propaganda, public relations, opinion and political communication. Seminar paper presented at the Department of Mass Communication, University of Lagos, Nigeria.

Aledeh, K. 2011. Propaganda, public opinion and religion. Seminar paper presented at the Department of Mass Communication, University of Lagos, Nigeria, November.

Baran, S.J. and K.D. Davis, K.D., eds. 2006. *Mass Communication Theory: Foundations, Ferment and Future*. Belmont, CA: Wadsworth.

Bernays, E.L. 1952. *Public Relations*. Norman, OK: University of Oklahoma Press.

Daramola, A.C. 1994. Public relations and propaganda: An unpleasant association of terminologies. *Masscope* 2 (1): 10–22.

Daramola, A.C. 2003. *Fundamentals of Professional Public Relations: A Global Overview*. Lagos: Certified Marketing Communication Institute of Nigeria (CMCIN).

Herman, E. and Chomsky, N. 1988. *Manufacturing Consent: The Political Economy of the Mass Media*. Vintage: New York.

Kim, Seungkun Stephan. *University of Chicago: Theories of Media*. Winter 2007. 13 04 2012. Available at http://csmt.uchicago.edu/glossary2004/propaganda.htm#sthash.oyNJCMbK.dpuf

Levitin, T and Miller, W. 1979. Ideological interpretations of presidential elections. *American Political Science Review*. 73. pp 751–71.

Nelson, K.A. 1996. How consumers make socially responsible decisions. In Lee R. Beach (Ed.), *Decision Making in the Workplace: A Unified Perspective*. Mahwah, NJ: Lawrence Erlbaum Associates, pp. 165–80.

Petty, R.E and Cacioppo, J.T. 1981. *Attitudes and Persuasion: Classical and Contemporary Approaches*. New York: Westwiew Press.

Ross, Sheryl Tuttle. 2001. Understanding propaganda: The epistemic merit model and its application to art. *Journal of Aesthetic Education* 36 (1): 16–30.

Seitel, F.P. 1989. *The Practice of Public Relations*. Englewood Cliffs, NJ: Prentice Hall.

Watson, J. 2003. *Media Communication: An Introduction to Theory and Process*. New York: Palgrave.

Yusuf, F.A.O. 2009. An evaluation of mass media and propaganda. Seminar paper presented at the Department of Mass Communication, University of Lagos, Nigeria.

II
THE POLITICS OF ADVERTISING IN AFRICA

CHAPTER 8

ADVERTISING IN A GLOBALISING CULTURE: THE NIGERIAN EXPERIENCE

ROTIMI WILLIAMS OLATUNJI

Introduction

Culture comprises the totality of man's knowledge, beliefs, arts, morality, laws and technology. It not innate but is transmitted from one generation to the next. Culture is a historically transmitted system of symbols, meanings and norms (Collier 1994). The different aspects of culture are the ideological component, which focuses on beliefs and value systems, and the material aspect, which includes the architectural, technological and other visible aspects of development. A third critical component of culture relates to societal institutions which deal with the family, politics, the economy and other socialising agencies, such as educational and advertising institutions. The interrelationships of culture and advertising are discussed in this chapter.

History of Global Advertising

Formal advertising as a social and economic institution began at different times in different societies of the world. For example, the first formal (print) advertisement in the United Kingdom appeared in 1472, whereas the first print advertisement in the United States appeared in the *Boston Newsletter* in 1704. Ever since, the advertising industry in each country of the world has traversed distinct epochs of development before reaching the current level of global advertising practice. J. Walter Thompson (JWT), a US-based advertising agency, was the first to open a foreign office, which it located in London in 1899, a date commonly held to mark the beginning of global advertising practice (Maxcy 2008). Maxcy (2008) chronicles other stages in the evolution of global ad practice. He maintains that in 1923, JWT, using its London resources, developed the first campaign that was targeted at the British consumers of a US product. In 1927, General Motors employed the services of JWT to market its automobiles on a worldwide basis, beginning from the UK. Between 1927 and 1960, JWT acquired operations in over 40 countries worldwide, until the "eater" was itself "eaten up" in the 1980s, when JWT was acquired by the British advertising company, the WPP Group. Maxcy (2008) points out that "although JWT was an early innovator in international advertising, the rest of the advertising industry has followed this same pattern of expansion". One example was Young and Rubicam (Y&R), which opened its London office in 1940. By the end of 1999, Y&R had 331 offices in 64 countries and employed over 10,000 workers (Berg and Katz 1999, Olatunji 2005).

Three phases of global expansion of the advertising industry have been identified (Leiss et al. 1997). The first phase (1899–1950s) saw a small number of advertising agencies opening overseas offices to serve specific promotional needs of manufacturing clients in specific locations. This was followed in the 1960s and 1970s by major manufacturing companies exploring global markets and compelling their advertising agencies to equally expand their operations across major markets worldwide. The third and the final phase (1980s to the present) has seen the major US, European and Asian advertising agencies becoming global advertising powers, mainly through mergers and acquisitions, and providing diversified promotional services on a worldwide scale.

Leiss et al. (1997) identify two dominant strategies often adopted by advertising agencies to penetrate foreign markets: opening overseas offices and purchasing shares in existing overseas agencies, the latter step often serving as the prelude to a complete takeover. A third strategy is what Olatunji (2003) refers to as affiliation agreements between foreign and local advertising agencies. The goal of all three strategies is to broaden the scope of operations of the advertising agencies involved so as to harness the commercial potential of globalisation. The table presented below, adapted from Olatunji (2005), indicates the monopolistic nature of modern global advertising operations.

From Table 8.1, it is apparent that ad agencies such as Omnicom, WPP, Interpublic, and Young and Rubicam have become 'octopus' agencies. What the table does not reveal is that each of the identified subsidiaries also has a network of affiliate agencies in different nations of the world.

Table 8.1: Global Advertising Agencies

Conglomerates	World Rating	Subsidiaries/Remarks
Omnicom	No. 1	BBDO DDB Needham GGT Group TBWA International Network Diversified Agency Services (DAS) Others
WPP Group Plc	No. 2	J. Walter Thompson Millward Brown BMRD Grey Kanter Media Research Others
The Interpublic	No. 3	McCann Erickson Ammirati Puris Lintas The Lowe Group Western International Media Others
Dentsu Inc. (Japan)	No. 4	Not available
Young and Rubicam	No. 5	Burson-Marsteller

Global Integration of the Advertising Industry in Nigeria

Traditional forms of advertising existed in several of the pre-colonial societies that later constituted the Nigerian state. Advertising then largely involved the use of town criers, dance-drama groups, word-of-mouth, personal selling or hawking. In their various forms, traditional advertising strategies were used most effectively as attention-catching devices. But with the publication in 1859 of the first newspaper in Nigeria, classified forms of advertisement were introduced. Formal advertising practice in Nigeria began in 1928, less than a century ago, with the incorporation in the United Kingdom of West Africa Publicity Limited, an in-house advertising agency of the United African Company (UAC, now Unilever). The company inaugurated the advertising industry in Nigeria and later adopted the name Lever International Advertising Service or LINTAS. Ogilvy, Benson and Mather (OB&M), Graham & Gills (G&G), Advertising and Marketing Services and Grant Advertising were a few other examples of multinational advertising agencies that operated in Nigeria during the colonial era and for over ten years of Nigeria's independence. Thus, formal advertising practice in Nigeria began with foreign advertising agencies fully controlling the industry.

Olatunji (2003) identifies five distinct phases of the historical development of advertising in Nigeria: the pre-colonial period, the colonial and early post-independence era (1928–1971), the era of indigenisation policy (1972–1985), the era of structural adjustment programmes (SAPs) from 1986 to 1998 and, finally, the era of neo-liberalism (1999 to the present). Commenting on advertising during colonialism and the immediate post-colonial era, Olatunji and Laninhun (2009: 167) observe that "just as foreigners dominated Nigeria's colonial economy, so was their influence on the advertising industry during the same era". At political independence, "the stranglehold of foreign domination on the economy did not abate, even as foreign ownership of the advertising industry was the order of the day" (Ibid: 167). In 1972, however, the Federal Military Government issued the Indigenisation Decree, which excluded foreigners from direct participation in the advertising industry, among several others. This situation paved the way for Nigerian professionals to assume ownership and control of the advertising industry and previously foreign-owned advertising agencies. As Olatunji and Laninhun (2009: 178–9) observe: "[w]ith indigenisation, the advertising industry enjoyed an unparalleled form of government protection". In short, the indigenisation policy introduced a form of protectionism in the advertising industry. This led to increases in the number of Nigerians who participated in the advertising industry. Equally, the number of indigenous advertising agencies doubled within the first year of the policy (from 10 agencies in 1972 to 20 by 1973), and by 1983 the number of advertising agencies operating in the country that were owned by Nigerians had increased to 51.

The era of SAPs was introduced by the Federal Military Government of General Babangida in July 1986 and lasted up to December 1993. Much has been written and said about structural adjustment as an economic policy (Iwayemi 1995, Obadan and Ayodele 1998, Odejide 1996, Onimode 1989, Olatunji 2003). Olatunji (2003, 2005, 2007) and Olatunji and Laninhun (2009) extensively discuss the influence of SAPs on the advertising industry in Nigeria, emphasising that the policy of indigenisation was reversed during this era, thus paving the way for the formal integration of the Nigerian advertising industry into the global industry during the neo-liberal era of economic development introduced by the civilian government of President Olusegun Obasanjo (1999–2007). The adoption of SAPs in Nigeria in 1986 prepared the ground for the re-emergence of foreigners in the advertising industry. However, there was no direct ownership of advertising agencies in Nigeria by foreigners either in the active years of structural adjustment (1986–1994) or in the years immediately following (1994–1996), a period we now recognise as the early phase of neoliberalism. During the full-blown era of neoliberalism that followed there has been increased affiliation of local agencies to global agencies (Olatunji and Laninhun 2009: 187–8). In summary, the formal practice of advertising began in Nigeria in 1928 with foreign advertising agencies serving as catalysts. From 1972, the advertising industry was indigenized, but with the adoption of structural adjustment in 1986 and subsequent neo-liberal economic policies of the ruling party in Nigeria (1999–2007), the advertising industry has been re-aligned within the global context.

Creative Advertising Strategies in a Globalised Environment

Three distinct creative strategies which are often adopted by global advertising agencies have been identified (Leiss et al. 1997). In the first, the central office of the ad agency sends its subsidiaries a completed advertisement, or a complete campaign, for wholesale use. There is no room for any form of modification. The ad or campaign is used 'as is'. The second strategy is referred to as the 'prototype' strategy. Here, the central office sends a range of copies, visuals and aural materials to the subsidiary. These materials are developed following a central 'idea'. In turn, the subsidiaries adapt the materials to the local culture. The third strategy allows subsidiaries to use the creative work plan of the central office as guides to create advertising campaigns for their specific markets. The first strategy can be called the globalisation or standardisation approach, while the other two can be referred to as the glocalisation approach, a term we borrow from Maynard (2003: 57). Adali et al. (2000), Hooper (2000), Maynard (2003) and Wilkins (2002) draw attention to the numerous creative strategies adopted by advertisers and their agencies in the era of globalisation.

Standardisation is necessitated by the fact that globalisation itself is seen as homogenisation, universalism and singleness. Accordingly, advertising standardisation sees advertising as a universal commodity, product or brand that must offer "one sight, one sound, one sell", according to Maynard (2003: 58). Thus, in addition to the product that is standardised, the logo, image, selling themes and other brand manifestations are equally standardised. These make the brand recognisable wherever it is sold globally. Examples include global brands such as Nike, Gillette, Coca-Cola, British Airways, McDonalds, American Express and Kodak. These global brands combine "consistent name, standardized product image and similar features" (Maynard 2003: 59).

Moreover, some benefits of standardisation of advertising are that it enhances consistent brand image and identity on a global basis; single, well-coordinated advertising campaigns across different markets; and considerable savings in costs of advertising production, illustrative materials and media.

While globalisation of advertising calls for a centralised approach, glocalisation operates within the framework of either the decentralised approach or adaptation strategy. In the centralised strategy, agencies and clients often operate from one location and set global marketing and communication objectives, including finished creatives, which they merely send to local agencies to execute. Internet systems are used for sending the finished ads, concepts and artworks to the local offices. In turn, local and regional markets implement the lead, taking cognisance of local competition.

In the decentralised approach, local affiliates of leading global agencies produce advertising messages based on their understanding and interpretation of the centrally-agreed ad strategy. Factors that recommend the use of the decentralised strategy include the need for "proximity to the market in order to reach even the narrower segments within it, flexibility, cultural sensitivity and faster response time" (Adali et al. 2000: 12). The decentralised approach is also popular because there are variations in product ranges globally. Most importantly, "consumers respond best to ideas that fully accommodate their values" (Adali et al. 2000: 12). The adaptation approach retains the use of brand name, logo, product specifications and positioning strategies globally, but allows local agencies to determine consumer promotions, media choices and the use of public relations or other promotional campaigns.

Wilkins (2002) identifies market, media and consumer differences as factors that militate against the effectiveness of standardised advertising. On the economic plane, he argues that, since all the nations and regions of the world are at different levels of development, what may be affordable in one country may not necessarily be so in others. This affects the tone and positioning of advertising. Moreover, media environments and advertising regulations differ from nation to nation. The available media in a locality determine the type of advertising the people consume, while different advertising regulations either open up or restrict the advertisements that may be available to consumers.

There are also cultural differences within and between the nations and regions of the world. The cultural heritage, values, ethics and habits of one country influence audience perception and reactions to creative styles and strategies. Similarly, the ways consumers use, consume and interact with brands differ across societies. Hence, one formula for advertising across all societies of the world may not fit.

This calls for alternative strategies, variously called hybridisation or glocalisation (Adali et al. 2000, Hooper 2000).

Glocalisation of Advertising

Glocalisation, an alternative concept to globalisation, is a process that has a high regard for the local content in advertising creation and production. Glocalisation also challenges "the top-down hegemony implicit in the term 'globalization'" (Maynard 2003: 57). Glocalisation refers to "the creation of products or services intended for the global market, but customized to suit the local culture" (Maynard 2003: 60). Whereas globalisation tends towards centralisation, glocalisation accommodates decentralisation. In advertising, glocalisation allows messages to be "both global and yet to be local" (Adali et al. 2000: 13). The brand positioning and creative strategies developed for the advertiser reflect the inputs of local regional markets. Glocalisation allows for separate messages to be used to reach buyers in different markets by fitting the message to each particular market or country, and it accommodates differences in cultural, economic, legal, media and product features between countries and within each country.

Adali et al. (2000: 14) observe that "in reality, very few totally standardized global campaigns exist. Even those campaigns that may appear identical contain subtle adaptations in creative executions". Maintaining that marketing the same product globally with the use of the same information and strategy has proved to be "ineffective", Adali et al (2000: 14) note that "advertising agencies are beginning to realise that they cannot 'cookie cut' ideas that worked for one client to another". Hence advertisers are being called upon to adapt universal messages to meet culture-specific local requirements. As Mooij (1998: 3) notes: "Markets are people, not products. There may be global products, but there are no global people. There may be global brands, but there are no global motivations for buying these brands".

Therefore, to ensure accessibility of a marketing campaign to different cultures, the practice of glocalisation or adaptation appears to be the most appropriate strategy.

Globalisation, Advertising Ethics and Regulations

As an institution in society, advertising is guided by three sets of ethics (Arens 1999). The most appropriate of the three deals with ethical standards which prescribe philosophical rules governing the behaviour of ad practitioners and other stakeholders in the advertising process. This is referred to as "professional ethics", which Arens (1999: 59) says comprises "two interrelated components:

the traditional actions taken by people in a community and the philosophical rules that society establishes to justify past actions and decree future actions". Under this category of ethics, the rights of the individual members of the group or association are subjected to widely accepted ethical standards within the group. The remaining two types of ethics of relevance to advertising are either society-wide in application or personalised forms of ethics. In the former, there are certain ethical standards in the wider society that prescribe measures about goodness or badness, justice or injustice and the like. These ethical measures may vary from one society to another. Personalised ethics relate to the personal beliefs every individual has regarding what is good or bad. These are based on personal feelings, attitudes and value judgments. Advertising is much more concerned with professional ethics than the other levels of ethics.

Globalisation, as mentioned earlier, represents the drive towards sameness or homogeneity in all aspects of life across the world's communities. We may ask at this point if it is possible to have global advertising ethics. This proposition is arguable. A school of ethics, commonly referred to as ethical absolutism, believes that universal morals exist. Okunna (1995: 16) summarises the ethical absolutist perspective: whatever is considered right should "be right in all places, at all times and in all circumstances". The philosophical basis of globalisation is in line with this school of ethics, as it uses the institution of advertising to advance universal ethical standards through the global media. This it does to the consternation and of anti-globalisation scholars. The relativist ethical school, on the contrary, maintains that "moral standards should vary according to cultures, circumstances, times, etc." (Okunna 1995: 17). Judgements on what is good or bad are dependent on context.

Notwithstanding such disagreements, practitioners agree that advertising should adhere to ethical standards, which, according to Arens (1999: 57) simply means "doing what the advertiser and the advertiser's peers believe is morally right in a given situation". This is different from social responsibility, which refers to "doing what society views as best for the welfare of people in general or for a specific community of people" (Arens 1999: 57). Thus, Arens (1999: 57) argues that "[t]ogether, ethics and social responsibility can be seen as a moral obligation of advertisers not to violate our basic economic assumptions even when there is no legal obligation".

As a result of the increasing globalisation of the advertising industry, advertisers now use similar campaigns or even the same advertisements in several countries of diverse cultural settings. The fact that messages perceived to be ethical in one society might be considered unethical in others has compelled governments to regulate advertising. Moreover, the need to protect consumers against unethical advertising has led to advertising regulation in different societies of the world. In the United States, advertising is regulated through laws, judicial interpretations and several government regulatory agencies. The agencies include the Federal Trade Commission (FTC), the Food and Drug Administration (FDA), the Federal Communication Commission (FCC), the Patent and Trademark Office, the Library of Congress, and a host of others. The situation is similar in Nigeria, where advertising regulation occurs through several laws, edicts, judicial decisions and governmental regulatory agencies. Apart from the Advertising Practitioners Council of Nigeria (APCON), which directly regulates advertising practice, other agencies responsible for the regulation of advertising in Nigeria, directly or otherwise, include the National Food and Drug Administration and Control (NAFDAC), the Nigerian Communications Commission (NCC), the Central Bank of Nigeria (CBN), which regulates advertisements of financial products, the Nigeria Copyrights Commission, the Consumer Protection Council (CPC) and others. Virtually all other countries of the world have similarly complex regulatory regimes (Arens 1999: 60).

However, advertising regulation in a globalised environment faces threats. It is, for instance, extremely difficult to regulate advertisements on the Internet. Similarly, regulating advertisements on interactive media such as digital television and other cable or satellite broadcasting systems, has proved problematic. These new media pose immense challenges to the enforcement of national laws and regulatory advertising frameworks. As an alternative, self-regulation of advertising (Boddewyn 1985), self-discipline or other regulatory measures put in place by advertising practitioners themselves might seem attractive. However, Olatunji (2005: 653) warns that "in spite of the attractiveness of the SRF (self-regulatory framework), experience and research findings demonstrate that practitioners often abuse this privilege". More and more, official sanctions against, and regulation of, advertising in a global era is proving difficult, if not impossible. Given this backdrop, "advertising self-regulation is highly beneficial for the development of both the industry and the profession at large," argues Olatunji (2005: 657). He concludes that the framework for bringing this about should be by giving more attention to "continuous education and training of extant and budding practitioners on issues of advertising ethics and social responsibility". Glocalised advertising, in the final analysis, adapts and adopts global best practices with due regards to cherished local cultural ethos, mores, morals and values.

References

Adali, E., Diaz, A., Page, P., Shanadi, A., Woo, C.M. and H. Zabad. 2000. *Global Best Practices*. Paper Presented to the International Advertising Association, New York.

Anyaoku, E. (2008a). Globalization and the developing countries. *The Guardian*.

Arens, W. 1999. *Cotemporary Advertising*. Boston, MA: Irwin, McGraw-Hill.

Boddewyn, J.J. 1985. Advertising Self Regulation: Private Government and Agent of Public Policy, *Journal of Public Policy and Marketing*, 129–41.

Collier, M. J. 1994. Cultural identity and intercultural communication. In L.A. Samovar and R.E. Porter, eds. *Intercultural Communication: A Reader*. Belmont, CA: International Thomas, 36–45.

Hooper, B. 2000. "Globalization and resistance in post-Mao China: The case of foreign consumer products. *Asian Studies Review* 24 (4): 439–70.

Iwayemi, A. 1995. Oil and the macroeconomy: A perspective on recent economic performance. In A. Iwayemi, ed. *Macroeconomic Policy Issues in an Open Developing Economy: A Case of Nigeria*. Ibadan: National Centre for Economic Management and Administration (NCEMA), 61–89.

Leiss, W, Kline, S. and S. Jhally. 1997. *Social Communication in Advertising*. New York: Routledge.

Maxcy, D. 2008. Advertising in a global context. In R. Dickinson, ed. *Postgraduate Programmes in Media and Communications Module 5 Guide*. London: University of Leicester.

Maynard, M.L. 2003. From global to glocal: How Gillete's Sensory Excel accommodates to Japan. *Keio Communication Review* 25: 57–75.

Mooij, M.D. 1998. *Global Marketing and Advertising: Understanding Cultural Paradoxes*. Thousand Oaks, CA: Sage.

Obadan, M. and S. Ayodele. 1998. Commercialization and Privatization Policy in Nigeria. Ibadan: National Centre for Economic Management and Administration (NCEMA).

Odejide, A.F. 1996. Beyond adjustment: The need to bridge the gap between theory and reality. In *Beyond Adjustments: Management of the Nigerian Economy*, Ibadan: NSE, 147–57.

Okunna, S.O. 1995. *Ethics of Mass Communication*. Enugu, Lagos & Abuja: New Generation Books.

Olatunji, R.W. 2005. Advertising ethics in a deregulated economy: The case of Nigeria. In E. Kaynak and T.D. Harcar, eds. *Global Business: The Challenges and Responsibilities in a World of Shifting Alliances*. Hummelstown, PA: The International Management Development Association (IMDA), 659–65.

Olatunji, R. W. 2003. The impact of the structural adjustment programme on the advertising industry in Nigeria (1986–1996). Unpublished PhD Thesis, University of Ibadan, Ibadan, Nigeria.

Olatunji, R.W. 2007. Advertising media planning, buying and selling in an open economy. In E. Kaynak and T.D. Harcar, eds. *Beyond Borders: New Global Management Development*

Challenges and Opportunities Hummelstown, PA: International Management Development Association, 767–73.

Olatunji R.W. and B.A. Laninhun. 2009. Neoliberalism: What Benefits for the Advertising Industry in Nigeria? In Anthony A. Olorunnisola, ed., *Media and Communications Industries in Nigeria: Impacts of Neoliberal Reforms between 1999 and 2007*. Lewiston, NY: The Edwin Mellen Press, 157–202.

Onimode, B. 1989. IMF and World Bank Policies in Africa. In B. Onimode, ed. *The IMF, The World Bank and African Debt: The Economic Impact*. London: Zed Books, 25–33.

Wilkins, J. 2002. Why is global advertising still the exception, not the rule? *Intercultural Communication Studies* 16 (2): 253–59.

CHAPTER 9

MEDIA LIBERALISATION IN KENYA: WHO BENEFITS?

JACINTA MWENDE MAWEU

Introduction

Following the gale of economic liberalisation programmes in much of Africa in the 1990s, breathtaking changes in the media landscape have remained the norm. Government monopoly has given way to private-sector competition with all its attractions – but not without some adverse consequences such "paid-for" news content and a blurring of the line between editorial and advertorial content. More than ever before, the media are more concerned with the profit motive at the expense of the public interest. This chapter examines the social, cultural and democratic implications in Kenya of the transformation of the media into a profit-seeking industry funded by advertisers to further the interests of capital. My main contention is that this commercialism has grave consequences. I argue that the media cannot function effectively as the people's watchdog under the pressure to compete for advertisers and audiences. The commercialisation of news media, in particular, reduces the quality of news content, leads to a loss of diversity of voices and hampers investigative reporting. The Herman and Chomsky (2002) "propaganda model" will guide this analysis of media performance and accountability in Kenya today.

Pre-Liberalisation Era

The mainstream media in Kenya started either as private businesses to serve colonial (white settler) interests or as state gazettes to spread colonial government propaganda. In 1901, Alibhai Mulla Jeevanjee, an Asian trader, established the first newspaper in Kenya, The *East African Standard*. He later sold it to individuals who were keen on serving settler interests. Much later, the colonial government established the Kenya Broadcasting Service (KBS), followed by the establishment, in 1958, of a television station (Makokha 2010). These early media ventures in Kenya exclusively served colonial interests. In response, Africans soon felt the need to start their own indigenous press through which they could express their grievances. The first African-owned press in Kenya, *Muiguithania*, was founded in 1928 by the Kikuyu Central Association, an anti-colonial political association. Its primary goal was to agitate for the socio- political empowerment of Africans. The indigenous press in Kenya was, therefore, a child of political expediency, as far as African freedom fighters were concerned. No wonder, therefore, that the pioneers of the indigenous media in Kenya were politicians rather than businessmen or media barons (Makali 2003). Nevertheless, by the time Kenya achieved independence in 1963, the mainstream print and electronic media were under foreign ownership. There were two main daily newspapers in English, the *Daily Nation* and the *East African Standard*), and one Kiswahili daily, *Taifa Leo*. There were also four weeklies, the *Sunday Nation*, the *Sunday Standard*, *Taifa Jumapili* and the *Weekly Review* and one television and radio station under the Kenya Broadcasting Corporation (KBC) which was owned by a consortium of British and American companies. The Aga Khan and Lonrho Ltd owned the *Nation* and *Standard* newspapers respectively (Ali 2009).

The new government saw the foreign ownership of the media as a threat to the nation's integrity and unity. The ruling class believed that foreign-owned media propagated foreign ideologies incompatible with the country's development agenda. They wanted the role of the media in newly independent Kenya to be defined by the ideals of unity and national development. The government, therefore, took control of the electronic media (KBC) but left the print media in private hands. Under a new name, "Voice of Kenya" (VOK), radio and television were to act as the government's mouthpiece while also educating, entertaining and informing the public. As part of the "nationalisation" process, new programs were introduced to promote African identity and cultural unity premised on Kenya's music and folklore, which were transmitted in Kiswahili (the national language). There was more focus on development journalism, and the media were supposed to help the new government in fighting the key development challenges: poverty, ignorance and disease.

But while the ruling elite proclaimed the role of the public broadcaster as a unifying and nation-building tool, in practice they used it to further their own narrow political agendas. They also manipulated the newspapers, which remained in private hands, especially through "the denial of import licenses for raw materials like newsprint and printing materials as well as sending signals to advertisers who advertised in newspapers critical of the government, that they risked losing their businesses" (Ali 2009: 54).

Era of Liberalisation (1990–2010)

The 1990s witnessed the wind of democratic change and attendant calls for the liberalisation and privatisation of the economy in Kenya. This situation was not an isolated development. Other countries in Africa were also experiencing similar changes. In 1991, the clamour for multiparty politics in Kenya occupied the front burner and eventually culminated into the adoption of multiparty democracy. Following the liberalisation of the political landscape, the media scene was also liberalized, and, between 1990 and 2010, there was an immense growth in both the print and electronic media in Kenya. At present, there are over 13 television stations, over 53 radio stations, eight daily newspapers and many weeklies (CCK 2008). All are privately owned except for the public broadcasting service, which resumed its original name, the Kenya Broadcasting Service (KBS).

Media Liberalisation: The Role of Advertising

One of the immediate effects of the liberalisation of the media in Kenya was that government could no longer interfere in the running of the media in a big way. Unlike in the pre-liberalisation era, the government could no longer be said to be a threat to the proper functioning of the media. Being almost exclusively in the hands of private entrepreneurs, the media in Kenya now depends fully on corporate-sector advertising revenue, which is fiercely competed for. Advertising is sourced from both local and international multinational companies. In effect, this means the advertisers arguably influence media content. As Otuma (2000: xvi) notes

> [M]ore threatening to the journalists' exercise of press freedom are the major advertisers who virtually hold some newspapers to ransom, given that most of them owe their survival to advertisers. There are some companies and parastatals whose negative stories cannot appear in particular newspapers regardless of the seriousness of the expose.

It is public knowledge that many negative stories about powerful multinationals in Kenya such as Safaricom, Coca-Cola, Delmonte and BAT, among others, are 'killed' or just 'fade away' due to fear of losing advertising revenue, no matter how important the stories may be to the public interest. A case in point occurred when one of the leading newspapers in Kenya, the *Daily Nation*, discovered that some mineral water packed by a leading multinational company in Nairobi contained harmful ingredients that posed significant health risks to consumers. Although the paper had a moral and professional obligation to publish such a story, it did not do so; the multinational company persuaded the editorial department to suppress the story by threatening to withdraw its advertising from all Nation Media outlets, not just the newspaper (Ali 2009: 183–4).

In the agricultural industry, a flower-exporting firm contaminated one of the leading fresh water lakes in Kenya, Lake Naivasha, causing the death of millions of fish. However, even after intense lobbying from civil society and even government intervention, the mainstream media houses gave the story a low profile because of pressure from the multinational polluter (Ali 2009: 183–4). Safaricom, the leading mobile telephone provider in Kenya, threatened to withdraw its KSh7 million (about US$90,000) per week advertising revenue from Royal Media Service after Royal published a negative story about the firm in the public interest. Not ready to lose such a large amount of advertising revenue, the top management forced the editor, Mwenda Njoka, to apologise to the firm in the same newspaper in which he had published the story (*Expression Today* 2008).

When Safaricom announced its initial public offer (IPO) on the Nairobi Stock Exchange in 2009, the public went into a frenzy in an attempt to own a piece of the lucrative company. Amid rumours of corruption, many small investors disposed of all their valuables to buy Safaricom shares, but, three years down the line, the share price is still below the buying price. It has been claimed that this is because of manipulation by a cartel that wants to frustrate the small investors, most of whom had taken out bank loans to buy the shares, in order to force them to dispose of their shares at a throw-away price. Shockingly, no media house has followed up on the story, presumably because Safaricom is among the leading advertisers in all media in Kenya.

It is also apparent that when big corporations perceive political competition as likely to result in a loss of business advantage, a reduction in profit or a policy change that does not favor them, they exercise their influence to whip media into supporting or undermining the appropriate candidates (Makokha 2010: 286), especially during general elections. Corporate interests collude with the media either directly or indirectly to ensure that their preferred political candidate sails through. This influence has transformed the media, supposedly founded on the principles of truth, objectivity and impartiality, into a marketing arm of big business characterized by public relations stories for the benefit of advertisers. As is often said, "he who pays the piper calls the tune".

The forces of corporate globalisation have no doubt profoundly influenced the Kenyan media in the post-liberalisation era both positively and negatively.

On a positive note, the media has proliferated, although this has not necessarily translated into a diversity of viewpoints, mainly due to cross-media ownership. On the negative, private media owners are increasingly concerned only with pursuing profits and selling audiences to advertisers. Only stories that are likely to bring in the money are fronted, while those that are not "client-friendly" rarely see the light of day.

The revenues at stake are enormous. A 2008 survey by international media monitoring and research firm Steadman calculated total media advertising revenue in Kenya at KSh17 billion (more than US$200 million) annually. This is a huge amount by any standard and if that is what sustains the media in a highly competitive market, compromises have to be made. This has, in effect, meant a shift in editorial policy due to the fierce competition for a share of this advertising spend. Advertising is now the main driving force in the media, the overriding goal being to deliver audiences to advertisers (Ali 2009). The increase in media channels has given advertisers plenty of options, so they can easily withdraw or threaten to withdraw advertising revenue from one outlet and invest it in a friendlier one. Advertisers are also able to target specific communities, age groups and other segments of the population with the increased audience segmentation that a proliferation of media provides. Thus advertisers, not consumers of media, are the main beneficiaries of the liberalised media market in Kenya.

The media, especially the electronic media, has been accused of focusing too much on entertainment, 'horse-race' political journalism and sensationalism at the expense of critical human-interest stories. For instance, most popular FM stations in Kenya, such as Classic 105, Easy FM, Kiss 100, Hot 96, Metro FM and even the public broadcaster KBC, focus on sex-related issues in their popular call-in talk shows instead of focusing on development issues such as poverty, ethnic strife, good governance and corruption, among others. There was once a public outcry about the ethics of talking about intimate sexual issues on national FM stations early in the morning when parents are taking their children to school. The media was quick to retort that sex talk sells and that whoever finds it offensive can switch to another station. However, it would be a mistake for media to think that this content reflects the public's preferences and free choice. After all, the public was never given the opportunity to approve or disapprove media liberalisation.

Political Economy of the Media in Kenya

The political economy of the media is often associated with macro questions of media ownership and control and examines the processes of consolidation, diversification, commercialisation and the operation of the profit motive in the hunt for audiences and or for advertisements and its consequences for media practice (Boyd-Barret 1995). One of the main concerns of this analytic tradition is that the media are increasingly being practiced as businesses with an emphasis on profit rather than as producers of culture with an emphasis on meaning and quality (Fourie 2007). Beyond the role of the media as commercial business institutions that produce and disseminate news, there is an undeniable need to analyse how economic and political interests influence how the media operates. As McQuail (2005: 218) observes:

> [The media] have historically grown up with a strong and widely shared image as having an important part to play in public life and being essentially within the public domain; their main commodity of trade – information, culture and ideas – are considered as the collective property of all.

As public watchdogs, the media have an implicit contract with the public to provide a public sphere to facilitate informed dialogue on critical and topical issues. The public interest should, therefore, supersede business or private interest in their operations. The media play a vital role in democratic societies. They are expected to reflect public opinion objectively, respond to public concerns impartially and make the public aware of important issues and policies. To fulfil these roles effectively, the media has to be free of any external coercion, whether from the government or market forces. However, with the increased commercialisation and corporatisation of the media, impartiality and objectivity are being blurred as the search for profits slowly but surely supersedes commitment to the public interest. Thus, corporate ownership and control of the media in Kenya in the post-liberalised era has resulted in a form of corporate censorship which has negatively impacted on the quality and diversity of the information disseminated to the public. There is a general feeling that the so-called fourth estate has colluded with economic and political interests at the expense of the citizenry, and investors in the industry are said to be treating the channels of democratic debate as their personal property (Kenya Media Debate Series 2005).

The political economy of the media in Kenya can best be analysed using the "propaganda model" developed by Herman and Chomsky. In *Manufacturing Consent: The Political Economy of the Mass Media*, Herman and Chomsky (2002) present a structural analysis of how the mass media works in a capitalist society. They outline the market forces, or "filters", which they believe determine what is to be considered newsworthy. Their model explains the mainstream media's behavior by examining the media's corporate character and its integration into the political economy of the dominant economic system (Herman and Chomsky 2002). Identifying five key filters, the propaganda model critically analyses the ways in which money and power are able to filter the news that is 'fit to print', as the famous motto of the *New York Times* puts it. These filters marginalise dissent and allow only the government and dominant private interests to get their messages across to the public. Herman and Chomsky (2002) argue that there are five filters which continuously interact with and reinforce one another to determine what is transmitted as news to the public. The five filters are: 1) the size, concentrated ownership, owner's wealth and profit orientation of the dominant mass media firms; 2) advertising as the primary income source of the mass media; 3) reliance of the mass media on information provided by government, business and 'experts' funded and approved by these agents of power; 4) 'flak' as a means of disciplining the media; and 5) 'anti-communism' as a national religion and control mechanism. Herman and Chomsky (2002) argue that the same underlying power sources that own the media and fund them as advertisers, that serve as primary sources and definers of news and that produce flak and proper thinking experts also play a role in fixing the basic principles and the dominant ideologies which govern what journalists do.

Our main focus here is on the first and second filters: the size, ownership and profit orientation of the mass media and advertising as the primary source of income for the mass media. The first filter emphasises the fact that "dominant media firms are quite large businesses; they are controlled by very wealthy people or by managers who are subject to sharp constraints by owners and other market-profit-oriented forces" (Herman and Chomsky 2002: 14). The second filter highlights the influence of advertising values on the news production process. The main argument is that, to remain financially viable, media must sell markets (readers) to buyers (advertisers) and that this dependency directly influences media performance. As McChesney (2004) notes, in a democracy, the relationship between advertising and the media is of paramount concern. For a significant part of the media, satisfying the needs of the advertiser is the most important task, and doing so can change media content dramatically; the needs of the audience have to be filtered through the much more important needs of the advertiser: "Advertising is the mainstay of both the media and the business community and whereas it is believed that the relationship is mutual, often the media end up as the junior partner forced to accede to the demands of the advertiser" (Otuma 2000: xviii).

Advertising also accentuates class bias in the media because, on balance, it tends to be interested in affluent consumers with disposable income. Therefore, media content is tailored to create a 'buying mood' in the upper classes, while the less marketable needs of the poor are marginalised or ignored altogether.

Due to commercial interests, the media in Kenya seem to be focusing more on urban consumers who attract advertisers at the expense of the plight of the poor and rural populations who are the majority. Rarely will you read, hear or see a news story that directly addresses the challenges of these marginalised groups. If content is not about the powerful political elite, then it is about the interests of the powerful business class. Over-dependence on advertising leads to the erosion of the public sphere. Investigative reporting and human-interest stories are replaced by entertainment, show biz pull-outs, sensationalisation and tabloidisation. Media outputs are commodified and tailored to serve market needs rather than public needs.

Competition for audiences is so stiff, especially in the electronic media, that if one station comes up with a new advertorial programme, the others will follow suit with similar programming on the same day at the same time. A case in point is 'KTN Business Weekly' (a Standard Media group TV programme on business issues) and 'NTV Business Journal' (a Nation Media Group programme on the same). These are the two leading TV channels in Kenya, and both programmes are aired the same day at the same time. The two stations also fiercely try to outdo each other on 'investigative' reporting. At one point, NTV showed for a week a preview of an investigative report in order to keep their viewers glued. What they did not know was that their main competitor, KTN, would 'scoop' (or steal) their story and start their prime news five minutes ahead of time on the material day. It was strange and awkward to watch both leading stations airing the same investigative story about money-laundering in Kenya. A critical observer is left to question the value added for viewers from such crude competition.

There have also been brand-sponsored news, an indirect way for advertisers to influence news content, especially when corporations receive insufficient positive publicity or when they want to 'soften' stubborn editors. And as Ali (2009) notes, news programmes are supposed to be factual, accurate, objective and reflective of the society without any slant. When sponsorships, which can arguably change the content, the angle and in some cases the accuracy of the news, become a major factor, such items can no longer be seriously considered as news. They have become promotional items.

My informal interviews with sub-editors, editors, reporters and former media personnel all confirm that advertisers exercise a huge influence on news coverage and that there is an endless war between advertising departments and editorial departments. Sometimes journalists are forced to cover major advertisers' functions no matter how un-newsworthy they may be because, as one candidly put it, "those are the guys who feed us". All those interviewed agreed that, as much as the media is supposed the public informer, no media house will publish a story that will negatively affect their main advertiser or other commercial activities that are part of a particular media house's empire. The most important thing for the media house, they note, is profit. It is money that matters, not truthfully informing the public. As one sub-editor told me:

> A negative story about a major advertiser – I mean those advertisers who place full-page colour adverts in the newspaper almost every other day – will be checked and cross-checked and then discussed before it is "carefully worded" to avoid upsetting the valuable client. If you are new in the media, you come to learn that a particular company is a valuable client if, every time a reporter brings a negative story about the company, the editor rejects it for "lack of adequate factual evidence" or for not being "newsworthy". It is then that you know you have to tread carefully; otherwise you risk being reprimanded for always coming up with "sub-standard" stories.

Some editors and managing editors in the two main leading newspapers in Kenya (*Daily Nation* and *Standard*) were adamant that they do not allow advertisers to influence their professionalism. However, a content analysis of the number of adverts in each paper before the editorial page and the sentiments from the junior staff seem to tell quite a different story.

In a content analysis of the number of adverts appearing in these two leading newspapers between 30 August and 30 September 2010, it was found that the the *Daily Nation*, with a daily circulation of about 200,000, had a total of 430 adverts with an average of about 14 adverts per day before the editorial page, which appears on page 12 of the newspaper. Thus, there is slightly more than one advert per page before the editorial page. An interesting trend is that there is at least a one full-colour full-page advert per day either on page five or page seven. The newspaper re-branded its look in July 2010 with numerous sponsored pull-out "features". In the *Standard*, with a circulation of about 80,000 daily, there were 247 adverts, an average of eight adverts per day before the editorial page, which appears on page 14 of the newspaper. As in the *Daily Nation*, there was at least one full-page colour advert either on page 9 or page 13 and sometimes even three full-page colour adverts on consecutive pages before the editorial page. As in the *Daily Nation*, there are many pull-outs, mostly on sensational entertainment stories, which account for about half the newspaper's content. It is apparent that adverts form a major part of these two newspapers, and it would be reasonable to argue that advertisers are major stakeholders in the final output of the newspapers. It can also be argued that the bigger (in terms of circulation) the newspaper, the more the adverts. In fact, the *Daily Nation* has close to twice the number of adverts as the *Standard*.

If the experience of the journalists interviewed that a negative story from a major advertiser has to be checked and cross-checked and then carefully worded or abandoned altogether is anything to go by, it suggests how many stories have to be carefully worded or abandoned simply because of the money factor. With government censorship out of the way, this new form of censorship dictated by profits is even more tragic for the public mainly because it is not immediately apparent to ordinary readers, listeners and viewers. It is subtle and more sophisticated and can easily escape even a keen observer.

Implications

Blumler and Gurevitch (1995) summarise the main functions of the media in a democratic society as surveillance of the socio-political environment, meaningful agenda setting, providing platforms for an intelligible and illuminating advocacy by politicians, providing mechanisms for holding officials to account and incentives for citizens to learn and principled resistance to efforts of forces outside the media to subvert media independence. Blumler and Gurevitch (1995) also note that one of the stumbling blocks for the media in fulfilling these roles is that the media themselves are constrained by their economic and institutional contexts. Christian et al. (2009) builds on Blumler and Gurevitch to posit four broad roles of the media: the monitorial role, which refers to all aspects of collecting and disseminating information, the facilitative role, which refers to journalism that is practiced as a means of improving the quality of public life, the radical role, which focuses on exposing abuses of power by raising popular consciousness of wrongdoing and the collaborative role, which specifies the tasks for the media that arise in situations of unavoidable engagement with social events and processes, such as collaboration between the media and the state during times of crisis or emergency. Although these roles and functions will be dependent on the particular society in which the media is based, there is near-universal agreement that a free and vibrant media is essential to democracy and to development in any society. In most developing countries, freedom of the media is interpreted to mean freedom from government control, but this overlooks the fact that, in the new, liberalised media market, there is a worse threat to media freedom and performance than government control.

Although there is no media policy framework in Kenya (Oriare 2010, Makokha 2010, Ali 2009), any time the media seems to have abused its power and there is call for a legal policy framework to govern the operations of the media,

media owners are always up in arms, claiming the government wants to muzzle the press. However, they never seem to complain about pressure from advertisers. My argument is that these pressures have led to widespread self-censorship in the media in Kenya and that this has negatively impacted on journalistic objectivity, impartiality and truth-telling. Although the proposed new constitution recognises that the media should be independent from control by government, political interests or commercial interests, there is need for good will from both the media fraternity and the government in order to check owners' influence on the performance of the media in Kenya and give editorial teams more independence in reporting instead of just protecting advertisers' and owners' interests.

Conclusion

While the remarkable growth of the media in Kenya is welcome, the commercial challenges that have come with this growth can no longer be ignored or wished away. The rigorous battle for audiences has often led to disregard of the key journalistic principles of truth, objectivity, accuracy and impartiality, leading to sensationalisation and trivialisation of news in order to create a buying mood for the target audience at the expense of serious issues such as poverty, corruption and ethnic strife, among others. Although the commercial media in Kenya cannot be forced to report on these issues without guaranteed economic return on their part, they still have a social responsibility to act as a genuine public sphere. The concept of the press as fourth estate recognise the fact that the media in a democracy is expected to act on behalf of the people in the public interest.

References

Ali, M. 2009. *Globalization and the Kenya Media*. Nairobi: Image Publications.

Blumler, J.G. and M. Gurevitch. 1995. *The Crisis of Public Communication*. London: Routledge.

Boyd-Barret, O. 1995. The political economy approach. In O. Boyd-Barret and C. Newbold, eds. *Approaches to Media: A Reader*. London: Arnold.

Christians, C., Glasser, T.L., McQuail, D., Nordenstreng, K. and R.A. White. 2009. *Normative Theories of the Media: Journalism in Democratic Societies*. Chicago: University of Illinois.

Fourie, P. 2007. *Media Studies: Institutions, Theories and Issues*. Vol. 1. Claremont, South Africa: Juta. Herman, E. and N. Chomsky. 2002. *Manufacturing Consent: the Political economy of the Media*. New York: Pantheon Books.

Kenya Media Debate Series. 2005. *Talking with Kenyans*. Nairobi: Media Council of Kenya.

Makali, D. 2003. *Media Law and Practice: The Kenyan Jurisprudence*. Nairobi: Phoenix Publishers.

Makokha, K. 2010. The dynamics and politics of media in Kenya: The role and impact of mainstream media in the 2007 general elections. In Karuti Kanyinga and Duncan Okello, eds. *Tensions and Reversals in Democratic Transitions*. Nairobi: Society for International Development (SID) and Institute for Development Studies (IDS), University of Nairobi.

McChesney, R. 2004. *The Problem of the Media: U.S Communication Politics in the 21st Century*. New York: Monthly Review Press.

McQuail, D. 2005. *Mass Communication Theory*. Fifth Ed. London: Sage.

Oriare, P. 2010. *Mass Media in Kenya: Systems and Practice*. Nairobi: Jomo Kenyatta Foundation.

Otuma, O., 2000. When the watchdog can't bark in its own backyard. *Expression Today Media Review*.

CHAPTER 10

REVISITING THE WOMAN QUESTION IN ADVERTISING

GILBERT MOTSAATHEBE

Introduction

Any serious discussion of advertising will inevitably lead to the question of its enigmatic relationship with women, especially the way in which women are habitually portrayed in advertising messages. For a long time, women were denigrated, stereotyped and objectified in advertising messages. However women's situation seems to have dramatically improved in recent years, and this is now being re-envisioned in the media with the image of a modern, sophisticated woman. In attempting to unpack this change, this chapter is guided by a number of assumptions. The first is that women are the biggest consumers of advertised products. The second is that advertising uses women more than men to sell products, and the third that advertising mostly targets women because they are more likely to respond to ad messages than men. The fourth assumption is that advertising has a tradition of negatively portraying women as mere objects to sell products and, in the process, has exploited women's images and bodies to entrench stereotypes and the oppression of women in society.

The purpose of this chapter is to take a closer look at advertising in relation to these assumptions, looking for both disjunctions and continuities. I use a content analysis of selected magazines to test the assumptions and, at the same time, to assess the extent to which advertising uses women more than men to sell products and undresses women in terms of exposing their naked bodies, breasts and thighs as compared to men. I also examine the gestures and behavioural patterns (facial expressions, sexually suggestive gestures, poise, exuberance and submissive positions) exploited in advertising messages in relation to both women and men and the types of bodies (athletic, full figure, slim, etc.) more likely to be used in advertising.

This chapter is divided into four sections. The first section takes a broad view of advertising and highlights the objectives of the chapter as well as describing the questions driving the research. The second section discusses advertising from an African cultural perspective, while the third describes the methodology of the research and the rationale for the choice of magazines. The fourth section discusses the research findings and concludes by proposing ways to contain some of the problems discovered.

Objectives

The overarching objective of this chapter is to re-examine and rethink advertising in relation to its depiction of women in order to see how much has changed (or not) in recent years. I assess to the extent to which the current wave of advertising messages are more likely to portray women as mere objects to sell products and to what extent such treatment entrenches stereotypes and the oppression of women in society. The chapter is driven by the following questions:

- To what extent does advertising undress women by exposing their naked bodies (breasts, thighs and so on) compared to men?
- What kind of gestures and behavioural patterns (facial expressions, sexually suggestive gestures and poses, exuberance and submissive positions) are exploited in advertising messages in relation to both women and men?
- What kinds of bodies (athletic, full figure, slim, etc.) are more likely to be used in the current wave of advertising?
- To what extent does advertising use women more than men to sell products?

Background

Historically, advertising does not have a good name in feminist theory. According to a United Nations report, advertising is "the worst offender in perpetuating the image of women as sex symbols and an inferior class of human being" (cited in Fagg 2008: 1). That is a serious indictment with serious implications for women, especially in the chauvinistic society that we live in today. However, in the last few years, many media professionals have taken steps to improve gender portrayals in advertising. In addition, the position of women in society has improved quite dramatically. The modern woman seems to be more sophisticated and have a more nuanced involvement in a variety of roles and responsibilities which were traditionally reserved for men. In South Africa, for example, the government has, since 1994, made a commitment to increase the number of women in parliament and senior government positions. The government's initial target was thirty percent, but, by 2009 the number of women in the National Assembly had increased to 45 percent, giving South African the third-highest proportion of women in parliament after Rwanda and Sweden (Mbola 2009). Similar progressive transformations have occurred in many other spheres. In parallel with this, the image of women seems to have improved drastically in many media programmes.

Given these developments, it seems an appropriate time to re-examine and rethink advertising in relation to its depiction of women. I therefore chose a number of popular magazines at random, namely, *True Love*, *Discovery*, *Move*, *Men's Health*, *Real*, *O Magazine*, *Bona*, *Soul*, *Runners' World*, *Soul*, *Shape*, *Fair Lady*, *Glamour*, *Eve*, *Marie Claire* and *Top Billing* to assess how women are represented in magazine advertising.

Advertising from an African Cultural Perspective

According to Okigbo (1995: 5), "Africa is the best illustration of the creative mixing of the traditional and modern mass media, on account of its rich traditional culture which is proving impervious to rapid change in the face of massive onslaughts from foreign culture". Nevertheless, advertising, like all other mass-media activities, has established a racialised and sexist discourse, promoting whiteness and Western notions of sex and beauty. As Benshoff and Griffin (2009: 13) explain, "historically, European culture judged itself to be superior to all other cultures on the globe. True culture was thought to be synonymous with Western notions of high art and other cultures were judged to be deficient by those standards". Through advertising, culture is packaged as a commodity and exported, and this has serious consequences in Africa, particularly in the cities where the majority of the population is exposed to the mass media. Consequently, most people in the cities look down on rural dwellers as simpletons, while those in rural areas look at city people as uncultured and disrespectful. As Ndlela (2006) puts it, "African countries are generally importers of cultural commodities, propelled by the domestic desire and taste for western entertainment and media products" (para. 6). Anything African is regarded as backward.

Although it is a well-documented fact that culture is not static, the majority of people across the world still associate anything that is deemed as backward with Africa, while anything grand is associated with developed countries. Such stereotypes are reproduced and entrenched through media messages on a daily basis. For instance, in South Africa, the Vodacom ad, "We have been having it", portrays the typical African leader as a pompous and ignorant dictator in full military regalia. Played by Kenyan-born actor Charles Bukeko, the dictator complains that he has been hearing stories about Vodacom's claims (regarding its service and products), which he says do not make sense since he manages well without them. To illustrate his point, he uses runners to deliver his mail, apparently to prove that the speedy delivery promised by the cellphone company is not an issue for his country. The ad triggered a flurry of complaints from viewers claiming that it portrays Africans as primitive, arrogant and stupid and that it amounted to a "commercial reinforcement of stereotypical perceptions of African countries as being of third world status" (MyBroadband 2008: para. 5). Nonetheless, the Advertising Standards Authority of South Africa (ASA) ruled that the ad did not contravene ASA guidelines. Indeed, the ad went on to win an award for "Campaign of the year".

The mass media are the most pervasive ideological structures in society, and, within the media, advertising plays a critical role in persuading consumers and raising awareness about what is modern and trendy. Inevitably, most people, especially those in the cities, shape their identity in a world constituted by fashion, glitz and glamour relayed by the mass media, particularly through magazine and television advertising. This is especially true for the youth, who are the major consumers of mass media. A cursory view will reveal that African youth are more likely to identify with American pop stars than African musicians, for example. On the other hand, advertising also enhances life, as more and more people rely on ad images not only to negotiate their identity, but also for guidance, health messages and other important information. Thus, advertising also plays a positive role by opening up new avenues for growth and self-expression. For instance, advertorials and adverts relaying HIV messages, such as the "Scrutinise HIV campaign", promote safer sex and have been highly effective.

According to the *PlusNews* and analysis, the "Scrutinise" ads are like no other HIV awareness adverts. Instead of earnest celebrities or solemn voiceovers imploring young people to abstain or practice safer sex, they feature attention-grabbing graphics and wise-cracking cartoon characters delivering HIV messages in catchy phrases. "Eliminate the element of surprise, scrutinise," screeches Victor, the main character. "Flip HIV to HI Victory!" he urges at the end of each of the seven ads. Recently, I saw a young lady buying a pack of condoms at a convenience store, whereupon the cashier, also a young woman, remarked, "I see you scrutinise!" This illustrated to me that people actually remember the powerful message relayed by the ad, although one cannot therefore conclude that they would act as advised in the ad when confronted with similar situations. Whereas in the past, it would have been difficult for the two women to talk openly about condoms, they now found it easier to converse about this life-saving product because it had been popularized in the ads.

Advertising and Women

The contention that women are now the biggest consumers of advertising messages is no longer debatable. According to Barletta (2003: 26), "there is so much support proving the power and wealth of the female market that it seems downright off that some companies sill resist the opportunity". This is clear if one looks at the way women have taken the job market by storm, entering professions that were traditionally reserved for men and often earning more than their spouses. Traditionally women's buying power was limited to mundane household products. This situation has changed dramatically. As Barletta (2003: 32), observes, "[t]hese days women are buying cars, computers, and carpeting, and shelling out the cash for insurance policies, investments and improvements to the home as well". In fact, Barletta argues that, in most cases, women have too much money to spend, since they not only have their own money but their spouses as well, having become the primary purchasers for everything the family needs.

However, women still appear to be given a raw deal. They are not only manipulated as consumers but also used to carry the ad messages that undermine them by portraying them as sex objects, even though there seems to be a realisation that this is unfair and entrenches stereotypes which reinforce women's oppression and marginalization. There is, at the moment, a media image of the 'new' or liberated woman, which is exploited to tap into women's vulnerable emotions. Also, women talk a lot, and so they spread the word whenever they learn about a new product, thereby becoming the biggest consumers of products, especially beauty and household products. The relationship between advertising and women can thus also be looked at from another perspective, i.e. from a uses and gratification point of view, which is unpacked below in the section on theoretical frameworks.

Theoretical Framework

In some quarters, advertising is perceived negatively not only because of the way it depicts women, but also because of the alleged exaggerations or falsifications in many advertising messages. Indeed, the idea of regulating advertising arose out of the need to ensure that the industry portrays genuine messages without falsifying or overly exaggerating information about the product. The ethical demand is that ad messages must be truthful and not be misleading. However, there are no fast rules to measure how misleading the information may be, as most of the time ads tend to exaggerate or overstate the usefulness of products. They also do not tell us about the negative effects of the products they advertise.

However, all is not doom and gloom. From both a functionalist perspective and a uses and gratification point of view, advertising can serve a positive function. It provides us with ideas about how we can look and gives us information about things we never knew we may need. In this age where knowledge is commercialised, with the result that you have to pay to get information, advertising gives us free information, although we must understand that it is selective. It helps to create awareness for products and create a favourable attitude towards the product. Advertising may also have a good effect on people. For instance, some advertising makes people laugh without stereotyping or degrading either of the sexes. It may also serve as a trendsetter, especially for people who rely on advertising to know what is out of date and what is fashionable. During the course of the study on which this chapter is based, I regularly asked people at random about their views of advertising. This is a sample of what some of them had to say:

- Ads persuade us to buy things, most of which we don't really need. They can be helpful, as they show us what is fashionable and what is outdated.
- They are misleading, especially with this money-back guarantee they preach. I doubt if anybody ever gets their money back if unsatisfied with a product.
- Most of the ads I like are those with humour. I find them entertaining, especially on TV, and enjoy them every time they appear, although I do not always buy the products they advertise.
- For me the point is that even if I don't purchase the product I would have more information about it and that makes it more likely that I would buy it in future.

Advertising conveys sentiments that are not only nostalgic but also futuristic. It is able to transport us into the future through an imaginary space. Hence, it is crucial that advertising be regulated to ensure that it does not move too far from the truth. Nonetheless, advertising continues to lure people into buying products through various persuasive techniques that include selective communication. For instance, it typically highlights the usefulness of the product and says nothing about its disadvantages. As Horowitz (1991: 155) puts it, "for the most part, advertising techniques can ill afford to engage in the complete truth." Indeed, the success of advertising today owes much to its deceptive techniques.

According to DeFleur (1995: 273), "some ads have traded on prestige; others have used fear. Some have promised glamour and the good life. Some have embraced fantasy, and others have been firmly fixed on reality." Due to such varied *modus operandi*, people tend to model their behaviours on the persuasive images they see in the media. Advertising can induce certain behaviours which are seen as cool and more sophisticated due to the glamour associated with the media. The modelled behaviour can be good or bad. People tend to forget that the media is not the real world and that the picture they see is very selective and only portrays those aspects that are appealing, while the dark side is invariably omitted. Yet everything has a dark side to it.

Through the exotic images it portrays, advertising becomes a cultural transmitter, especially in terms of clothing, etiquette and other behavioural patterns. The youth are the most affected. They see the world represented in the media as a paradise, whereas the one their grandparents inhabit is perceived as old-fashioned, boring and uncivilised. Advertising has also played a role in perpetuating risky behaviour, such as drinking alcohol and smoking. For this reason, in South Africa, strict measures have been introduced on risky products such as cigarettes, where manufactures are now forced to warn people about the dangers of cigarettes and not just say that, "it gives you a great feeling and great taste." Previous research has shown that advertising does play a role in encouraging people to indulge in unacceptable behaviour, such as drinking and promiscuous sex leading to HIV/AIDS. Due to their glamorous appeal, advertisements have the ability to put individuals in a state where they can suspend the veracity of the real world and live the exotic life portrayed in the fictional world of advertising. Equally, advertising can also serve a positive function through advertorials, for instance, that create awareness about health issues and other matters of critical public importance, which some members of the public might otherwise not readily access. The effect of advertising is even more pronounced on children, since they do not yet fully know the real world around them. Thus, they tend to believe everything they are told; if children see a toy in an advert, they are more likely to cry for it when they see it at the shops. Since we want our children to feel exceptional, chances are that we will buy that toy if we can.

Questions about the effect and power of advertising are of particular interest to feminist communication scholars both from an agenda-setting and an interest-stimulation perspective. Since the media influence public opinion, as the agenda-setting theory maintains, the frequency of adverts portraying women as sexual objects, for example, is seen as negative socialisation which will inevitably affect the perception and treatment of women in the real world. Thus, the representation of women in advertising as objects, or as dependent on men, dovetails with patriarchy in society. The same applies to advertising's tendency to liken connect products with sex. As the advertising mantra says, "sex sells," and sexually explicit images stimulate interest. However, viewers, especially young ones, might end up indulging in risky behaviours as a result. Such ads not only stimulate interest in the product but also in the (sexual) context in which the advertising message in presented.

Another concern is that, while, in the past, the producers of media messages were exclusively male, these days women have made inroads into the media due to legislation's and an array of women symposia, conferences and other international platform, such as the 1995 Beijing Platform of Action and have thus become involved in the production and crafting of media programmes. However, there are still concerns in some quarters that, even where women are involved, they still produce media programmes which are just as scandalous as the ones produced in male-dominated media. This concern is echoed by Ogunleye (2005: 126): "It is distressing to find that even female producers champion such damaging stereotypes." He concludes that "there is a need for consciousness-raising among female producers (media practitioners) to help them understand who they are and what role they ought to play in furthering the feminist agenda".

Design and Method

With a clearer understanding of the debates on women, culture and advertising, and of the theoretical framework driving the issues raised in this chapter, I turn now to the research methodology. This consisted of examining various magazines in South Africa on the basis of the following characteristics, which also form some of the core assumptions driving issues raised in this chapter:

- Popularity with women.
- Replete with advertisements.
- Informative and entertaining.
- Accessibility to the researcher.

That magazines are popular with women is not debatable. Everyone knows that women buy magazines. This explains why there are so many more magazines targeted at women than at men. The quantity of women's magazines can also be linked to feminism. Feminists have encouraged women to create their own publications in order to counteract the mainstream media's devaluation of women through under-representation, misrepresentation and stereotyping. Women's magazines can thus be seen as products of feminism. Indeed, magazines are arguably the only example of mass media predominantly produced and edited by women for women. This is definitely the case in South Africa.

Magazines have lots of advertisements. This is not surprising, since women are the biggest consumers of healthcare, household and beauty products, precisely the type of products that feature most in magazine advertising. There is a symbiotic relationship here; magazines need advertising for economic survival, and advertising needs this form of mass media to reach a mass audience. According to Magazine Publishers of America "allocating more money to magazines in the media mix improves marketing and advertising ROI across a broad range of product categories" (cited in Phere 2007: 9).

It is widely believed that women also feature in advertising more than men. To test this hypothesis, I watched some television advertisements and observed that women were dominating. Then I browsed through the magazines I had chosen and found the same. One reason for this is suggested by Lee (1988: 168):

> It seems that whenever someone has something to sell to women—be it clothes, careers or contraception – we are urged to change ourselves in to the "new women" of the moment, by adopting whatever definition of liberation or modernity is current and buying whatever signifies that we have not been left behind as the 'old woman.

Lee's observation touches the core of my argument. Advertising may have adopted the feminist imagery of the "new woman" from contemporary identity politics, but the exploitation of women in advertising continues.

Categories of Analysis

In my analysis, I deployed the categories outlined in Table 10.1. I chose "revealing" as one of the categories because many previous studies of women and advertising complain that advertising portrays women as sexual objects by parading their nakedness for male gaze. I wanted to see what extent this was still the case.

Through the second category ("facial expression"), I wanted to problematise which facial expressions were prominent and what this might suggest. Similarly, through the category "sexual invitation", I wanted to examine gestures or other signs that might be construed as sexually suggestive. Through the category "confidence", I wanted to see if the women depicted in these ads are shown as less confident than the men depicted. "Body size" was an unavoidable category for this appraisal; the media has often been accused of promoting the "ideal" of extreme slimness at the expense of more full-figured women. Finally I was also interested in seeing which type of products dominate magazine adverts and products are more likely to be associated with, or promoted by, women.

Table 10.1: Categories and Characteristics of Analysis

Category of portrayal	Operationalisation
Revealing	Thighs, chest, cleavage, buttocks, half-naked
Facial expression	Eye contact, serious, smiling, laughing
Sexual invitation	Sexually suggestive gesture, mannerism, display, position
Confidence	Poise, displaying confidence, exuberance, indifference, submissive positions
Body size	Full figure, slim, average
Products	Type of products mostly featured

Findings

A total of 103 adverts from 16 magazines were analysed using the categories from Table 10.1. In Table 10.2 below, I record the number of instances in which adverts appeared to display: (a) images that are revealing; (b) facial expressions that appear to be passive; (c) poses that appear to be sexually inviting; (d) images that appear to portray the model as being passive as opposed to being confident; and (e) body types *other* than slim or athletic for both female and male models featuring in the adverts.

As can be seen from Table 10.2, the tabulation of findings generally indicates that the adverts in all the magazines were not as revealing with regard to the nakedness of the models featured; that women were more likely to be portrayed as being passive, submissive or less confident compared to men; that women were more likely to be portrayed in sexually inviting positions compared to men and that only slim to average men and women were used. Each category of these results is discussed in detail below.

Adverts in all the magazines were not as revealing as initially assumed. *Marie Claire* and *Men's Health* had the most revealing adverts compared to other magazines, but even here, the practice was somewhat mute compared to what previous studies have revealed. This could indicate that there has been a conscientization about the objectification of bodies.

Table 10.2: Analysis of Magazine Advertisements

Magazine	Nakedness		Facial Expression		Sexual Orientation		Confidence		Body size	
	M	F	M	F	M	F	M	F	M	F
True Love	3	4	3	6	—	3	2	6	—	—
Move	1	2	—	3	—	2	2	6	—	—
Men's Health	3	3	—	4	—	6	—	4	—	—
Real	—	3	1	3	—	1	1	3	—	—
O	1	2	1	4	—	—	2	5	—	—
Bona	3	3	1	3	3	3	—	3	—	—
Soul	3	1	—	4	3	4	—	2	—	—
Runners' World	2	3	—	4	2	3	1	3	—	—
Soul	3	3	1	3	2	2	1	4	—	—
Shape	3	3	—	1	3	3	—	3	—	—
Fair Lady	1	5	—	3	—	1	—	3	—	1
Glamour	3	3	2	5	3	5	—	4	—	—
Eve	3	3	2	4	3	3	—	3	—	—
Marie Claire	2	3	—	4	1	3	1	3	—	—
Top Billing	3	3	—	3	3	2	—	2	—	—
Discovery	2	3	—	2	—	3	—	3	—	—

Nevertheless, a sexual objectification of women's bodies was apparent in several ads. In *Marie Claire*, for example, a Ralph Lauren Blue fragrance advertisement showed a young and beautiful woman with very long hair looking suggestively at the camera in a skimpy blouse. The blouse is unbuttoned, revealing her breasts and abdomen. *Eve*, an ad for a unisex Calvin Klein fragrance shows a man caressing a woman, tenderly kissing her below the neck, with his nose appearing to sniff her upper chest just above the breasts. The woman is shown as completely overpowered by erotic emotions. Her eyes are closed and her mouth slightly open. She is wearing what appears to be a silk sleeveless nightdress, and her entire chest is completely exposed. No part of the man's body is exposed except his face. The same strategy is followed in an ad in *Men's Health* promoting the David Beckham signature fragrance. Interestingly, most of the people I spoke to when preparing this research this predicted that pictures of a topless man would not be as common as those of a topless woman.

With regard to the second category, "facial expression", men were mostly portrayed with more serious expressions than women. In most of the adverts, the men were looking directly at the camera, while the women looked slightly away. Also, facial expressions were prominent in all the ads reviewed, presumably because they were mostly advertising beauty products and because the face is the first feature people look at to assess beauty. Facial expression can also be linked to our third category, "sexual invitation". The way poses were struck were usually appealing or even inviting, to put it more crudely, especially when women were portrayed. The ads in *Men's Health* were very conspicuous in this regard. In one instance, for example, the ad displayed a woman wearing only a blouse and 'sexy' underwear, which were slightly exposed, while she looked suggestively at the camera. Nevertheless, in terms of sexually inviting poses, the images were rather restrained on the whole, compared to what previous literature has found.

With regard to body size, in all the adverts reviewed no full-figured woman was used, with one exception promoting a diet product where a picture of a full-figured woman was used alongside the slim woman to illustrate the change that could result if the product was used – the slim woman being the ideal, of course. In all the other ads, only slim-to-average women were used. However, they were all suggestive of fitness and health, not the 'anorexic' types that ads have sometimes been accused of featuring. The results confirm that advertising favours slim women, but, although this can be seen as discriminating against full-figured women, it can also be seen as encouraging the overweight to lose weight and avoid the health problems associated with obesity.

Thus, the depiction of slim models can be seen from two antagonistic positions. The media are a major socialising agent in our society, and so the more people see slender people portrayed in the media as exotic, glamorous and beautiful, the more that are likely to internalise the idea that full-figured people are ugly and unhealthy. Already, many people feel they are discriminated against or ridiculed based on their weight. For instance, there have been increasing reports of overweight people being discriminated against when using public transport becuase they are seen as taking up too much space. This is when the images portrayed in the media become problematic. Overweight children also grow up in an environment where they are ridiculed by their playmates because the socialising agents in society do not paint any positive image of this group.

In looking at the kinds of products mostly featured in magazine advertising, I found that the most common products in the women's magazines were fragrances, underwear, beauty products, health products, food, cleaning products and technological gadgets such as mobile phones. Men's magazines such as *Men's Health*, on the other hand, tend to advertise alcohol, sporting goods, banking services, holidays, cars and bikes. None of these products were appeared in the women's magazines. However, women were more likely to be used to advertise these products compared to men, except in the case of alcohol. This confirms previous research on advertising. In her study on magazine advertising, Fagg (2008: 12), for example, observes:

> Not only do magazine advertisements often portray women's beauty as their sole valuable characteristic to men, throwing intelligence and worth aside, but these images also harm women themselves. They cause women to focus intensely on how to remain beautiful at all points in their life.

It is clear that a typical advert poses questions, sometimes directly but more often implicitly, that viewers are not expected to be able to say "no" to. For example, do we want to be look sexy, beautiful, successful, fabulous, sophisticated? Few can answer in the negative to such questions. One ad posed the following series of questions:

> Any of these niggles apply to you?
>
> Dry mouth?
>
> Dry, red itchy, sore eyes?
>
> Hearing problems?
>
> Degenerative eye disorders?
>
> Night sight problems?

For most people, it is difficult not to answer "yes" to one or more of such questions. This ad advertised health products, but the picture was a close-up portrait of a very beautiful young woman (*Discovery Health Magazine*: 6). In another example, the ad starts with a compelling statement painting a scenario that everyone wants to be part of:

> Life is sweet.
>
> Introducing "Pleasures Delight".
>
> Estée Lauder.

The irresistible new fragrance.

As in the previous example, the picture accompanying this fragrance ad was that of a very beautiful woman carrying an assortment of followers and niceties. A third example used the following phrases: "Fast and clean. Dries out imperfections in only 5 hours". This was an ad advertising facial cleansing pads from Garnier, again with a close-up of a young and beautiful woman with pure skin. As a form of persuasive communication, advertisements are designed to have an impact. They play with our strongest emotions, and research shows that women are more emotional than men and, hence, are more likely to respond to such messages.

In preparing this chapter, in addition to reading magazines, I watched a lot of television, looking at advertisement, advertorials and anything highlighted in relation to advertising. In one episode of the soap opera *Generations*, South Africa's most-watched soap and by far the most-watched television programme in the country, a male character criticises an ad for using a cartoon to promote a sports car. He says they should have used a sexy woman instead of the cartoon. When a female character responds that the ad is humorous and works quite well for her, he cynically responds, "I didn't realise you are a feminist. If you want to fight for the cause, go and do it somewhere. There is no room for feminists in advertising. The bottom line is sex sells." Presumably, the soap's creators included this in the script to highlight the sort of problems raised in this chapter and to conscientise viewers, so they should be applauded!

Based on my analysis, I propose that a typical ad can be conceptualised, with regard to message composition, in terms of the following six stages:

i. Contextual stage, which provides context about the product that is to follow or its usefulness or presents a problem that needs a solution (the problem is usually exaggerated).

i. Awareness stage, which introduces the product in relation to the context (the product is offered as a solution to the existing problem).

ii. Advocacy/promotion stage, in which the message is reiterated and the viewer is given more reasons why she needs the product, often through discrediting other products and showing how this one is better.

iii. Interest stimulation stage, in which the viewers develop interest in response to the persuasiveness of the message.

iv. Reinforcement, in which the viewer feels the "rush" of an immediate urge to acquire the product.

v. Sealing the deal, in which the advert closes the deal, either by offering a discount (usually time-limited) or by making a compelling statement, often in the form of a rhetorical question that which leaves the viewer thinking about the product and realising her need for it.

Summary and Recommendations

To summarise, I will return to the research questions and some of the assumptions mentioned earlier. The assumption that advertising uses women more than men to sell products was proven to be correct. Of all the adverts reviewed here, 92 percent used women. Men were more likely to be used for items such as shaving products and men's fragrances. In general, women were widely used to advertise household products. With regard to the assumption that advertising portrays women as objects to sell products, and in the process exploits women's images, bodies and other traits, further entrenching gender stereotypes and the oppression of women in society, I found that women were, in some cases, portrayed in a sexually suggestive manner, and in a way that could be viewed as stimulating the male gaze. However, this phenomenon was not as pervasive as I initially anticipated. Images of semi-naked women were also not as prevalent, mostly occurring in ads for underwear. Therefore, I tentatively suggest that the depiction of women in contemporary advertising has slightly improved, although there is still much room for further improvement. To keep abreast with contemporary developments and future challenges, I make the following recommendations:

Ways to Improve the Portrayal of Women

Advertisers should consider developing a style book or set of guidelines on gender representation to ensure that neither sex is portrayed negatively in advertising messages. The regulatory bodies should then enforce these guidelines rigorously and use punishments as a deterrent to ensure that women are not marginalised and objectified. As mentioned elsewhere in this chapter, research shows that advertising has a tradition of negatively portraying women as mere objects to sell products, and has in the process exploited women's images, body and other traits, further entrenching gender stereotypes and reinforcing the oppression of women in society. The tendency of advertisements to portray women in roles or through behavioural patterns that may be construed as demeaning further entrenches assumptions made about women and how they are treated in society. This was confirmed by my research, although it should be noted that, at the moment, the media seem to be pandering to feminist consciousness, especially in portrayals of the "modern" woman, who, as Lee (1988: 169) notes is depicted in the media as "cool, stylish and rich".

Ways to Identify Damaging Images

Producers should consider involving a range of voices from women's groups, gender experts, the models who participate in these adverts, as well as ordinary women who consume advertising messages, during post-production so that damaging images can be identified before the ads come out. It is also important that people from religious groups, cultural activists and gay communities be included, as all these groups play an important role in modern society. A discussion of embryonic gender-related issues will go a long way in ensuring that damaging, disparaging and stereotypical images are eliminated from advertising messages.

Full-figured people should be used more regularly in order to deconstruct body-image stereotypes that entrench slim figures as the ideal at the expense of full-figured people. Advertisers should explore ways of selling their products through more positive messages and images that deconstruct stereotypes. They need to acknowledge that people are influenced by media messages, as research proves, and that certain messages and muted values lingering in advertising images may encourage certain behaviours, such as marginalisation, objectification and abuse of women, or indulgence in risky sexual practices.

Ways to Improve Racialised Portrayals

Issues of race, ethnicity and xenophobia are an ever-present concern in many communities across the world. The Rwandan genocide, the Holocaust, apartheid and the recent xenophobia attacks in South Africa are just some of the more vivid examples of destruction that has resulted from racial and ethnic hatred, fuelled by stereotypes and prejudices often entrenched through media messages such as those in advertising. It was for this reason that the Vodacom ad "We have been having it" was pulled off the air due to its stereotypical messages about African leaders. Those involved in producing adverts should be sensitised and made aware of the potential damage their messages can do if not framed properly and responsibly. To address the problem, advertisers need to ask themselves questions such as the following when developing ideas for ads:

- What kind of message am I relaying through this ad, both overtly and covertly?
- Is there any indication that the background information or context of the message may be misconstrued?

- Where people from different races, ethnicities or cultures are featured, are they all presented in a manner that is not denigrating or stereotypical?

Much of the research conducted on advertising does not suggest solutions to address the identified problems. As a start, reception studies should be conducted for each and every major advert not only to determine its usefulness in selling the product but, more importantly, to determine its potential to entrench damaging stereotypes. Research addressing these questions will help to refine advertising strategies and bring about a nuanced understating of certain images and their functions as interpreted by consumers of advertising messages. Such understanding is necessary because advertising is such an essential feature of society despite its shortcomings. It is a burgeoning multi-billion dollar industry and an integral feature of the mass media, which relies on advertising for survival.

In conclusion, when conducted responsibly, advertising can animate life and serve as an essential tool to inform, educate, mobilise, conscientise and entertain, while marketing different products at the same time. Well developed advertising campaigns and advertorials have contributed immensely in promoting healthy lifestyles, mobilising communities and providing crucial information to consumers. A case in point is the "Scrutinise" campaign cited elsewhere in this chapter. To ensure positive advertising messages, efforts must be made to design messages that are free from denigrating, racial and gendered content. Adoption of the recommendations made in this chapter will go a long way in helping advertisers sell their products without entrenching undesirable stereotypes.

References

Barletta, M. 2003. *Marketing to Women: How to Understand, Reach, and Increase Your Share of the World's Largest Market Segment.* Chicago: Dearborn.

Benshoff, H. and S. Griffin. 2009. *America on Film: Representing Race, Class, Gender, and Sexuality at the Movies.* Hoboken, NJ: Wiley-Blackwell.

DeFleur, D. 1995. *Understanding Mass Communication.* 3rd ed. Boston: Houghton Mifflin.

Fagg, L. 2008. Women's images in magazine advertisements: How far have they come? http://belisima.i.ph/blogs/belisima/2008/08/18/women%E2%80%99s-images-in-magazine-advertisements-how-far-have-they-come/ (retrieved 28/03/2010)

Horowitz, I.L. 1991. *Communicating Ideas: The Politics of Scholarly Publishing.* London: Transaction Publishers.

Lee, J. 1988. Care to join me in an upwardly mobile tango? Postmodernism and the "New Woman". In L. Gamman and M. Marshment, eds. *The Female Gaze.* London: The Women's Press.

Mbola, B. 2009. Women in parliament on the rise. *BuaNews,* 6 May. http://www.southafrica.info/about/democracy/parlyw-060509.htm (retrieved August 7, 2012).

MyBroadband. 2008. Vodacom's been having it. http://mybroadband.co.za/news/Cellular/4690.htmlNonetheless (retrieved 25/03/2010).

Ndlela, N. 2006. Alternative media and the global popular: Youth and popular culture in Zimbabwe. http://www.glocaltimes.k3.mah.se/viewarticle.aspx?articleID=73&issueID=7 (retrieved June 16, 2010)

Ogunleye, F. 2005. Gender stereotypes and reconstruction: A feminist appraisal of Nigerian video films. *Acta Academica* 37(3): 125–49.

Okigbo, C. 1995. Media and sustainable development: A prologue. In C. Okigbo, ed. *Media and Sustainable Development*. Nairobi: Litho, 2–24.

Phere, M. 2007. The effect of magazine covers on the reader's decision to buy a magazine. Unpublished thesis. Cape Peninsula University of Technology.

South Africa: Scrutinize! An in-your-face HIV prevention campaign. 2009. PlusNews Global HIV/AIDS news and analysis, March 4. In http://www.plusnews.org/Report/83283/SOUTH-AFRICA-Scrutinize-An-in-your-face-HIV-prevention-campaign (Retrieved August 7, 2012).

CHAPTER 11

REPRESENTATIONS OF WORK IN TELEVISION ADVERTISING IN SOUTH AFRICA: THE EMPLOYMENT EQUITY ACT OF 1998

SYDNEY FRIENDLY KANKUZI

Introduction

The South African labour market is characterised by a long history of racial and gender discrimination. In an effort to address such discrimination, the South African parliament passed the Employment Equity Act in 1998. Over the years, the act has featured prominently in the country's labour market discourse to the extent that it is now almost impossible to talk about the distribution of jobs in the country without alluding to it as a benchmark. Against this backdrop, the present chapter explores the possible implications of using the act to regulate television advertising representations of work. I start with a brief historical background of work, and of television advertising representations of work in South Africa to contextualise the discussion appropriately. Thereafter, I critically explore the theoretical and methodological assumptions behind the proposed use of the act by linking them to cultural indicators theory and the cultivation hypothesis. I pay particular attention to the relationship between cultural indicators theory and the method of content analysis to highlight the methodological constraints of cultivation analysis. Against this background, my discussion highlights how the cultural aspects of advertising would clash with those of the economy if the act were to be used as an index for monitoring advertising representations of work. Finally, I propose a way forward for monitoring advertising representations in general and representations of work in particular, using experiences from

South Africa. The reader is expected to develop a critical understanding of the ideological relationship that obtains between the cultural and economic aspects of advertising and, as a consequence, be enabled to critique the role that theory and methodology play in the study of advertising as culture and the implications for the study of advertising.

Historical Background

In South Africa, apartheid laws were used to manipulate the labour market to the advantage of the White minority. The Population Registration Act (No. 30) of 1950, for example, created a labour market where race was used as a criterion for employment. Consequently, many skilled jobs and managerial positions were reserved for Whites (and some lucky qualified Indians), while Africans were relegated to low-wage employment by virtue of their race. Similarly, the Bantu Education Act (No. 47) of 1953 provided for the allocation of separate educational facilities for Africans to prepare them for low-paying jobs in the semi-skilled sector. Although apartheid was primarily a racial ideology, it intersected with conservative class and gender ideologies. Afrikaner women, for instance, were victims of Afrikaner patriarchal conservatism which enjoyed the support of the apartheid state. They were discouraged from participating in the employment sector because it was regarded as a specialised area for men (Msimang 2001: 5). The inequitable distribution of jobs on gender and racial grounds crossed over into post-apartheid South Africa. For instance, in 1998, a huge gender-racial divide characterised the distribution of managerial positions in the public sector. White males and White females occupied 56 percent and 5 percent of all managerial positions respectively, while their African counterparts occupied 29 percent and 7 percent. Indian males and Coloured males occupied 4 percent and 3 percent respectively and their female counterparts only 1 percent each (Orkin 1998: 4).

Since the introduction of democracy in 1994, South Africa has tried to redress employment inequalities by passing a number of statutes, of which the most critical is the Employment Equity Act of 1998.[1] The act recognises that it is not enough to abolish discriminatory labour laws without taking steps to correct the inequalities caused by these laws. Section 6 (1), therefore, promotes fair treatment of workers by prohibiting unfair discrimination on grounds such as race, class and gender. The act also attaches great importance to the actual number of workers from a specific sexual or racial group who are employed to do particular types of work in any organisation. Section 20 stipulates that any designated employer

---

1. Act No. 55 of 1998. Available at www.labour.gov.za

is required to draw up an employment equity plan as an additional requirement of affirmative action. Among other things, an employment equity plan must "set numerical goals to achieve the equitable representation in occupational category and level in the work force". To date, the Employment Equity Act of 1998 is the backbone of socio-economic policies of the country's labour market.

In South Africa, television advertising was launched in 1978 during the government of Prime Minister B. J. Vorster, when work was also a highly sensitive issue. Consequently, television advertising was designed to promote apartheid ideologies in the job market. For example, advertisements aired on the first channel, TV1, tended to portray pejorative stereotypes of Blacks, who were more often than not depicted as menial workers (Van der Walt 1989: 58). It was not until a year later that television advertising began to undergo positive transformation when the new regime of P. W. Botha decided to use it as an ideological apparatus to replace the use of coercion. In 1979, for example, the regime authorised partial racial integration in advertising content on TV1 by allowing Blacks and Whites to appear in the same advertisements, though not necessarily in the same camera frame (Holt 1998). This partial racial integration in advertising content had important implications for the ways in which work and employment were represented in advertising. By the mid 1980s, beer advertisements had fully integrated images of Blacks and Whites and depicted them as social equals, although advertisers were prohibited from using English in advertisements targeted at Black audiences (Holt 1998). Eventually, the prohibition of English in advertisements targeted at Blacks led to the introduction of two new categories of advertising stereotypes: ethnic stereotypes that conformed to those aired on Radio Bantu[2], and stereotypes that emphasised an emerging Black middle class (Holt 1998). Advertising on TV1, TV2 and TV3[3] took a new turn when M-Net was launched

---

2. Radio Bantu was established in 1959 to broadcast in the vernaculars of the homelands. The implication was that its programming and advertisement content featured stereotypes that were wrongly believed by the South African government to reflect the needs of each target ethnic group. For example, if members of a particular ethnic group were believed to be lazy, advertisements on radio Bantu would repeatedly use the belief to represent them in that way, consequently exaggerating reality.

3. In 1982, Botha's regime opened TV2 and TV3 to cater for Blacks (Collins 1993: 86, 99). Both stations were guided by a language policy that all programming be in the vernacular of their target ethnic groups. TV2 was targeted at Zulu, Xhosa, Swazi and Ndebele groups, although, to begin with, programming was only in Zulu and Xhosa. TV3 broadcast to the Tswana, North Sotho, South Sotho and Venda, although programming started with Sotho only.

in 1986 as the first pay-channel in South Africa (Currie 1991). M-Net did not use much local content in its programming. However, its advertising content tended to display more racial integration than was found on SABC channels. The higher representation of integration possibly suited M-Net's commercial imperatives.

Holt (1998) observes that the practice in the 1980s of having separate television channels for Blacks and Whites, and different languages for different ethnic groups, sharply structured consumer markets along racial and ethnic lines, a development which did not reflect the reality on the ground. Market research, for example, had established that many urban Black viewers of TV1 and TV2 were more conversant with English than with any of the African languages in which the stations were broadcasting. Research also showed that Blacks were willing to adopt some elements of the Western lifestyle in order to compete effectively in an industrial society dominated by Whites.

Television advertising representations witnessed radical positive transformation during the regime of F.W. de Klerk (1989–1994). The regime made considerable efforts to reform the country's media industry. Pejorative racial stereotyping of Blacks was almost phased out, and racial integration in advertisement content was intensified (Holt 1998). The de Klerk regime felt the need to promote a positive image of the then-emerging democratic South Africa to the international community. Similarly, the regime tried to respond to pressure from groups such as the Film and Allied Workers Organisation (FAWO), which demanded that broadcasting should be "re-organised in the best possible way for all people in South Africa, both as consumers and citizens" (Currie 1991: 11).

Reforms in advertising representations in general, and television advertising representations in particular, were carried over into post-apartheid South Africa. The country's advertising industry has come under sustained pressure to address unfavourable racial representations in its advertising content and, specifically, to reflect the ideals of the new democratic dispensation. In 2001, for instance, the South African Advertising Research Foundation (SAARF) stopped using references to race after being criticised for promoting racism in the consumer market.[4] In connection with this move, a senior member of SAARF, Paul Haupt, is on record as saying that, although the role of SAARF is not that of a watchdog, it is necessary for the organisation to promote transformation in the

---

4. See Portfolio Committee on Communications Hearing into Transformation of the Advertising and Marketing Industry. http//www.gsci.gov.za/docs/portcom/02saarf. html/#intro

advertising, media and marketing industries.[5] On 6 and 7 November 2001, the Portfolio Committee on Communications (Parliamentary Monitoring Group) held public hearings on racism in the advertising and marketing industry and accused the advertising industry of displaying racial imbalances in its content, among other racially discriminating employment practices (Portfolio Committee on Communications 2001).

The Employment Equity Act as an Index for Analysing Culture

The long-standing expectation that advertising representations in general, and of work in particular, should conform to the racial and gender realities of the labour market highlights a critical ideological relationship between culture and the economy within the advertising industry of South Africa. Against this backdrop, it is tempting to think that the 1998 Employment Equity Act, which is aimed at addressing, among other things, race, class and gender inequalities in the very same labour market, should be a legitimate benchmark for monitoring advertising representations of work in the new South Africa. The present section critically explores some of the cultural and economic implications of this supposition, which is rooted in cultural indicators theory.

Cultural Indicators Theory

Cultural indicators are indices used for monitoring culture. They measure cultural dynamics such as values, motives, beliefs and ideas, which find expression in ideological texts and the ways in which different groups of people internalise these texts (Reijnders and Bouwman 1984). Considering that culture is essentially abstract, these indices enable researchers to collect and analyse cultural material "in a way that renders a small set of stable statistical time-series measures that can be used to indicate the content of the products of communication presented to the public" (Peterson and Hughes 1984: 444). The central aspect of cultural indicators is the periodic analysis of trends in the composition and structure of message systems (Gerbner 1970). The term "cultural indicators" was coined by George Gerbner in 1969 "as a way to measure the pervasiveness of violence in [American] television programming" (Namenwirth 1984: 93). However, although cultural indicators tend to be associated with television violence, they may be related to other types of media and social aspects. A multi-disciplinary Swedish project entitled *Cultural Indicators: The Swedish Symbol System 1945 –1975 Research*

---

5. See "Race Must Go, Says SAARF," Media Toolbox. 09.12/2004. http://www.mediatoolbox. co.za/pebble.asp?p=40&relid=3004

Program (CISSS) was concerned, for example, with various newspaper genres such as advertising and obituaries (Reijnders and Bouwman 1984). Other well-known cultural indicators include the sex, age, professions/occupations and race of the persons "in the world of television" (Reijnders and Bouwman 1984: 33).

Rosengren (1984) identifies three dimensions of cultural indicators: substantive, theoretical and methodological. The substantive dimension is concerned with the substance of cultural processes manifested in all kinds of media. Substantive cultural processes include violence, religion, politics, the economy and inter-group relationships (for example, those existing between elites and the masses and between women and men). The theoretical dimension deals with three theoretical problems, namely the nature, causes and effects of culture. The nature of culture is concerned with elements of culture and their internal relations. A researcher concerned with the causes of culture seeks to understand the factors responsible for cultural change, while the effects dimension is concerned with the functions of culture in our mass media-saturated societies. It holds the view that the most important thing about media messages is how they affect audiences in the long run. The methodological dimension of cultural indicators recognises three widely known research traditions in the human and social sciences: content analysis, survey research and secondary statistical analysis. In a typical scenario, each of these methodological approaches tends to focus on a specific theoretical problem. Survey research and secondary statistical analyses are associated with the causes of cultural change and the effects of culture respectively. Content analysis is mostly associated with the nature of culture.

Reijnders and Bouwman (1984) identify two divergent approaches within the cultural indicators tradition: the broad sociological approach and the mass communication approach. The broad sociological approach is mainly concerned with cultural change in general and particularly with cultural trends in the media. It analyses these by relating cultural development to wider social and economic changes, hoping to obtain insights into the cohesion of the social and economic fields (Reijnders and Bouwman 1984). A perfect example of the broad sociological approach is the Swedish project, which drew researchers from psychology, sociology, political science, theology and philosophy from the Universities of Lund and Stockholm. The project, which started with a focus on daily and weekly newspapers, attempted "to construct cultural indicators for different areas of post-war Swedish society – to construct standardised instruments for measuring various aspects of the symbol system in the cultural environment as conceived in a broad perspective" (Reijnders and Bouwman 1984: 42).

The mass communication approach is mainly associated with the work of Gerbner. It mainly emphasises how mass media messages influence the way society understands the world, particularly in the long-term. Reijnders and Bouwman (1984: 39) put forward three ways in which the approach analyses the media, namely institutional process analysis (IPA), message system analysis (MSA) and cultivation analysis (CA). The IPA is concerned with aspects of television production. It assumes that television production receives pressure from various stakeholders, such as investors, writers, political figures and audiences. For instance, shareholders of a given television station are likely to encourage the station to broadcast only those programmes that are not detrimental to their profit motives. The aim of message system analysis is to generate an in-depth understanding of media content. For instance, one may want to understand issues that television producers emphasise, tendencies that characterise programming or how television structures phenomena. Methodologically, MSA employs the research tradition of content analysis (Reijnders and Bouwman 1984). The rationale is that content analysis produces content indicators that reveal "shared representations of life, the issues, and the prevailing points of view that capture public attention, occupy people's time, and animate their image-making in communications" (Gerbner 1973: 562).

Cultivation analysis is based on the view that "the message systems of a culture do not only inform, entertain, and satisfy the public but they also form common images, create publics, and shape a range of attitudes, tastes, and preferences of the public" (Gerbner 1973: 567). Gerbner sees television as the dominant medium in the symbolic environment and concludes that it is "not a window on or a reflection of the world, but a world itself" (McQuail and Windahl 1993: 100). Typical cultivation analysis involves identifying prevailing televised images of violence and correlating them with data collected from audience research using surveys. Apart from images of violence, cultivation analysis is also interested in establishing other images that dominate various sectors of the world of television, as is the case in the present discussion.

A critical examination of the assumption that the Employment Equity Act of 1998 could be used as an index for analysing television advertising representations of work reveals that it is theoretically and methodologically informed by cultural indicators theory.

> Cultivation is about the implications of stable, repetitive, pervasive and virtually inescapable patterns of images and ideologies that television provides …. Cultivation research approaches television as a system of messages – a system whose elements are not invariant or uniform, but complementary, organic and

coherent – and inquiries into the functions and consequences of those messages as a system, overall, in toto for its audiences. The focus of cultivation analysis is on the correlates and consequences of cumulative exposure to television in general over long periods of time (Shanahan and Morgan 1999: 5).

Similarly, Gerbner's alternative "resonant thesis", which is based on the cultivation hypothesis, argues that television messages tend to be more powerful when they reflect the viewer's social experience, a situation, which Clifford et al. (1995: 6) call the "double dose effect". Gerbner found, for example, that heavy viewers of television violence are far more likely to overestimate their chances of being victims of violence in high-crime neighbourhoods.

The assumption at hand is concerned with the substance of cultural processes that take the form of inter-group relationships based on race, gender and class in television advertising. It subscribes to message system analysis in so far as it assumes that it is possible to identify content indicators that reveal shared representations of race, class and gender within the symbolic labour market of television advertising, representations which capture public attention, occupy people's time and animate their image-making. It also assumes that survey research and secondary statistical analysis could be conducted to detect the causes of existing trends in television advertising representations of work and their possible cultivation effects. This does not necessarily mean that cultural indicators subscribe to the effect tradition in the pejorative sense. As Ruddock (1998: 119) argues:

> When cultivation analysis speaks of the process of homogenisation, it does not argue that TV produces uniformity. Mainstreaming refers to a reduction of difference, which is very different to the idea of the direct effect. It is not an "empiricist" concept in its pejorative sense, since it assumes that neither the meaning nor the effects of television content are transparent.

Possible Challenges of Using the Employment Equity Act of 1998 to Analyse Advertising Representations of Work

From a critical cultural studies point of view, the use of the Employment Equity Act of 1998 as an index for analysing television advertising representations of work would be an uphill task. Firstly, the expectation that advertising representations should reflect the realities of the real labour market directly conflicts with the conceptual framework of the genre of advertising, because it is inevitable for the genre to construct reality: "Advertising … draws deeply from the dispositions, hopes and concerns of its audiences, but it reformulates them to suit its own purposes, not reflecting meaning but rather reconstituting it" (Leiss et al. 1990: 200).

Requiring advertising to represent work in ways that conform to reality as conceptualised by the Employment Equity Act would be tantamount to forcing advertising to abdicate its conceptual rules for the sake of conforming to existing dominant ideology. This unnecessary conflict between the economy and culture is illustrated by a controversial television advertisement called "Another look at the Mzansi", which was used on SABC 1 as a signature device in 2003 and 2004. The advertisement reverses racial stereotypes by portraying Africans as living under what are usually believed to be the socio-economic conditions of Whites and vice versa. One cannot read the advertisement without noticing the racial tension between Blacks and Whites in the subtext. This, in turn, evokes memories of stereotyped media images of Black and White economies during the apartheid era. Ironically, the advertisement does not do any justice to previously disadvantaged groups. Instead, it promotes a form of escapism among them and reinforces negative stereotypes, racial tension and stigmatisation. If applied to product and service advertisements, the reversal of character roles on racial, class and gender grounds would also be economically detrimental to the television advertising industry. It is one thing to create advertisements which conform to existing socio-economic policy; it is another to have these advertisements interpellate target consumers in ways that can reward the advertising business financially. An advertisement which carelessly reverses character roles on racial and/or gender grounds is unlikely to meet the financial goals of the advertising business.

A semiotic communication test (Griffiths 2001) of a television MTN airtime competition advertisement popular on e.TV and SABC in 2003–4 supports the above claim. The advertisement features a male African taxi driver buying MTN airtime from a female African grocer. The characters and setting of the advertisement indicate that it is targeted at working-class South Africans, most of whom are Black and live in townships and other high-density areas. However, for the sake of conforming to the race and gender ideals of the Employment Equity Act, the male African taxi driver could be substituted by a White female taxi driver, and the female African grocer by a White saleslady who works at a middle-class shop such as Morkels. Apparently, the advertisement would not be able to interpellate its originally intended audience, because many Africans would not be able to identify themselves with the female White taxi driver, considering that, in reality, Whites, let alone female Whites, do not "normally" drive minibus taxis. Similarly, many working-class South Africans would not feel that the advertisement was targeted at them, because they do not identify themselves with up-market shops such as Morkels. Sooner or later, advertisers would not be able to satisfy their clients and would consequently lose business.

The use of the Employment Equity Act as an index for analysing advertising representations of work is also likely to be faced with significant methodological challenges. Cultural indicators theory over-depends on content analysis, a method which does not satisfactorily address the question of researcher objectivity and tends to be obsessed with quantitative aspects of data at the expense of qualitative ones.

Content Analysis: Uses and Limitations

In its simplest terms, content analysis is a "research technique that involves measuring something … in random sampling of some form of communication" (Berger 1998: 117). Berelson, the father of content analysis, conceptualised it (1952: 18) as "a research technique for the objective, systematic, and quantitative description of the manifest content of communication". The technique may be used for describing patterns or trends in media portrayals, testing hypotheses about the policies or aims of media practitioners, drawing inferences about media effects, comparing media content with the real world or assessing the representation of particular groups in society (Wimmer and Dominick 1983). Gunter (2000) contends that content analysis is systematic because it employs explicit, consistent rules to select and code, thereby giving each item an equal chance of being selected for analysis. The principle also applies to evaluation of data. As Wimmer and Dominick (1983: 138) point out, "systematic evaluation simply means that one and only one set of guidelines for evaluation is used throughout the study". This way of perceiving objectivity is based on the claim that, ideally, the personal biases and idiosyncrasies of the researcher are not allowed to influence the results of the study (Wimmer and Dominick 1983: 138). Thus, it is expected that, when a study is replicated, the same results will be produced. To ensure that this happens, the researcher is required to explain clearly all operational definitions and rules for classifying variables (Gunter 2000):

> Unless a clear set of criteria and procedures are established that fully explain the sampling and categorisation of method, the researcher does not meet the requirement of objectivity, and the reliability of the results may be called into question (Wimmer and Dominick 1983: 139).

Content analysis is conducted through a series of clearly defined steps, which may vary from one study to another (Bowers 1970: 291–314). It may start with the formulation of a hypothesis or a research question. In either case, one needs to explain clearly the broad issues under investigation and their corresponding research questions to avoid aimless data collection and counting. This includes an operational definition of the topic under study. Next, the researcher defines the population in the question and specifies the boundaries of the body of content to be considered. Finally, the researcher selects a sample on which to base the analysis.

Sampling usually involves two stages (although it may entail three). The researcher begins by sampling content sources and then selects dates on which content will be collected. This is usually determined by the research goals (Dominick 1983). For example, a comparative study is expected to select dates from different periods of the year in which the issue under investigation occurred. Then the researcher needs to select specific content for analysis. Usually, the researcher is faced with vast amounts of content, hence the need to decide how much of it he or she needs (Bowers 1970). The actual selection of media texts is one of the most challenging procedures of content analysis. Thus the question of objectivity naturally arises. Larger samples, if chosen randomly, usually run less risk of being 'atypical' (Gunter 2000: 66). Furthermore, researchers must ensure that they make a random sampling of whatever they are analyzing, while still providing a representative sample which may not be accused of researcher bias (Berger 2001: 182).

The fourth step of quantitative content analysis requires the researcher to select a unit of analysis. This unit is "the thing that is actually counted. It is the smallest element of a content analysis but it is also one of the most important" (Wimmer and Dominick 1983: 146). The unit of analysis may be as big as a whole television programme or as small as a single word in a television advertisement. It may also be abstract, such as the theme of an advertisement. A study may also have more than one unit of analysis. In any case, one needs to give a clear operational definition of each unit of analysis to avoid confusion when coding data. Defining the unit of analysis also helps the researcher to sift through the data more easily and eliminate irrelevant aspects of the data. After explaining the unit of analysis, the researcher describes the system for classifying media content. The classification system is "an analytical framework that [classifies] attributes of content of interest in the research" (Gunter 2000: 60). Wimmer and Dominick (1983) call it a category system and observe that it must be mutually exclusive, exhaustive and reliable.

A study of representations of beauty in television drama may use the following categories: (1) male beauty (2) female beauty (3) old-age beauty (4) African beauty (5) American beauty. To ensure the exclusivity of a category system, the researcher is required to provide an operational definition for each category (Berger 2000). When a category system is exhaustive, the researcher must be able to put every unit of analysis into a predefined category (Leiss et al. 1990). In the above example about different types of beauty, the researcher is not expected to get into a situation whereby a certain character fails to fit in any of the categories of beauty. However, if such a thing happens, they may create new categories and label them "other" or "miscellaneous". Finally, a category system is said to be reliable when it allows for inter-coder reliability, meaning that most coders reach a consensus on the proper category for each unit of analysis as they use the categories (Wimmer and Dominick 1983). The next step requires the researcher to code the content. Coding means "placing a unit of analysis into a content category" (Wimmer and Dominick 1983: 148). Coders use standardised sheets that allow them to classify data simply by marking relevant sections of specially designed coding sheets.

Despite these procedures, the objectivity of content analysis is debatable, since it is based on an unsustainable positivist view of science. For example, the researcher cannot completely exclude his or her value judgements during sampling, coding and analysis of data. The researcher needs to make value judgements when deciding which media product should be subjected to content analysis and to determine the relationship between various categories of data. Similarly, the researcher relies on common sense, pre-testing and experience to determine the number of categories in a coding system (Wimmer and Dominick 1983: 148). For instance, a study of representations of religion in the media might be said to have inadequate categories if it labelled one of them "Christians". The problem would be that there are many Christian sub-groups, such as Pentecostals, Presbyterians, Evangelicals, Catholics and so on. Conversely, the study may be said to have too many categories if only a small number of subjects fell into a certain category. For example, if Pentecostals scored 43, Presbyterians 53, Evangelicals 2, and Catholics 2, the researcher may need to decide to combine the categories of Evangelicals and Catholics and re-label them "other". The researcher may, however, maintain the categories if they have a strong motivation to do so (Wimmer and Dominick 1983). No wonder the major challenge of MSA is to objectively define the concepts the researcher wants to measure and to determine units of analysis, and corresponding measuring categories. Owen (1972) criticises Gerbner's definition of violence for being too broad, but a critical look at the criticism reveals that this is not a challenge for message system analysis per se but of content analysis' over-reliance on "common sense".

Thus, the proposed use of the Employment Equity Act of 1998 as an index for analysing television advertising representations of work would be faced with an endless task of addressing the question of objectivity. One possible way of dealing with the problem would be to ascertain the degree to which the researcher's intrusion into the process affects the results. However, even this task would face problems associated with the researcher's subjectivity, since culturally different people tend to interpret the same situation differently. Similarly, the preoccupation of content analysis with quantitative data has prompted some critics to argue that the methodology offers only a superficial analysis of media content (Gunter 2000). Ruddock (1998) observes that the methodology of cultivation analysis is often accused of using quantitative methodologies that deal with meaningless abstractions, thereby articulating generalisations that are not necessarily related to the positioning of television in a social world. Where content analysis may only identify quantitative data in television advertising, qualitative approaches such as semiotics may detect the use of covert aspects such as framing, lighting, distance, angles and so on, and use them to establish how camera work is used to generate preferred meanings in a given text. For example, Zettl (1999) observes that, when compared with the detachment and distance of long shots, close-ups have the effect of intensifying the event that is depicted on the screen, thereby creating a different feel altogether. Messaris (1997) adds that close-ups increase both the attention and involvement of the viewer.

The methodological weakness of content analysis is illustrated by a study the present author conducted in 2004. The study was based on content analysis of a sample of 54 television advertisements on the theme of work which were broadcast over a four-week period (2–30 May 2004) on SABC 1, 2 and 3, and e.TV. Using the race and gender of workers as units of analysis, it head-counted the number of people from each race and their sex who were depicted doing a particular type of job such as bricklaying, driving and office work. The results revealed that advertising representations of work did not conform to the ideals of the labour market as promoted by the Employment Equity Act. Male workers tended to dominate the advertising representations, accounting for 66.8 percent of the representations. Similarly, males dominated high-status roles which require high intellectual capacity. For example, the appearance of male life-science professionals and male business professionals was two times and five times greater than that of their female counterparts respectively.

When race was factored in, it was found that African females dominated average-status roles which require average intellectual capacity. The visibility of female African nurses, for instance, was twice that of their male counterparts, while that of female African shop salespersons was three times greater than that of their male counterparts. Overall, although Africans emerged as the most dominant group in the advertising representations of work in general, they tended to be marginalised in certain high-status roles that require high intellectual capacity.

However, when a semiotic test was applied on some of the advertisements, the results revealed different tendencies. Semiotic analysis was able to detect many subtleties which had gone unnoticed during content analysis. Two advertisements from the sample ably highlight the results of this semiotic test.

The first example is drawn from a Nescafe advertisement in which the camera deliberately draws viewers' attention to an African business professional who is working with four White colleagues and one female African colleague. Firstly, the advertisement uses a level-angle medium shot to depict a male African wearing a suit and travelling on a minibus taxi. Thereafter, it shows the African man without his jacket in a boardroom meeting delivering a presentation to his colleagues. Only the back of his body and head are shown first in close-up. He then turns around and shows his face to the audience in a suggestive manner, as if saying, "Look at me. I am the same man you saw earlier travelling in a taxi."

There is no doubt that the close-up makes the viewers give this African business professional more attention than any other character in this scene, especially since the camera is also out of focus on the faces of his three male White colleagues seated directly opposite to him. Upon watching this scene, one cannot help but feel as if the camera is directing the audience not to worry about the three White gentlemen and concentrate on the African business professional who is the main character in the scene. When content analysis alone is used, one may be misled to conclude that the advertisement discriminates against African males simply because the African males are out-numbered by White males.

A similar phenomenon can be observed in the depiction of a White female character and her Black female counterpart who are attending the presentation. The camera draws most of the viewer's attention to the female African. This is done by showing only part of the face of the White business professional through a close-up that pays more attention to her nose, eyes and mouth than to her status as a business professional. In contrast, her female African counterpart is shown seated behind a desk next to a male White colleague. Significantly, her face is not out of focus like that of the male White colleague. Thereafter, in a closing scene, the female African business professional is shown drinking Nescafe coffee while seated behind a large office desk. All this subtlety, which is used to emphasise the presence of the African female executive, went unnoticed by quantitative content analysis.

The last example can be found an advert for Sunlight Auto Powder. The advertisement features a White gynecologist examining an African woman in the presence of her husband/boyfriend. Eventually, he tells the couple that the woman is pregnant with triplets. The advertisement then shows the husband/boyfriend at home in the kitchen loading the washing powder in a washing machine as a voiceover explains that Sunlight Auto Powder washes three times more than other soap powders. As far as content analysis is concerned, the viewer only sees one worker who happens to be a White doctor because the advertisement explicitly portrays him as such. However, if one applies the principles of semiotics on the same advertisement, one would see that viewers may use their knowledge about social and cultural codes to decipher that the husband/boyfriend is also a worker, although the advertisement does not explicitly present him as such. The man's jacket and necktie, and the glamorous kitchen where he is shown, indicate that he is a middle-class African male who probably has a high-status job.

Recommendations

It is doubtful that the problem of pejorative stereotypes of designated South Africans in the labour market can be addressed successfully without interference from the law. However, both theoretically and methodologically, the use of the Employment Equity Act of 1998 would be undesirable. Even if the act could be used reliably as an index for analysing advertising representations of work, changing a symbolic environment does not automatically yield changes in the real environment. On the contrary, the symbolic environment is the one that is likely to conform to changes which occur in the real world, because a symbolic system does not exist in a vacuum. This is why advertising as a business tends to be sensitive to the socio-economic environment and easily adapts to existing socio-economic conditions to secure its commercial interests.

The history of television advertising in South Africa supports this claim. Holt (1998) observes that, in the 1980s, racial integration in television advertising was possible because more Blacks had begun contributing to the economy, both as white-collar and blue-collar workers and as consumers. Consequently, it became imperative for advertising representations to tone down pejorative racial stereotypes in order interpellate Blacks as a non-ethnic middle-class reflecting an emerging business sector that was supposedly based on a non-racial class structure. This is why the prohibition of English words such as "chips" and "toothpaste" in advertisements targeted at Blacks in an effort to use more "culturally appealing" language ironically caused communication breakdown; Blacks had already adopted these words into their vernaculars.

Similarly, the reforms which the de Klerk government initiated in the 1990s were partly in response to new market dynamics which previous regimes had ignored. By the end of the 1970s, for example, Black consumption expenditure had surpassed that of Whites in many ways. In 1979, the All Media Products

Survey (AMPS) carried out by the South Africa Advertising Research Foundation (SAARF) had revealed that Blacks topped the consumption of some products, for example, whiskey and deodorants, along with a number of selected services (Cassim 1987). Furthermore, projections had been made that, by the mid-1980s, Black consumer expenditure was going to surpass that of Whites (Brits and Reekie 1985). There is also historical evidence that financial competition among advertising companies tends to cause them to go through a self-righting process which encourages them to use content which is in tandem with the socio-economic environment of the real world. During the second half of the 1990s, for example, M-Net's use of more racially integrated advertising content posed a threat to SABC television. The latter reacted by revisiting its advertising restrictions and allowing advertisers to depict an emerging Black middle-class without necessarily including the ethnic stereotypes that had been ubiquitous hitherto (Holt 1998).

Now that South Africa is a fully fledged democracy which allows everyone, including previously disadvantaged groups, to participate freely in the economic sector, including the advertising industry, it is even more plausible to expect the advertising industry to regulate its content through self-censorship and market competition instead of resorting to legal interventions such as the use of the Employment Equity Act. Culture is both conservative and dynamic and, as a result, naturally tends to be self-regulatory. When culture is regulated using state apparatuses, the strategy tends to serve the interests of dominant groups. This does not mean that the state cannot make any contribution towards regulating advertising representations, but it should be encouraged to play a minimal role by using democratically appointed advertising complaints bodies which can encourage viewers to read advertising representations critically and bring to the bodies' attention any stereotypical representations they notice for possible redress. These bodies should also be tasked with providing media literacy services to the general public in an effort to create critical television viewers who can challenge the advertising industry to produce more acceptable representations.

Conclusion

The discussion in this chapter has revealed that the direct use of the law to monitor advertising representations of work is not only culturally undesirable but also spells out disastrous economic consequences for the business of advertising. Using experiences from South Africa, I have elaborated the theoretical and methodological constraints which would be encountered if state machinery such as the Employment Equity Act of 1998 were to be used as an index for monitoring advertising representations. As a business, advertising has internal and external mechanisms which regulate its content, thus precluding the need for direct intervention by the state. However, the importance of civic education and mediatory roles of democratically appointed independent monitoring bodies cannot be overemphasised.

References

Berger, A. 1998. *Media Research Techniques*. Thousand Oaks: CA: Sage.
Berger, A. 2000. *Media and Communication Research Methods: An Introduction to Qualitative and Quantitative Approaches*. Thousand Oaks, CA: Sage.
Berelson, B. 1952. *Content Analysis in Communication Research*. Glencoe, IL: The Free Press of Glencoe.
Bowers, J.W. 1970. Content analysis. In E. Philip and W. Brooks, eds. *Methods of Research in Communication*. Boston: Houghton Mifflin.
Brits, R.N. and W.D. Reekie. 1985. *Marketing in South Africa: Decision Analysis, Theory and Practice*. London: Macmillan.
Cassim, S. 1987. A study of the opinions and attitudes of Indian women towards specific strategies in advertising. Unpublished MA thesis, University of KwaZulu-Natal, South Africa.
Clifford, B., Gunter B., and J. McAleer. 1995. *Television and Children: Program Evaluation, Comprehension and Impact*. Hillsdale, NJ: Lawrence Erlbaum Associates.
Collins, R. 1993. Broadcasting policy for a post Apartheid South Africa: Some preliminary proposals. In P.E. Louw, ed. *South African Media Policy: Debates of the 1990s*. Bellville, SA: Anthropos.
Currie, W. 1991. The control of broadcasting: Transition period. In J. Balch et al., eds. *Jabulani! Freedom of the Airwaves*. Amsterdam: African European Institute.
Dominick, J. 1983. *The Dynamics of Mass Communication*. New York: McGraw-Hill.
Gerbner, G. 1970. Cultural indicators: The case of violence in television drama. *Annals of the American Academy of Political and Social Sciences* 388: 69-81.
Gerbner, G. 1973. Cultural indicators: The third voice. In G. Gerbner, ed. *Communication Technology and Social Policy*. New York: John Wiley.
Griffiths, M. 2001. Children's toy advertisements. Unpublished PhD thesis. University of Wales, Aberystwyth, UK. http://users.aber.ac.uk/lmg/chapter_4.html (retrieved 15/01/2003).
Gunter, B. 2000. *Media Research Methods*. London: Sage.
Holt, A.R. 1998. An analysis of racial stereotyping in South African Broadcasting Corporation television in the context of reform. Unpublished PhD thesis. University of Natal, South Africa. http//www.ukzn.ac.za/ccms (retrieved 15/04/2004).
Leiss, W., Kline, S., and S. Jhally. 1990. *Social Communication in Advertising: Persons, Products and Images of Well Being*. Second Ed. New York: Routledge.
McQuail, D. and S. Windahl. 1993. *Communication Models for the Study of Mass Communication*. London: Longman.

Messaris, P. 1997. *Visual Persuasion: The Role of Images in Advertising*. Thousand Oaks, CA: Sage.

Msimang, S. 2001. Affirmative action in the new South Africa: The politics of representation, law and equity. *Women in Action*, 1: 36.

Namenwirth, J. 1984. Why cultural indicators? A practical agenda. In G. Meleschek, et al, eds. *Cultural Indicators: An International Symposium*. Osterreichische Acadamie der Wissenschaften.

Orkin, F. 1998. Women and men in South Africa. *Africa Policy Electronic Journal*. http://www.Africaaction.org.docs 98/gen9809.htm (retrieved 15/01/2004).

Owen, B. 1972. Measuring violence on television: The Gerbner Index." Staff Research Paper, Office of Telecommunications Policy, OTP-SP-7.

Portfolio Committee on Communications. Hearing into transformation of the advertising and marketing Industry. http//www.gsci.gov.za/docs/portcom/02saarf.html/#intro (retrieved 15/07/2004).

Reijnders, N. and H. Bouwman. 1984. Cultural indicators: Some states of the art. In G. Meleschek et al., eds. *Cultural Indicators: An International Symposium*. Osterreichische Acadamie der Wissenschaften.

Rosengren, K. 1984. Cultural indicators for the comparative study of culture. In G. Meleschek et al., eds. *Cultural Indicators: An International Symposium*. Osterreichische Acadamie der Wissenschaften.

Ruddock, A. 1998. Doing it by numbers. *Critical Arts* 12(1&2): 115–37.

Shanahan, J. and M. Morgan. 1999. *Television and Its Viewers: Cultivation Theory and Research*. Cambridge: Cambridge University Press.

Van der Walt, D. 1989. Specific inferior and superior role portrayals in multi-racial television advertisements. *Communicare* 8 (1): 53–60.

Wimmer, R. and J. Dominick. 1983. *Mass Media Research: An Introduction*. Belmont, CA: Wadsworth.

Zettl, H. 1999. *Sight, Sound, Motion: Applied Media Aesthetics*. Belmont, CA: Wadsworth.

CHAPTER 12

THE RISE OF POLITICAL ADVERTISING ON TELEVISION IN SOUTH AFRICA

SIBONGILE SINDANE

Introduction

During election time, there is normally a buzz about which political party will gain the most votes, as the parties campaign to get the most crosses next to their names on election day. Various appeals are used in order to make the electorate aware of the parties and their policies. South Africa has recently seen the rise of political advertising on television. The debate around the assessment of political advertising has focused on the question of whether political advertisements concentrate on images rather than political issues and thus hinder well-informed voting decisions (McNair 1999, Kaid and Holtz-Bacha 1995, Scammell and Langer 2006, Fourie 2008, Fourie and Froneman 2003). This chapter investigates the rise of political advertising on television in South Africa and its implications for democracy. My focus is on the 2009 South African election campaign and, specifically on the political advertisements that appeared on national television during the pre-election period from 30 March to 20 April 2009. I explore the themes that were covered in the advertisements and the extent to which these advertisements focused on images rather than issues. The investigation in this chapter is interesting and timely because television political advertising is a relatively new phenomenon in South Africa. The study of the rise of political advertising is also important because, in first-world countries such as the United States, the impact of television political advertising has been more unfavourable than favourable for democracy. Thus, if television political advertising is going to develop in South

Africa in the same way as in the first world, this is cause for concern. I am, therefore, concerned here with the implications of television political advertising for democracy in South Africa. Qualitative research is used in the investigation and, as a means of interpreting the data collected, a thematic content analysis is used.

I begin with definitions of political advertising and then of democracy, focusing on liberal democracy and deliberative democracy. My key argument is that deliberative democracy is a better option than liberal democracy. I argue for a correlation between deliberative democracy, the public sphere and political advertising on television. I then describe the research method and discuss the results. Three categories of analysis are identified: the themes and images in political advertisements on television, the emotional appeals and the character appeals. The chapter concludes by discussing how the political parties articulated their political manifestoes in their television political advertisements and the different approaches they took in communicating their messages. In a majority of the political advertisements, the content was packed with sufficient and clear information. Thus, the advertisements were by no means superficial and dealt with important issues in the South African situation. Nevertheless, I argue that implications television political advertising on for democracy in South Africa are both positive and negative.

Defining Political Advertising

According to McNair (1999: 86), political advertising is the purchase and use of advertising space, paid for at a commercial rate, in order to transmit political messages to an audience. However, McNair argues (1999: 96–7) that it detracts from rational decision-making by concentrating on emotional features rather than political issues. He claims (1999: 92–3) that the focus in political advertising tends to fall on the image, which results in emotional rather than logical voting choices, whereas a rational voting decision is presumed to be linked to logical and issue-oriented information. When political advertisements detract from rational decision-making and participation, they could be considered "unethical" (McNair 1999: 93) as well as disadvantageous to democracy in the sense that the advertisements may not necessarily make room for the principles and characteristics of a democracy.

Kaid and Holtz-Bacha (1995: 3) view political advertising as "a means through which parties and candidates represent themselves to the electorate mostly through mass media". They argue that political advertising is sometimes referred to as "paid media". "Free media", that is, free coverage, is constrained by the usual journalistic constraints, while paid media allows candidates, parties and sometimes other interest groups to decide how they want to present themselves to the voters (Kaid and Holtz-Bacha 1995: 3–4):

> Political advertising is a controlled, non-mediated campaign channel, meaning that responsibility for the ads lies with the political actors, and they do not run the risk of their messages being altered by the media production process.

Kern (1989: 52) suggests that advertising allows candidates to reach uninterested and unmotivated citizens – those who pay little attention to news reports, debates and other campaigns. Thus, political actors determine how they are represented on television and dictate the shape and content of the political advertisement.

However, the definitions of political advertising of both McNair (1999) and Kaid and Holtz-Bacha (1995) carry some weaknesses within. For example, McNair fails to acknowledge that the purchase and use of advertising space is through the mass media. Hence, political advertising can be understood and defined as a controlled and non-mediated campaign channel which purchases and uses advertising space, mostly through the mass media, in order to transmit political messages to a potential electorate.

Image vs Political Reality

One of the major criticisms of modern political advertising is that it is emotive and manipulates people's feelings. As Young (2002: 88) argues, political advertising is "essentially trivial, exploiting emotions and substituting catchcries and slogans for real political debate". Idealists may hope that political advertisements will encourage informed decision-making, educate voters, stimulate debate and promote participation. However, political parties are less concerned about these civic functions; for them, the primary aim of political advertisements is to win votes (Young 2002: 88). There are also concerns that the lack of quality information in television advertisements "dumbs down" political debate, that the increasing use of negative advertising fosters public cynicism and that false and misleading claims are made in political advertising (Ansolabehere and Iyengar 1995, cited in Young 2002: 90).

Kaid and Holtz-Bacha (1995) argue that the central characteristics of American election campaigns are 1) the prevailing role of the different campaign channels, 2) the predominance of images instead of issues, going hand in hand with a personalisation in the presentation of the political process, and 3) a professionalization, as a consequence of increased media orientation, of political actors in the development of their media strategies (Gurevitch and Blumer 1990, cited in Kaid and Holtz-Bacha 1995: 59). Like Young (2002) and Norris (2005), Kaid and Holtz-Bacha (1995: 9) observe that political actors increasingly rely on professional consultants from the advertising industry and that, as a consequence, one of the typical characteristics of symbolic politics is personalisation, going hand in hand with a predominance of images over issues. Slogans and value-laden rhetoric are used to distract from political problems. In addition, the messages that candidates pack into thirty-second spots are superficial, deceptive and increasingly nasty. As a result, campaigns offer citizens little hard information with which to make a reasoned choice, and the information that the voters do acquire is slanted and negative (Gurevitch and Blumer 2000: 153). Borchers (2002: 307) illustrates that the line between image and issue is generally blurred. He notes that the image is often the overall perception that voters have of the candidate or political party: "The candidates image is based on a variety of factors; manner of speaking, appearance, and character". Borchers (2002: 307) argues that the image the candidate portrays is increasingly important in political campaigns and that images are created through careful planning by campaign staff. Thus, the advertising creative play a key role in developing the candidate's image.

Importantly, however, the images themselves can be based on issues. Candidates not only talk about their image and their opponent's image, they also talk about their positions on various issues (Borchers 2002: 308). Some of Borchers' findings show that "winning candidates speak more often about policy issues than their opponents, who spend more time speaking about character, or image (2002: 308). Bogart (1998: 8) considers the printed text the best way to communicate political matters:

> [W]hile visual images may convey expressions and evoke empathy more vividly than words, printed text is unsurpassed in its ability to arouse indignation and stir the reflection and deliberation that are essential to the democratic process.

Bogart and Borchers both argue that text is better than image at communicating a democratic massage. However, I argue that the image can make a viable contribution to political communication depending on how it is communicated.

Political Advertising in South Africa

In the South African context, no research has been done on political advertising on television. Presumably, this is because such advertising is still a new phenomenon in South Africa. However, some South African research has dealt with the issue of political communication in newspapers and on billboards and other outdoor media. Research on political communication is also limited; only a few academics have focused on it. Most of the political communication research that has been done in South Africa has looked into the concept of issue versus image. For example, David (2004) and Herzenburg (2004) conducted an analysis of the different party manifestos, and their results showed that the major parties agreed on what the important issues were, but they tried to address the concerns of their specific constituents in different ways. Herzenburg (2004: 16) also argues that the politically less sophisticated voter often looks to media for information to enable him or her to analyse the policies of the different parties.

In her research entitled 'A Salient Revolution: South-African voters, 1994–2006', Schulz-Herzenburg (2007) confirms that the levels of political engagement are low and that large percentages of voters are uninformed on policy issues. She looks into the trends and patterns in partisanship over time. Schulz-Herzenburg (2007: 114) makes use of eight national public opinion surveys from 1994 to 2004 to explore the changes in the demographic support bases of parties and the motivations of voters. As she argues (2007: 114):

> when voters have little information they rely on 'information short cuts' often in the form of clues supplied by a candidates dress, race and accent, which provide information as to the potential attitudes and performance of that party in government.

Fourie (2008: 224) investigated the role of election campaign communication in a young democracy. She began with the assumption that political parties in developing societies have a normative obligation to do more than canvass for votes during election campaigns. She argues that they should also be instrumental in fostering a democratic political culture by communicating democratic values, encouraging participation and enabling voters to make informed electoral choices. Thus, like Norris (2005), Fourie (2008) acknowledges the role of the political party and what it should entail. Her results show that posters contribute mainly to image-building, the reinforcement of party support and the visibility of the party, and that posters are the agenda-setters (or headlines) of a party's campaign. Her argument is that political parties in developing societies need to design political posters responsibly, in order to sustain democracy. Furthermore, Fourie (2008) argues that, in general, the poster campaigns of parties have matured since 1999, in the sense that there is now less emphasis on democratisation issues and campaigns conform more to the norms of Western political campaigning. As a research method, Fourie (2008) focuses on the political posters of the main political parties that contested the 1999 and 2004 national elections, as well as the 2004 and 2006 local elections in North-West Province. She did a qualitative content analysis according to the following categories: policy issues, identification messages, party leaders and democratic leaders (Fourie 2008: 227). It would be interesting to see whether the analysis of political advertising on television would produce similar results.

Fourie and Froneman (2003: 189) investigated emotional political advertising in South Africa, with a particular focus on the use of persuasive emotional appeals and negative messages in political newspaper advertisements in the North-West Province during the South African general elections in 1999. They argue that the over-emphasis on party image in advertisements could lead to the neglect of important political information for voters and that emotional and negative advertisements could, therefore, be detrimental to any young democracy. However, Fourie's and Froneman's (2003) results show that, although the parties in their study used emotional appeals, they mostly connected them to policy issues. Nevertheless, these policy issue were not elaborated on. They maintain that the opposition parties mostly used appeals of uncertainty, fear and rage, while the ANC "concentrated on appeals of hope and achievement" (Fourie and Froneman 2003: 187). Overall, Fourie and Froneman (2003) deduce that the ANC virtually abstained from using negative messages, while the DP, the NP and the FF (Freedom Front) attacked one another in order to emphasise their differences. They argue that the political advertisements did not harm the sustainability of South African democracy as such, but that they also did very little to promote it actively.

Fourie's and Froneman's findings were based on a qualitative content analysis limited to North-West Province "to increase its feasibility". They analysed advertisements from newspapers published between 15 March and 9 June 1999, from the date of announcement of the elections until a week after the elections. Fourie and Froneman (2003: 191) argue that a qualitative approach enabled a more in-depth and descriptive analysis of a small but comprehensive data set:

> To ensure reliability, the advertisements were analysed systematically according to the following categories: character appeals, emotional appeals (including appeals of sympathy, uncertainty, anger and fear), positive identification and policy messages, negative messages (harsh reality techniques and political blunders) and comprehensive messages.

Defining Democracy

Fundamentally, democracy is a form of political decision-making conducted in public. It is associated with the liberal tradition which views humans as free and as having the right to self-determination (Oosthuizen 2001: 133). The key objective of democracy is to promote social and political conditions in which people can exercise choice and become freer. Democracy, therefore, depends on "freedom of speech, religion, movement, as well as freedom to form economic associations (Roelofse 1993: 4–5). Thus, as Berger (2001: 151) observes, democracy also requires "a pluralism of media that includes significant political independence from government", while Alger (1989: 6–7) argues that alternative choices competing for public acceptance are central to the idea of an operative democracy. Indeed, Alger sees choice as the core of democracy and, like others such as Roelofse (1993), Oosthuizen (2001), Keane (1999) and Berger (2002), he acknowledges that, without choice, democracy is meaningless. Alger, therefore, considers education a vital element in democracy, since it enables the public to make good choices (also see McNair 1999). In this respect, democracy in South Africa may be somewhat disabled, because there are many South Africans who are illiterate. A solution would be to enforce a deliberative democracy instead of a liberal democracy. This can be done by requiring citizens to state the reasons they are choosing a particular political party. Furthermore, Cunningham (2005: 163) describes democracy as "a necessary condition for attaining legitimacy and rationality with regard to collective decisions". Thus, democracy can be summarised as a form of decision-making conducted in the public by citizens based on majority rule which is exercised by a way of a process based on the equal rights of the citizens.

Cunningham (2005: 1) argues that the problem of democracy is that it "involves majority tyranny, and … is beset by irrational decision-making procedures and other challenges". He acknowledges (2002: 2) that most studies of democratic theory are organised around themes such as freedom and equality, rights, collective decision-making, legitimacy, justice, democracy and so on and criticises the fact that nearly all aspiring democracies are described as liberal democracy, pointing out that "[n]ot all theorists believe liberal democracy to be the best or [most] feasible form of democracy" (2002: 27). Furthermore, Dryzek and Berejikian (1993: 48) acknowledge that empirical democratic theory flowered in the 1950s and 1960s, when new technology, most notably the opinion survey, enabled summary judgement concerning the capabilities and dispositions of mass publics. Such theories have evolved and developed to include 'digital' democracy, which can be defined "as a collection of attempts to practise democracy without the limits of time, space and other physical conditions, using ICT or CMC [computer-mediated communication] … [in addition to] traditional 'analogue' political practices" (Hacker and Van Dijk 2000: 1).

Liberal vs Deliberative Democracy

It is only in the twentieth century that liberalism and democracy were freely spoken about. By the end of the twentieth century, they had become the world-dominant political ideologies (Cunningham 2005, Dryzek 2000). However, the historical changes that contributed to the emergence of modern liberal-democratic thought were immensely complicated (Cunningham 2005: 56), involving struggles between the monarchs and estates over the domain of rightful authority, peasant rebellions against the weight of excessive taxation and social obligation, the spread of trade, the development of commerce and market relations, changes in technology, the consolidation of national monarchies (notably in England, France and Spain), the growing influence of Renaissance culture, religious strife and challenges to the universal claims of Catholicism and struggles between the Church and the state.

Essentially, liberal democracy refers to a political system which allows democratic rule and political liberties (Bollen and Paxton 2000: 59). The first dimension, democratic rule, exists when the national government is accountable to the general population and each individual is entitled to participate in the government directly or through representatives (Bollen and Paxton 2000: 60, Duncan and Seleoane 1998: 3). Political liberty, the second dimension, exists when citizens have the freedom to express a variety of political opinions in any media and the freedom to form and participate in any political group (Bollen and Paxton 2000: 60). Thus, a liberal democracy should be both representative and participatory, and it should guarantee freedom of speech. Thus, Duncan and Seleoane (1998: 13) suggest that, while citizens forego certain freedoms through a social contract when consenting to be governed, "natural" rights such as the right to freedom of expression should be above government interference (Duncan and Seleoane 1998: 13). Rozumilowicz (cited in Moyo 2006: 38) stresses that participation and competition are key aspects of an "operational" definition of democracy. Competition among political actors ensures that the electorates have a meaningful choice, while participation ensures that those choices are representative of the larger political community:

> Participation is … essential to democratic theory in the sense that participatory democrats look beyond the instrumental conception of people as voters or choosers of their leaders to view them as active participants in the decision-making process at all levels (Moyo 2006: 39).

Thus, participatory theorists emphasise the need for direct participation by citizens in the regulation of key institutions in society, including the workplace and local community (Pateman 1970, cited in Moyo 2006: 39).

However, many theorists argue that liberal democracy is insufficient on its own to govern today's democracies (Cunningham 2005, Dryzek 2000), and some (Dryzek 2000) argue for deliberative democracy instead:

> [D]eliberative democracy by definition is open to preference transformation within political interaction, while liberal democracy by definition deals only

in the reconciliation and aggregation of preferences defined prior to political interaction (Dryzek 2000: 8).

Dryzek argues that liberalism is a flexible doctrine, noting that some liberalists allow that there are circumstances in which individuals can be open to deliberative persuasion. Thus, he argues:

> The deliberative conception of democracy turns out to facilitate a more effective reconciliation of liberal and democratic principles in connection, moreover, with the specifically constitutional aspects of liberalism long thought most resistant to democracy (Dryzek 2000: 10).

Cunningham (2005: 163) also voices a critique against liberal democracy by suggesting that liberal theory (or social choice theory) pictures citizens entering a democratic political process with fixed preferences that they aim to further by the use of democratic institutions and rules. He also suggests that these institutions and rules function to aggregate citizens' differing preferences and are legitimate when people at least tacitly consent to being bound by them. The deliberative democracy alternative takes issue with this picture on the issues of legitimation, fixed preferences and aggregation (Cunningham 2005: 163). As suggested by Cunningham (2005: 53), some theories, for instance, about human nature or the political economy of cultural industries, will at least point one in the direction of favoured hypotheses, while liberal-democratic theory by itself does not do this.

An emphasis of deliberation is not new; antecedents can be found in the polis of ancient Greece, in the political theories of Edmund Burke and John Stuart Mill and in theories from the early twentieth century such as John Dewey's (Dryzek 2000: 2). Deliberation as a social process is distinguished from other kinds of communication in that deliberators are amenable to changing their judgements, preferences and views during the course of their interactions, which involve persuasion rather than coercion, manipulation or deception (Dryzek 2000: 8). The sense of democracy itself is now widely taken to be deliberation, as opposed to voting, interest aggregation and constitutional rights. The deliberative turn presents a renewed concern with the authenticity of democracy: the degree to which democratic control is substantive rather than symbolic and engaged by competent citizens (Dryzek 2000: 8). This authenticity means that deliberative democracy's welcome of forms of communication is conditioned. The exact content of these conditions is a matter of dispute. The only condition for authentic deliberation is the requirement that communication include reflection upon preferences in a non-coercive fashion (Dryzek 2000: 11). This domination rules out domination via the exercise of power, manipulation, indoctrination, propaganda, deception, expression of self-interest, threats (of the sort that characterise bargaining) and attempts to impose ideological conformity (Dryzek 2000: 11).

Cohen (1997, cited in Cunningham 2005) argues that deliberation under the right conditions is an ideal model which democratic institutions ought to strive to approximate. Deliberation is a type of democracy that does not refer only to preference or choice (voting), but it calls for a forum where there is communication and good reasons are expected for the choice opted for. Thus deliberative democracy resonates with the idea of the public sphere as a reservoir of democratic authenticity (Cunningham 2005: 4). Thus, in a deliberative democracy, citizens need to be intellectually stimulated through communication. To be intellectually stimulated, they need to be well informed. One of the best means to do this is through the media, but, if the media does not fulfil this important role, it leaves citizens in a vulnerable position. For example, Cunningham (2005: 164) argues that democratic processes are legitimate only when they permit and encourage reasoned deliberation both over specific issues and also over 'the very rules of the discourse procedures and the way in which they are applied. "In order for such deliberation to confer legitimacy on democratic procedures and their results, reasons must be publicly given and exchanged in forums suitable for this purpose, and participants must be able, freely and equally, to arrive at informed preferences and to acquire and exercise the abilities required for effective participation in the forums" (Cunningham 2005: 164). Thus, instead of holding a public vote, citizens should rather bargain with one another in order to come to a solution. In a deliberative democracy, people do not merely give their views, they must give reasons for their views and, in turn, they should hear other people's views also in the attempt to persuade people to take their view. Therefore, in this type of democracy, reciprocity is important (Cunningham 2005: 164). People engaged in deliberative democratic practices must be prepared to question and to exchange their own preferences and values. Thus, Cunningham (2005: 164) states that "I cannot expect you to entertain my reasons respectfully and with mind open to change your views unless I am prepared to entertain your reason in the same-spirit".

Therefore, it can be concluded that deliberative democracy allows free and reasoned agreement amongst equals and that an ideal deliberation requires participants to state their reasons for or against proposals. Kaposi (2006: 11) argues that the principle of reciprocity expresses a sense of mutuality that the citizens should bring to their deliberation, and, thus, "principles of publicity and accountability are shaped by the principle of reciprocity". Deliberation then views political discussion as a central role in the democratic process. For example, "deliberative potential can occur in any situation where citizens engage in political discussion precisely through the act of their engaging in such an exercise". It is this alternative that we need in South Africa so that people do not merely choose but also state why they have made their choices and try to convince others to make the same choices. Thus Kaposi (2006: 13) acknowledges that some have argued that such deliberation among political representatives and experts suffices for a healthy democracy (see also Bessette 1994).

Deliberation, the Public Sphere and Political Advertising on Television

It is evident that a deliberative democracy supports the notion of the public sphere. According to Habermas (1989: 24):

> the ideal public sphere is largely separated from economic concerns because it is a discursive model of interaction whose function is to integrate various levels of society into a realm of common interaction.

Thus, the public sphere can be understood as a platform where people gather together to freely express their views. Like deliberation, it complements the exchange of ideas or opinions. The public sphere also views people as equals sharing a common right to take part in determining public policy and state practice, as does deliberation. It also advocates that the media should not treat its audience as consumers but rather as citizens (Berger: 2002: 35). Furthermore, as Berger says (2002: 31):

> ...the notion of "public" as in "public opinion" refers ... to a collection of politically significant shared common interests – which collection is seen as impacting ideologically upon the exercise of state power. The word "sphere" draws from spatial terminology and suggests a discrete – or, rather, distinctive – realm where public discussion takes place. Less often stressed is the point with particular value for analysing southern African conditions, namely that the notion of the "public sphere" can be contrasted to that of a "governmental sphere" and to that of a "private sphere".

In addition, Berger (2002: 24) acknowledges that Habermas, in his later writings, theorised that class, gender, social and cultural interest groups could develop their own different public spheres. He also points out critiques by others that Habermas focused on individualised (and neglected group) inputs into political life, failed "to recognize the exclusion of women" and wrongly assumed the "triumph of reasoned discourse in this realm" (Berger 2002: 24, and see Mak'Ochieng 1994, Calhoun 1992, Curran 1991, Garnham 1990, Ronning 1994, cited in Berger 2002). However, we do not need a discrete public sphere. In order for deliberation to work, there is a need for an extensively "public" public sphere. Thus, political advertising on television could hinder this standpoint, as it makes the public sphere "private", in most cases leaving discussion only to family members as they watch. This also calls into question the ability of television to mobilise voters, as Norris (2005: 13) acknowledges.

Research Method

This study is qualitative and is both exploratory and descriptive. It is exploratory because advertising on television in South Africa is a new phenomenon, and it is descriptive because it describes the data set collected. Thematic content analysis is employed as the methodology. A purposive sample is drawn from the political advertisements which appeared on the national broadcaster channels, SABC 1, SABC 2, and SABC 3. Furthermore, the sample consists of English advertisements from the six most prominent political parties in South Africa which placed political advertisements on television during the 2009 pre-election period. The sample was selected from 30 March 2009 to 20 April 2009.

Qualitative research involves several methods of data collection, such as focus groups, field observation, in-depth interviews and case studies (Wimmer and Dominick 2000: 4). The word "qualitative" can refer to "1) a broad philosophy and approach to research, 2) a research methodology, and 3) a specific set of research techniques" (Wimmer and Dominick 2000: 113). According to Du Plooy (2001: 29) "qualitative research has been assigned many different labels such as field research, naturalism, ethnography, anti-positivist approach, an alternative approach and constructivism". She mentions that these concepts all share a common focus: to interpret and construct the qualitative aspects of communication experiences (2001: 29). Furthermore, as Bruhn-Jensen and Jankowski (1991: 5) point out:

> various forms of qualitative analysis acquire general explanatory value, despite their "non-representatative" empirical samples, because, as part of the analytical procedures, continuous cross-reference is made between the theoretical and other levels of analysis.

Along with these qualitative methods, a thematic content analysis was also used for this paper as a means of interpreting the data. The emotional appeals and character appeals were also analysed. A purposive sample was used, whereby the political advertisements were selected from the six major political parties in South Africa: the African National Congress (ANC), the Democratic Alliance (DA), the Independent Democrats (ID), the Congress of the People (Cope), the African Christian Democratic Party (ACDP) and the Freedom Front Plus (FF+). The investigation relied mainly on thematic content analysis, which has both strengths and weaknesses. One of its great strengths is cost-effectiveness. It can also handle large amounts of data and is effective for longitudinal studies when one wants to study phenomena over a long period of time (Wigston 2009: 35). A more interesting aspect of content analysis is that it "allows us to research situational, semantic and political aspects of massages" (Wigston 2009: 34). When doing a content analysis, no one really needs to be interviewed, and there is no need for a questionnaire, although content analysis combines very well with other methods. The main weaknesses of content analysis are that the method is limited to examining material that has been recorded in a retrievable format and cannot tell how the audience reacts to a message. Thus, content analysis is beneficial for a descriptive or explanatory study, but it cannot be used for an experimental study (Berg 1989: 125–126).

The study employed open coding in thematic content analysis. Coding in thematic analysis is the process of identifying themes or concepts that are in the data. The researcher attempts to build a systematic account of what has been observed and recorded (Ezzy 2002: 88). Theory emerges through this coding process, and coding links the data to an emergent theory (Ezzy 2002: 88). Thematic analysis aims to identify themes within the data; it is inductive, as the themes are not predetermined, which was the case in this study, although there was a vague initial idea of what theme to expect prior to the analysis. Significantly, thematic analysis "may take the researcher into issues and problems he or she had not anticipated" (Ezzy 2002: 88). Thus:

> [W]hen using coding one can explore the data; identify the units of analysis; code for meanings, feelings, actions; make metaphors for data; experiment with codes; compare and contrast events, actions and feelings; break codes in subcategories; integrate codes into more inclusive codes; and identify the properties of codes" (Ezzy 2002: 89).

Other prominent studies in the field of political advertising have used categories in analysing the data. Although categorising data is systematic, I preferred open coding for this investigation because it also assists in building theory. It is also inductive, whereas when data is analysed using predetermined categories, it becomes deductive. As for purposive sampling, Bornman (2009: 447) acknowledges that "purposive or judgemental sampling implies that elements are selected on the basis of knowledge of the population and the aims of the study". According to Du Plooy (2001: 100), "sampling involves following a rigorous procedure when selecting units of analysis from a larger population" and is not only applicable when generating or collecting new data but is also relevant when conducting historical research.

As mentioned earlier, South Africa currently has four broadcasting channels, two publicly owned channels dedicated to public service broadcasting (SABC 1 and SABC 2), one publicly owned commercial station (SABC 3) and one private commercial channel (e.TV). The political advertisements in question were aired on all these channels, but, for the purpose of the study, only the political advertisements on SABC 1, 2, and 3 were considered. During the pre-election period, SABC 1 had a viewership or cume (cumulative) reach of 87.2 percent of adults older than the age of 16 during the month of March 2009, and in April 2009 it had 74.6 percent. SABC 2 had a cume reach of 85.6 percent in March 2009 88.1 percent in April. SABC 3 had a cume reach of 85.9 percent in March 2009 and 85.3 percent in April (http://www.saarf.co.za). Cume reach means that the stated percentage of adults 16 years and older viewed the station at least once during that particular month.

SABC is considered to be the hub of South African television. SABC 1 is targeted specifically at the youthful segment of the population and is considered to be South Africa's biggest television channel, with more than 14.5 million adult viewers. SABC 2 is seen to reflect the multi-faceted nature of South African families, and its purpose is to fulfill a nation-building role. SABC 3 is aimed at reflecting a successful and stylish South Africa, "with viewers who have their hearts rooted in South Africa, but have their heads in the world" (www.sabc.co.za). It is a contemporary adult channel targeted at living standard measurement (LSM) 8–10, with viewers in the 25–49-year bracket (www.sabc.co.za). LSM is a bracket that is used in the media to ascertain the audience class and buying power. It uses a scale of 1–10. 1–4 is considered to be the lower class, with minimum buying power, and 4–7 is considered to be the middle class, with medium buying power. 8–10 is considered to be the upper class, with the best buying power and also the highest levels of education.

As a method of data interpretation, thematic content analysis is used mainly to analyse the themes and issues that appear in the political advertisements on television in South Africa. Content analysis is both quantitative and qualitative research:

> Content analysis attends to the repositions of frequency of features, their proportions within a text, and consequent assumption about significance. The percentage of advertisements of a certain type within a newspaper may, for instance be significant (Burton 2005: 49).

It is a research technique that is based on measuring the amount of something (violence, negative portrayals of women, or whatever) in a representative sampling of some mass-mediated popular art form, such as a newspaper comic strip

(Berger 1993: 25):"Content analysis may be defined as a methodology by which the researcher seeks to determine the manifest content of written, spoken or published communications by systematic, objective and quantitative analysis" (Zito 1975: 27).

Thus, one can also conduct content analysis of phenomena such as personal letters, telephone conversations and classroom lectures, which are not mass mediated.

Content analysis is a direct way of making inferences about people. As Berger explains, "when we do a content analysis, we try to obtain a substantial amount of material to examine, and we always do it from a comparative point of view" (Berger 1993: 26). It is a method by which researchers can keep their fingers on the collective pulse, so to speak, and study phenomena as they develop – facts, fashions, crazes and social movements (Berger 1993: 28). Finally, content analysis provides numbers, since the technique is based on counting and/or measuring and the findings are given in numerical form (Berger 1993: 28). As Du Plooy (2001: 191) points out, a "common use of content analysis is to record the frequency with which certain … [thematic units] appear in messages … [such as] repeating patterns of propositions or ideas related to issues such as sex, violence, AIDS, equality, gender or stereotyping based on age, race and disability". This study mainly employs thematic units as the unit of analysis, although physical units, syntactic units and propositional units were also considered. Physical units include the medium of communication, number of pages, size and space in print media and time duration in broadcast media. Syntactic units involve the analysis of paragraphs, sentences, phrases, clauses or words, and proportional units involve questions, answers, statements, assertions or arguments (Du Plooy 2001: 191).

As mentioned earlier, content analysis involves the analysis of policy documents, so a document analysis is conducted as well to ensure reliability. The final stage of content analysis is the interpretation of the results. The results are compared with the predictions of the pre-existing theory, and conclusions are drawn. Thus, content analysis is a useful way of testing or confirming a pre-existing theory: When the research questions are clearly defined and the categories of analysis have been well established by pre-existing research, content analysis may be an extremely useful method of data analysis" (Ezzy 2002: 84).

Content analysis begins with predefined categories, while thematic analysis allows categories to emerge from the data. However, when new theories or interpretations are required, the researcher typically requires a more inductive methodology, such as thematic analysis (Ezzy 2002: 84). Since content analysis assumes that the researcher knows what the important categories will be prior to the analysis, it has a weakness; it severely limits the extent to which the "other" can have a voice as part of the research process (Ezzy 2002: 85). For this reason, "in qualitative research content analysis is always used in conjunction with other forms of data analysis that are more inductive and sensitive to emergent categories and interpretations" (Ezzy 2002: 85). Thus, in this study content analysis was used to analyse the themes and images, and, in addition, the emotional appeals in the political advertisements were also analysed using content analysis. The main research questions were the following. What implications does political advertising on television have for democracy? What messages (themes) are covered in the political advertisements on television? And to what extent do the political advertisements focus on the images rather than the messages (themes) in the content?

Discussion of the Results

Themes and Images

The debate around political advertising has centred on the question of whether political advertisements concentrate on images rather than the political issues of the time and hinder well-informed decisions about which political party to vote for (McNair 1999, Kaid and Holtz-Bacha 1995, Scammel and Langer 2005, Fourie 2008, Froneman 2003). In the South African case, there were various themes that the political advertisements on television unpacked. Some political advertisements addressed the same themes while others covered different themes. For example, the themes that appeared prominently in the African Christian Democratic Party (ACDP) advertisements included hope, crime, murder, violence, rape, fear, intimidation, hatred, security, freedom, HIV/AIDS, disease, death, the elderly, orphans, poverty and family values. The main themes in the African National Congress (ANC) advertisements were freedom, race, hope, fear, violence, black economic empowerment (affirmative action), poverty and education. In the Democratic Alliance (DA) advertisements, the main themes were poverty, prosperity, crime, security and hope, while the Independent Democrats (ID) featured themes of family values, motherhood, security, crime, poverty, housing, drug-abuse, choice, human rights, the constitution, hope and government accountability. The Freedom Front Plus (FF+) mainly covered issues of crime, featuring themes of murder, rape, highjackings, residential burglaries, stolen vehicles, and non-residential robberies. The main themes which appeared in the Congress of the People (Cope) advertisement were new beginnings, prominent leaders, safety, family values, electricity, housing, government accountability, health care education and disease.

As suggested by Young (2002: 28), one of the main criticisms of modern political advertising is that it is emotive and manipulates people's feelings. It is seen, therefore, as essentially trivial, exploiting emotions and substituting catchphrases and slogans for political debate. Although idealists may hope that political advertisements will encourage informed decision-making, educate voters, stimulate debate and promote participation, it has been said that political parties are less concerned about civic education than winning votes (Young 2002: 88). However, this was not the case for the political advertisements on television in South Africa. Instead, they proved to be very informative, although they took different approaches in communicating their messages.

As Young (2002: 88) suggests, it would be difficult to have a yardstick as to how political advertisements on television encourage informed decision-making, because the ultimate decision lies with the voter. Nevertheless the political advertisements analysed in this study were generally informative. Most of them articulated themes which also appeared in the party manifestos. The most informative advertisement was that of the ACDP, because most of the themes that were outlined in its elections manifesto were also spelled out in the political advertisement on television. For example, the ACDP states in their manifesto that they want to bring South Africa hope and build a strong, healthy, prosperous nation which recognises family values as the building blocks of society. They also state that hope lies in Christian values. Furthermore, the ACDP points out that it will focus on addressing critical challenges such as poverty and unemployment, education, housing, health, justice and crime, moral regeneration and integrity. Likewise, its television political advertisement reflected themes of hope, crime, murder, violence, rape, fear, intimidation, hatred, security, freedom, HIV/AIDS, disease, the elderly, orphans, poverty, family values and godly governance. Hence the themes which were covered in the ACDP manifesto were well represented in the political advertisement that appeared on television.

For its part, the ANC, in its manifesto, noted that it would build on the achievements and experiences since 1994, which it stated to be an equitable, sustainable, and inclusive growth path that brings decent work and sustainable livelihoods, education, health, safety, secure communities and rural development. However, although the ANC provided other political advertisements on television, this English advertisement did not discuss all these themes. The advertisement reflected themes of freedom, race, hope, fear, violence, black economic empowerment, poverty and education. The themes of health and rural development were not presented in the ANC English political advertisement on television. However, the themes of inclusive growth, sustainable livelihoods, education, non-racialism and safe and secure communities were represented. It was only the FF+ advertisement which focused mainly on crime, although its elections manifesto presented other themes.

Randall (1998: 1) acknowledges that television communication depends on images whose emotional impact can be intense but whose informational content is often unclear. However, when considering the selected sample in the study, what Randall (1998) suggests is not entirely true. For instance, television communication does depend on images whose emotional impact can be intense, but most of the political advertisements analysed in this study were packed with sufficient and clear information for decision-making. This was evident in the advertisements by the ACDP, DA, ID and Cope, although the last two carried the most emotional impact compared to the others. The advertisements from the remaining two political parties, the ANC and the FF+, did not have clear informational content; these advertisements did not establish all the themes that the parties stood for as articulated in their manifestos.

Nevertheless, the political advertisements selected for this study were not (pace Gurevitch and Blummer 2000: 153) "superficial": they focused on themes which are a reality in the South African political situation, such as HIV/AIDS, crime, unemployment, affirmative action, violence, poverty and education. In addition, none of the political advertisements featured negative appeals or were nasty to their opponents. Indeed, the majority of the political parties stressed the theme of "hope". The political climate just prior to the election (September 2008 going into 2009) was one of despair. The ANC was split into a Thabo Mbeki camp and a Jacob Zuma camp, and a breakaway party, Cope, which was seen to be in support of Thabo Mbeki, had entered the scene. Interestingly, this is the party that focused most on the theme of hope in its television political advertisement. The advertisement constantly repeats "I hope, I hope" and so forth. At the end of the advertisement the slogan "Vote for hope, vote for Cope" appears. Thus, the general informational content of the political advertisements on South African television was not negative or slanted.

On the other hand, the slogans used by the political parties at the end of their advertisements were rather emotive: "Hope for South Africa" (ACDP); "Working together we can do so much more" (ANC); "One nation one future" (DA); "Be part of the solution" (ID); "Stand up against crime" – Vote Freedom Front Plus"; "Vote for hope, vote for Cope". Only the Freedom Front Plus did not rely heavily on emotive language, as their slogan is based on a critical theme in the political reality of South Africa. Hints of propaganda can be seen in these slogans, most especially in the ANC's and the DA's. Both play on the notion of patriotism. Propaganda is the manipulation of symbols as a means of influencing attitudes on controversial matters. The media can systematically manufacture propaganda under the guise of "facts" to elicit consent from a mass audience for patently undemocratic and often scurrilous practices (Laswell 1942: 106, Duncan and Seleoane 1998: 14).

Images in the political advertisements were emotive but also helped in communicating the messages better (Borchers 2002: 307). For example, in the ID advertisement, as Patricia de Lille speaks, images of what she is speaking about appear. The same concept is also evident in the DA advertisement: the images appearing on the screen support the themes. This is also in the FF+ advertisement, although here the images appear in silhouette, and some of them do not address the themes directly. However, the link between the theme and image is not as clear in the ANC, ACDP and Cope advertisements. This proves that the images are important in political advertisements and should not be taken for granted; fusing them with the theme (text) can help to bring forth a better understanding.

McNair (1999: 92–3) argues that the focus in political advertisements on imagery results in emotional rather than logical vote choices. Bogart (1998: 7) argues that advertising introduces a dazzling and constantly changing array of fresh images into everyday life, thus continuously raising aspirations, challenging the status quo and, in this respect, fostering democracy. However, the political advertisements on South African television did not focus on the images; there was more writing on the screen than images. In most of the advertisements, the images were presented as background information supporting the text. Nevertheless, as much as the political advertisements proved to be very informational in their content, they also presented images which provided an emotional appeal. For example, the advertisements used images of children, the elderly and the disabled (ACDP, DA, ID and Cope). Images of women were also used extensively (DA, ACDP and ID). The use of such imagery makes an emotional appeal, because these groups of people are usually regarded as vulnerable.

Emotional Appeals

In its advertisement, the ACDP relies on black and white instead of colour, creating a feeling of seriousness, urgency, despair and sadness. It also shows a child covering his eyes. The viewer may want to save the child from despair or hurt. A disabled man is then shown in a wheel chair in the middle of the street, making the viewer want to help him to a safer place. The ACDP advertisement also shows a lady holding babies in her arms, with more children standing around her, creating an emotional appeal to sadness and shame and, at the same time, making the viewer want to remove the woman from the situation. The ID used a similar image in its advertisement, as well as the image of a black child holding a barbed wire fence, with his dusty hands hanging down and his eyes looking at the camera to express hopelessness and poverty. However, as much as these images are emotive, they are also images that relate to the actual experiences of people in South Africa.

Appeals to happiness and success are also shown in the political advertisements. Here, the ads play on the idea of dreams and dreams coming to reality. For example, in the DA advertisement, the theme song says "somewhere, over the rainbow, blue birds fly". This creates an image of harmony and peace. Throughout this advertisement, it is only the song that plays; no one speaks, but the images and the song speak for themselves. Similarly, the ACDP advertisement shows a young girl running towards her father and jumping into his arms while he spins her around. Although the other three advertisements had an emotional appeal, these were not so intense. The ANC only used an image of a girl of mixed race in the Cape Flats. The Cope advertisement used images that did not correlate clearly to the themes, and in the FF+ advertisement, the images could not be clearly seen because they appeared in silhouette.

Character Appeals

Character appeals were used minimally. Only the ID, ANC and ACDP showed their leaders or president in their advertisements. The ID used character appeals the most, as Patricia de Lille is shown throughout the ID advertisement. She is presented as a simple, ordinary citizen wearing a simple shirt and skirt with her hair tied back. She also speaks throughout the advertisement and presents herself to the audience as an ordinary person, saying, "most of you know me as a politician, but I am also a mother. And like you I have a family, and like you every day I have to work". Thus, de Lille's character is presented as sympathetic and one with the people. The advertisement shows her as knowing what the ordinary person on the street goes through. In the ACDP advertisement the president of the party is shown wearing a suit and sitting in an office with a cabinet full of blue and green books. Thus, he is presented as educated and hard-working. He refers to the audience as friends, which suggests love, loyalty, honesty and commitment. This can be seen as a form of propaganda. Meanwhile, in the ANC advertisement, the ANC (and state) president is also presented wearing a suit, although he does not say much, only the slogan of the party, "working together we can do more". The articulation of only this slogan helps to reinforce the notion of propaganda, since the topic which the ANC opts to use also makes the slogan stick in one's mind.

Conclusion

Although political advertisements on television are generally seen as emotive and manipulative, the advertisements in South Africa proved to be informative. The political parties articulated their manifestos, and, in most cases, the content was packed with sufficient and clear information. Thus, the political advertisements were not superficial and provided themes that are a reality in South Africa's situation. None used negative appeals or were nasty to their opponents, nor did they concentrate on images but rather on themes. There was more text than imagery, and most of the advertisements used imagery to support the themes or messages. Nevertheless, it goes without say that emotional appeals were present in these advertisements, with the use of images of children, woman and the disabled to create an influential emotional appeal. Interestingly, the advertisements also appealed to emotions of happiness and success, especially the idea of making dreams come true. Character appeals were used minimally, with only three parties relying on or showing their leaders. It was only in one of the advertisements that the party leader was shown throughout the political advertisement.

Thus, the implications of television political advertising for democracy were both positive and negative. The positive aspect was that the political advertisements created room for choice. Citizens no longer have to rely only on newspapers, pamphlets, radio and billboards to get information about political parties and what they stand for. The negative aspects are that these advertisements make the public sphere more private, emotional appeals are still present. Moreover these advertisements do not allow for a deliberative democracy, because they are confined to the television room, although through the aid of media effect they can possibily escape the television room. However, the results of this study cannot be applied to all the political advertisements that appeared on television during the 2009 pre-election period but only to the selected sample. It is recommended that a more comprehensive study be done again, including a study of audience reception by means of focus groups.

References

Alger, D. 1989. *The Media and Politics.* Englewood Cliffs, NJ: Prentice Hall.

Berger, G. 2002. Theorising the media democracy relationship in Southern Africa. *International Communication Gazette* 64 (1): 21–45.

Berger, G. 2001. Deracialization, democracy and development: Transformation of the South African Media 1994–2000. In K. Tomaselli and H. Dunn, eds. *Critical Studies of African Media and Culture: Media Democracy Renewal in South Africa.* Colorado Springs, CO: International Academic Publishers.

Bogart, L. 1998. Media and democracy. In E. Dennis and R. Snyder, eds. *Media and Democracy*. New Brunswick: NJ: Transition.

Bollen, K.A. and P. Paxton. 2000. Subjective measures of liberal democracy. *Comparative Political Studies*: 33 (1): 58–86.

Borchers, T. 2002. *Persuasion in the Media Age*. Boston: McGraw-Hill.

Bornman, E. 2009. Questionnaire surveys in media research. In *Media Studies, Volume 3: Media Content and Media Audiences*. ed, Fourie, P.J. Kenwyn: Juta.

Bruhn-Jensen, K. and N. Jankowski, N. 1991. *A Handbook of Qualitative Methodologies for Mass Communication Research*. London: Routledge.

Burton, G. 2005. *Media and Society: Critical Perspectives*. London: Open University Press.

Cunningham, F. 2005. *Theories of Democracy: A Critical Introduction*. London: Routledge.

Davids, Y.D. 2004. The people's agenda vs. election manifestos of the political parties. *Election Synopsis* 3(1): 12–15.

Duncan, J. and M. Seleoane. 1998. *Media and Democracy in South Africa*. Pretoria: HSRC.

Du Plooy, G.M. 2001. *Communication Research: Techniques, Methods and Applications*. Claremont, SA: Juta.

Dryzek, S.J. 2000. *Deliberative Democracy and Beyond: Liberals, Critics, Contestations*. Oxford: Oxford University Press.

Dryzek, S.J. and J. Berejikian. 1993. Reconstructive democratic theory. *American Political Science Review* 97 (1): 48–60.

Ezzy, D. 2002. *Coding Data and Interpreting Text: Methods of Analysis. Qualitative Analysis*. London: Routledge.

Fourie, L. 2008. South African election posters: Reflecting the maturing of a democracy? *Communication: South African Journal for Communication Theory and Research*. 34 (2): 222–37.

Fourie, L. and J. Froneman. 2003. Emotional political advertising: A South African case study. *Communicare* 22 (1): 188–210.

Gurevitch, M. and J.G. Blumer. 2000. Political communication systems and democratic values. In D.A. Graber, ed. *Media Power in Politics*. Washington, DC: CQ Press.

Habermas, J. 1989. *Jurgen Habermas on Society and Politics: A reader*. Ed, Seidman, S. Boston: Beacon Press.

Hacker, K.L. and J. Van Dijk. 2000. What is digital democracy? In K.L. Hacker and J. van Dijk, eds. *Digital Democracy: Issues of Theory and Practice*. London: Sage.

Herzenberg, G. 2004. Party support in South Africa's third democratic election: Set in stone or up for grabs? *Election Synopsis* 1(3): 15–20.

Kaid, L. and C. Holtz-Bacha, eds. 1995. *Political Advertising in Western Democracies: Parties and Candidates on Television*. Thousand Oaks, CA: Sage.

Kaposi, I. 2006. An Ethnography of Online Political Discussion in Hungary. Unpublished PhD thesis. Central European University, Budapest, Hungary. web.ceu.hu/polsci/dissertations/Ildiko_Kaposi.doc (retrieved 20/01/2010).

Keane, J. 1999. Crisis of the sovereign state. In M. Raboy and B. Dagenais, eds. *Media, Crisis and Democracy: Mass Communication and the Disruption of Social Order.* Thousand Oaks, CA: Sage.

Kern, M. 1989. *Thirty-Second Politics: Political Advertising in the Eighties.* New York: Praeger.

Lasswell, H.D. 1942. Communications research and politics. In *Print, Media and Film in Democracy.* ed., Waples, D., Chicago, IL: University of Chicago Press.

McNair, B. 1999. *An Introduction to Political Communication.* Second Edition. London: Routledge.

Moyo, D. 2006. Broadcasting policy reform and democratisation in Zambia and Zimbabwe, 1990–1995: Global pressures, national responses. Unpublished PhD thesis, University of Oslo, Norway.

Norris, P. 2005. *Political Parties and Democracy in Theoretical and Practical Perspectives: Development in Party Communications.* Washington DC: National Democratic Institute for International Affairs.

Oosthuizen, L.M. 2001. Media, ownership and control. In P.J. Fourie, ed. *Media Studies, Volume 1: Institutions, Theories and Issues.* Kenwyn, SA: Juta.

Roelofse, J.J. 1993. *Towards Rational Discourse: An Analysis of the Report of the Steyn Commission of Inquiry into the Media.* Pretoria: Van Schaik.

Scammell, M. and A. Langer. 2006. Political advertising: Why is it so boring? *Media, Culture and Society* 28 (5): 763–84.

Schulz-Herzenburg, C. 2007. A salient revolution: South African voters, 1994–2006. In State of the Nation: South Africa 2007. eds, Bahlungu, S. Southall, J.D.R and Lutchman, J. 114–43. Cape Town HSRC Press.

Wigston, D. 2009. Narrative analysis. In P.J. Fourie, ed. *Media Studies, Volume 3: Media Content and Media Audiences.* Kenwyn: Juta.

Wimmer, D and J.R. Dominick. 2000. *Mass Media Research: An Introduction.* Belmont, CA: Woodsworth.

Young, S. 2002. Spot on: The role of political advertising in Australia. *Australian Journal of Political Science.* 37 (1): 81–97.

Zito, G.V. 1975. *Methodology and Meanings: Varieties of Sociological Inquiry.* New York: Praeger.

CHAPTER 13

A DISCOURSE-ANALYTICAL INVESTIGATION INTO THE NATURE OF AFRIKAANS AND ENGLISH RADIO ADVERTISEMENTS IN SOUTH AFRICA

ANGELIQUE VAN NIEKERK & MARISKA BERTRAM

Introduction

In this investigation, discourse analysis is used to explore the nature of radio advertisements and advertising awards in Afrikaans and English during 2005–2006, namely, the Loerie Awards (English and Afrikaans: www.theloerieawards.co.za) and the Pendoring Awards (only in Afrikaans: www.pendoring.co.za). A selection of eleven advertisements was made from each category based on the visibility of linguistic variables (for example, dialogue, code switching, rhyme and word games) and of variables that are related to language (for example, shared knowledge, humour and intertextuality). Radio advertisements were analysed in terms of their distinguishing features and their correlation with real spoken communication. The investigation has a didactic-academic purpose, namely, to describe the linguistic and language-related strategies that are characteristic of radio advertisements.

An exploration by means of discourse analysis into the recursive linguistic patterns in radio advertisements could contribute towards workable guidelines for writing credible advertisements that echo word-of-mouth advertising. Although language and sound are the basic instruments for creating a radio advertisement, the primary focus of the current literature on copywriting is either the nature of the advertising medium or the specific marketing principles for copywriters and advertising texts, for example, identifying who the target market is. Sadly, a linguistic approach is generally missing and whenever linguistic analyses have in fact taken place, the focus has been primarily on print advertisements, leaving a gap in this field of investigation.

An empirical approach was followed in this discourse-analytical investigation into radio advertisements. Its aims were to uncover the linguistic strategies (such as dialogue and code switching) and the language-related strategies (such as humour and intertextuality) which are characteristic of radio copy in English and Afrikaans advertisements in South Africa.

Theoretical Framework: A Discourse-analytical Approach

There is no well-defined difference between text linguistics and discourse analysis. According to Carstens (1997: 9), discourse analysis is often used as an expression that complements the term text linguistics. The concept of discourse can be understood in at least three ways. In the American tradition, it is used to refer to refer to matters such as conversations, narratives etc. The analyses of discourse are done by means of formulated theoretical points of departure. In the more general convention, discourse refers to the broad framework that enables communication. Lastly, discourse is sometimes used as a complementary term for the text (Carstens 1997: 10). Salkie (1995: xi) maintains that text is what one speaker says, while discourse involves two or more speakers having a conversation.

As for discourse analysis, Stubbs (1983: 1) uses the term primarily to refer to the linguistic analysis of written or spoken discourse which takes place naturally. He adds that "discourse analysis is also concerned with language in use in social contexts, and in particular with interaction of dialogue between speakers". Crystal (1987: 11) adds interviews, commentary and speeches to Stubbs' list. On the basis of this assumption, the analyses of this study belong mainly to a discourse-analytical approach in the sense that radio advertisements in the dataset pretend to be true conversations taking place within social contexts. There is also dialogue, or at least communication, between a speaker and the intended target market or listener.

Discourse analysis concentrates on broader communication principles, while text linguistics focuses more on the textuality of a text (Carstens 1997: 12). Yet there is inevitably a certain amount of overlap between the two; both approaches concern the analysis of sections of language usage that are usually more than a single sentence. Only the focus on the sections of language usage differs (Carstens 1997: 12). During this study, the differences between the linguistic and the language-related characteristics have been based on Van Jaarsveld's (1987: 204) linguistic and communicative assumptions and also on Carstens's differentiation between textual linguistics and discourse analysis. According to Van Jaarsveld (1987: 204), the first supposition is the shared assumption that a speaker and a listener both speak the same language and that both fully control and understand this language. His second assumption is that a speaker always has a specific, recognisable purpose in mind when making each utterance. The linguistic characteristics are closely related to the communicative assumption as a prerequisite for successful communication. Carstens (1997: 105) shows his agreement with Van Jaarsveld by referring to constitutive and regulatory principles. He maintains that the first principle creates and defines the form of language behaviour that is known as textual communication. The second principle controls existing forms of behaviour and has, as its point of departure, the idea that this behaviour will indeed occur even though there are no clear rules which can be applied.

Advertising as a Unique Genre

Advertising can be regarded as a unique genre because it relies on an established code between the communicator and the target market (Fourie 2001: 59). Genres can be regarded as the patterns, forms, styles, structures, analyses, narratives and content that the expression/encoding of communication by means of the mass media covers and also the encoding of these by the target market (Fourie 2001: 60, cited in Myers 1994). However, there are certain additional factors that contribute to the definition of genres:

- Genres represent points of reference.
- Genres contribute to the development and preservation of textual forms.
- Genres establish certain expectations in the sense that a certain genre has to conform to a certain format on which the target audience will base its expectations.

Myers (1994: 3–10) suggests six reasons why advertising can be regarded as a unique genre:

- Advertisements consist of patterns of textual choices, for example, the interplay or rhyme of parallel syntactical forms.
- Linguistic characteristics in one text are interpreted in relation to those of other texts (intertextuality).
- Advertisements are stereotyped actions of commutation that are regarded as a genre.

- Advertisements create a role for the target market to play.
- Target markets interpret advertisements in different ways.
- Advertisements create a relationship between the advertisers and the target market. The relationship is based on associations evoked by the meaning of the products.

Characteristics of Radio as an Advertising Medium

As a medium – and as an advertising medium in particular – radio has unique advantages that competing media do not have. Radio is seen as a "theatre of the mind" (Felton 1994: 225). It can be regarded as a "blind" medium because it contains no images; it is immediate and relies only on hearing. Thus radio stimulates the listeners' imaginations because they have to visualise the situation and try to "see" the speaker in their thoughts (De Beer 1998: 151). Radio creates a personal bond with the listener. It is one of the few media that successfully bonds with individual listeners and, in so doing, creates more personal contact than television. For this reason, it can be regarded as a one-to-one medium (Felton 1994: 225 and De Beer 1998: 152). Radio not only serves individuals but also a mass audience and is successful in making the outside world part of one's everyday existence (Oosthuizen 1996: 328).

As a result of radio's close link with the target market, it has a word-of-mouth quality. Word-of-mouth advertising take place whenever someone that you trust makes a recommendation about a matter in which he or she is an expert (O' Day, n.d.: 1). For example, a radio advertisement using a friend as an advisor within the context of friendship is convincing.

Radio can also focus on certain demographic groups – teenagers, older people, Yuppie New Age listeners etc. – more narrowly than other media by means of market segmentation (Meeske 2003: 111). Advertisers choose a radio station whose target market shows the greatest agreement with the profile of the market to which the product is being directed. On the other hand, radio is also more flexible because of its mobility. Radio can be listened to at home, in the car, at the office, on the beach etc. (Meeske 2003: 111). Another aspect of its flexibility is that radio advertisement can be created quickly and easily on impulse and broadcast immediately.

According to De Beer (1998: 152), radio has the widest coverage in the whole of Africa, and it can take on a huge diversity of forms. The reason that there are so many radio stations is because there are so many target markets that various programming options can reach. At the same time, radio deals with "invisible" target markets, and a radio station is not always aware of which people or groups are being targeted.

Finally, radio is relatively cheap and can act as a good supplement to other media. For example, radio and television complement each other well because prime time for watching television is normally in the evenings, while radio is listened to mainly during the day.

Different Genres of Radio Advertisements

Radio copywriters make use of various textual options (choices of genre) in order to create a unique radio advertisement which will draw a listener's attention despite the overdose of 'white noise' which surrounds him or her. Accordingly, the following types of radio advertisements can be identified:

- Dialogue format: Such advertisements attempt to create the impression of a credible everyday conversation between two or more people.
- News flash format: These advertise things for sale at discounted prices or bring important marketing events to the attention of the target market.
- Jingles: These render the slogan of a shop or company with the aid of music. Often, the advertiser has its own jingle for its own series of advertisements. For example, the jingle associated with Shoprite-Checkers is repeated as: "Checkers, better and better!"
- Advertisements using a storyline to sell their product. Emotion plays a major role in gaining attention in such advertisements.
- Witnesses: Sometimes advertisers use witnesses to emphasise a product's success, advantages, characteristics etc. In this way, they hope to convince people in the target market to buy the product. There are different ways in which witnesses can be used (Felton 1994: 283).
- "Man-in-the-street": These advertisements use a "satisfied consumer" (Meeske 2003: 127) who has the same needs and longings as those of the target market. The aim is to make the target market identify with this person.
- Unknown expert: Although the people comprising the target market do not really know the expert, they understand that he or she is an authority. This knowledge gives them confidence in the product.
- Executive director: This person recounts his long experience of the product and the improvements which have been made over the years for the comfort and convenience of the people who comprise the target market.

- Famous person (Meeske 2003: 127): As soon as a well-known person acts as a spokesperson for a product, the members of the target market become convinced of the validity of the promises made in the advertisement.
- Anonymous well-known person who acts as a witness: This is a well-known person whose name is not mentioned in the advertisement. Consequently, the desired reaction "Isn't that so-and-so?" is elicited. This technique makes the target group feel more involved in the advertisement than would otherwise have been the case.
- Fictional witness: Often, when a new children's film comes on circuit, a restaurant such as MacDonald's uses one of the characters in the film as a spokesperson to lure children to the restaurant.
- Comparative advertisement: Such advertisements are often used to compare advertisements for the same product or to compare elements within the same advertisement etc. (Felton 1994: 295). Different types of comparisons in advertisements encompass:
  i. A new versus old version of a product.
  ii. Comparisons that have no relationship with each other. For example, a Lipton Iced Tea advertisement with the slogan "It is like seeing your ex-girlfriend after five years and she has put on weight".
- Advertisements with a sequel: Such advertisements involve a series of two or more advertisements with stories that have a sequel. Their success lies in stimulating the curiosity of the people to whom the advertisement is being addressed to find out what happens in the next episode.

Creativity in Radio Advertisements

The most important principles for good radio advertisements are discussed below. A good advertisement should consider the following guidelines:

- Sell the results and not the product: According to O' Day (n.d.: 15), the focus should be on selling the effects of the product and not the product itself. The people who make up the target market are not really interested in the product per se, but rather in what the product offers them. Therefore, advertisers need, first, to identify a need to be fulfilled or a problem needing to be solved, then focus the target market's attention on the fact that they need the product to resolve the problem and, finally, prove to the target market how their need will be fulfilled or how their problem will be solved by using the product (O' Day n.d.: 16).

- Concentrate on the problem from the target market's point of view. A radio advertisement has to be written from the perspective of the people who make up the target market (O' Day n.d.: 17, 34). During the communication with people within the target market, successful advertisements consider daily human behaviour that is experienced by almost everyone (O' Day n.d.: 18). In so doing, the advertisement is linked to credible behaviour (human truth) and reinforces a strong marketing message at the same time.
- Use credible language and emotion: Credibility is a key concept in advertising. Without it, an advertisement loses its value. There are ways to make an advertisement plausible by linking it to mundane human behaviour without depicting a specific daily situation (O'Day n.d.: 20). This is achieved by using the same language used daily by the target market. Lewis (2004: 219) warns that copywriters should not use an advertisement as an opportunity to show off their vocabulary. Moreover, they should avoid adjectives or descriptive words that consist of more than three syllables. This creates difficulties in processing the information. Lewis uses the metaphor that the ear is the surrogate for the other four missing senses. In other words, the copywriter should create a mental image without having to demonstrate it (Lewis 2004: 225). An advertisement is also made credible by reflecting human emotions with which the target market can identify. Before an advertisement is written, the copywriter must have decided what the emotional point of departure will be. (O' Day n.d.: 37–8).
- Promote product advantage over product property. Radio advertisements should sell the advantages of the product rather than its properties.
- Provide a logical justification for consumer behaviour. The target market should also be given an excuse to "justify" to themselves and to other people exactly why they should buy a certain product. The advertisement should provide them with this justification (or excuse). This is done in two steps: (1) offer the target market a true, measurable price (in other words, a sale) and (2) make the consumer fully aware that he or she should hurry or miss the opportunity (in other words, set a time for the sale or special offer) (O' Day, n.d.: 35–6). The target market's decision to buy has an emotional base. Thus, the copywriter should give them reasons to justify their purchase.
- Stick to the facts and the creative brief. It is always important that certain questions be considered before attempting to write an advertisement. The answers to some of these questions should be available in the list of information containing the facts and details of the product. These questions concern, inter alia, the following (O' Day n.d.: 41–4) questions. Who makes up the

target market? Who would be interested in the advantages of the product? Is the product aimed at an active or passive market? What would the product mean to the target market in inflated terms? What would the product mean to the target market in realistic terms? What are the precise reasons that a prospective consumer would buy this particular product? (O' Day n.d.: 47). All the necessary facts have to be gathered to create an effective advertisement (O' Day n.d.: 46).

- Make your writing unique and do not follow a formula: The copywriter should avoid writing cookie-cutter copy. According to O'Day (n.d.: 53–4), many radio advertisements sound as though they have been cast in the same mould. In other words, it seems that the same recipe or formula has been used repeatedly for different advertisements.
- Focus on one message only. The fact that radio is fleeting in nature means that the radio message should be as short and simple as possible. It should never contain more than one message (Felton 1994: 226).
- Direct the behaviour of the target market. It has been found that people are more inclined to react when an advertisement tells them what to do (O' Day n.d: 59).
- Overcome product prejudice. Consumers may react with scepticism towards promises that advertisers make about their products. O' Day (n.d.: 62) suggests that the problem can be solved in the following way: "When advertising a product or service to which a substantial percentage of your target audience is likely to have an objection, deal with that objection within the commercial".
- Avoid too much text. The copywriter should never have too much copy, because listening to a radio advertisement is secondary. Consumers are usually only half-listening. Their main focus of attention is on the traffic, their work or their own inner dialogue (O' Day n.d.: 66).
- Tell a story. Each copywriter should tell a story in each advertisement (O' Day n.d.: 67–8). This makes the target market pay greater attention to what is being said, because a story is easier to recall and automatically summons up the marketing message (O' Day n.d.: 68).
- Avoid a shopping list (also known as a laundry list). The copywriter should avoid merely listing all the facts (in other words, the advantages of the products, in the form of a list). Truman Capote said: "That's not writing. That's typing" (O' Day n.d: 74).

- Maintain a balance. It is important for radio to maintain a balance (Oosthuizen 1996: 333). Radio is not a medium that can successfully deal with extremes or quick changes, because this could lead to the disintegration of the medium.
- Use humour. Meeske (2003: 128) advises that humour should be used with great circumspection, because, although it can be very effective, it can also be disastrous. In order to write successful copy, the copywriter should consider the following questions (Meeske 2003: 128):
  i. Can the target market recognise the humour?
  ii. Will the humour help to sell the product? Or will the consumers remember the comedy, but not the product?
  iii. Will the comedy survive constant repetition during broadcasts?

  The advantage of humour in an advertisement is that the name of the advertiser or product does not need to be repeated constantly. Only the story needs to be repeated. This is because the trademark or the product is automatically called up in the consumers' thoughts (O' Day n.d.: 81). A great mistake that is often made is to interrupt the humour with the marketing message. The aim is not to create a funny advertisement but rather to deliver the marketing message with the aid of humour. In order to write humorous copy, the copywriter should bear the following in mind (Meeske 2003: 130): use a credible setup (a general human truth) and extraordinary characters, or create an extraordinary situation with ordinary characters.
- Develop credible characters. Some radio advertisements work well when special characters are used. However, it is essential that they should be representative of the target market. It is important both that the characters should be 'attractive' and that the target market should be able to identify with them.
- Use voice to its full potential. It is important that one specific voice be used for the whole series of advertisements (campaign) for a specific trademark (Felton 1994: 105). As a result, consumers recognise a particular voice and associate it with the trademark. They then anticipate the advertisement which will follow. In addition, the voice contributes to create the feel, the so-called mood or ambience, of the specific advertisement. For example, if the advertisement deals with someone who is unhappy about something, the audience should be able to identify this from the tone of voice. In addition, elements such as music and background noise contribute to the atmosphere (and thus the recognition of the trademark). The voice should preferably transfer the message in the first or second person in order to suggest the

personality of a real-life person (Felton 1994: 114). There is an implicit distance between the speaker (the voice) and the audience. Consequently, the relationship of the voice with the audience should be made clear. In the copywriting industry, it is common for a client to insist on using his or her own voice in the advertisement. Some manage very well, but others should rather leave this in the hands of the copywriters. The solution would be to compromise in order to solve the client's inability to transfer the message of an advertisement himself or herself (O' Day n.d.: 87). This involves making clips of the client's voice in the advertisements. In other words, a professional person is used to do most of the speaking and clips of the client's voice are added. Another way of doing this is to interview the client about his or her product and then use excerpts of the interview in the advertisement. It must be remembered that using a child's voice in radio advertisements is a risky business. It is often amusing, entertaining, evokes emotion etc. but, incorrectly used, this technique can cause the whole advertisement to fail. This is because the audience focuses on the unusual element. It is important that the child or his or her voice is responsible for delivering the marketing message.

Radio is the only medium with the unique ability to transform ordinary sounds into lively visual images in the mind's eye of the audience. The human brain contains no prescriptions about what these images should look like; they are infinite. However, there should be a distinction between a real and a created image. According to O' Day (n.d.: 12–3) a real image can be defined as something that can be physically seen by the eye and then stored in the brain. This is a real memory in the form of an image. A created image is a visual memory that is never really seen. It is drawn so clearly by means of sound and descriptions that it is stored in the brain as a visual image. It is important to remember that sound may be an advertisement's greatest friend or worst enemy (O' Day n.d.: 95). The background sound determines the mental image that the target market forms. For this reason, copywriters should be aware that the sounds in the background should not be allowed to distract the audience from the advertising message.

The opening line of a radio advertisement is the most important element in the whole advertisement. O' Day (n.d.: 10–12) suggests several ways in which to create a "compelling, attention-getting headline":

- Start with a question.
- Give a command.
- Surprise the listener (the target market).
- Stimulate the listener's curiosity.

- Give the listener something to think about.
- Appeal to the listener's emotions or feelings.

Depending on the particular opening line, background sounds may be used to make this introduction more successful. As soon as the opening line becomes too long, the target market loses interest, their attention flags and the message becomes lost.

Another way to win the audience's attention is to use controversy to sell a product (Felton 1994: 309). This can be achieved, for example, by inverting the slogan of an advertisement and, in so doing, saying the opposite of what is expected. A slogan that previously read "Think big" would be effective and unexpected if it were changed to "Think small" in a subsequent advertisement.

Radio copywriters also need to be aware of the 'negative space' of the product: If the negative space of the product is discovered, it may be turned to the advantage of the product (Felton 1994: 311). In such a case, the focus should be on the people who would not use the product or the places where you would not be able to buy the product. These are then manipulated to work *for* the product. Other examples are unusual uses for the product and mentioning the advantages that the product lacks. One can even focus on the competition, identifying and comparing the disadvantages of the competitors' products with those of the product being advertised.

In any case, it is important, when writing a radio advertisement, to favour the active form of the verb over the passive. Sentences written in the active voice motivate the targeted consumers to move to action and also make them feel as if they are being addressed individually. In addition, metaphors create positive, interesting associations. In the case of radio advertising, products are not experienced via the sense of vision. This is the reason why they must be described metaphorically in order to appeal to other senses. An example of this is the name of a new fragrance for a deodorant, "Ocean Breeze." Because it is being advertised on radio, there is no way that visual images can be used, so the sound of waves breaking on the beach and gulls in the background evoke much more than the words. This allows the targeted consumers to smell the fragrance that is described in this way.

Linguistic Characteristics of Radio Advertisements

The following section considers the language-related characteristics of radio advertisements.

Characteristics of Dialogue

Cloete (1992: 69) explains that the simplest form of dialogue involves two people – a speaker and a listener – who are in a specific temporal and contextual relationship with each other. Dialogue plays an important role in radio advertisements because it is one of the few auditory elements available to the target market to interpret and deduce aspects of the product being advertised.

- **Forms of Address.** Speakers continuously use different forms of address. Carstens (1997: 412) maintains that a speaker's interpretation of a given context and the (social) context implicit in the relationship between the speaker and the listener greatly affect the style and form of language that characterises the communication taking place. It will also specify the particular form of address being used by the speaker in that situation.

- **Turn-taking.** Turn-taking in a conversation is a typical characteristic of spoken language. According to Crystal (2006: 477–8), "Conversation is seen as a sequence of conversational turns, in which the contribution of each participant is seen as part of a co-ordinated and rule-governed behavioural interaction".

  However, turn-taking in conversation differs from culture to culture (Cutting 2008: 27).

- **Hesitation.** Hesitation occurs in any real conversation when a speaker gets stuck or contradicts him or herself. Consequently, hesitation is used as a technique in radio advertisements to create the impression that a true and real conversation is taking place.

- **Use of Crude Language.** Crude language in an advertisement can be used to reflect the speaker's attitude, background and level of education.

- **Lexicon.** A speaker's lexicon refers to his or her choice of words. The lexicon plays an important role in advertisements in order to indicate the context and, in so doing, increase the credibility of the advertisement.

- **Interruptions.** Together with turn-taking and hesitations, interruption during a dialogue is a characteristic that is inherent in a successful conversation and, thus, in a successful radio dialogue. During turn-taking, the speakers interrupt each other continuously when one starts speaking before the other has finished saying what he or she wanted to.

- **Forms of Slang.** Slang is often used to stereotype a certain group of people. Matthews (1997: 343) explains the use of slang as follows: "vocabulary specific e.g. to a particular generation of younger speakers; also, as in ordinary usage, specific to a group of profession (e.g. army slang), to colloquial style, etc." The use of a different register that is implied by the use of slang contributes to making an advertisement sound credible.

- **Tone of Voice.** Tone of voice is a characteristic that reveals a lot about the speaker. It can reveal matters such as demographic information (e.g. the speaker's age, race, his or her mood or state of mind, levels of formality etc).
- **Pronunciation.** Pronunciation contributes to creating a context for the advertisement. This is because it is one of the few available auditory elements in the absence of visual elements. However, according to Cutting (2008: 155), differences in pronunciation could have the unfortunate result that an advertisement might be unsuccessful; the different variations in language might play an alienating role.
- **Interjections.** The primary aim of using interjections or exclamations during an advertisement is to express the speakers' emotions. Matthews (1997: 169) defines interjections as follows:

    > Traditionally, an exclamation refers to any emotional utterance, usually lacking the grammatical structure of a full sentence, and marked by strong intonation, e.g. Gosh! Good grief! Semantically, the function is primarily the expression of the speaker's feelings – a function which may also be expressed using other grammatical means, e.g. what on earth is she doing? (When it is obvious what is being done).

    Interjections are part of convincing dialogue.

- **Abbreviations, Contractions and Assimilation.** Assimilation is a characteristic of spoken language. As Matthews (1997: 390) explains, "… units are sometimes referred to as 'reduced', such as phrases (e.g. phone's ringing) and words (e.g. it's him)". These elements make up everyday conversation, and so they are included in dialogue in radio advertisements in order to create the impression of a plausible conversation.
- **Repetition.** Halliday and Hasan (1976: 278–84) distinguish between different types of lexical repetition, but, of the four they mention, only one is applicable to a dataset, namely, the verbal repetition of the same lexical item (Carstens 1997: 321). This refers to the repetition of the same item within a sentence or even in the following sentences. It is a strategy that is used to reinforce the trademark of a product.
- **Code Switching.** Crystal (2006: 79) defines code switching very clearly:

    > The linguistic behaviour referred to as code-switching (sometimes code-shifting or, within a language, style-shifting), for example, can be illustrated by the switch

bilingual or bidialectal speakers may make (depending on who they are talking to, or where they are) between standard and regional forms.

The particular situation within a radio advertisement often results in code switching. For example, it often occurs that an educated person wants to adapt to the speech of someone whose level of education is lower than his or her own.

- **Code Mixing.** "Code-mixing involves the transfer of linguistic elements from one language into another: a sentence begins in one language, then makes use of words or grammatical features belonging to another" (Crystal 2006: 79). Matthews (1997: 58) maintains that code mixing takes place when two speakers regularly (but for no apparent reason) jump from language to language or from one dialect (or register) to another.
- **Rhyme.** Cloete (1992: 460) explains that the definition of rhyme in poetry is the similarity in sound between two or more words or syllables. In terms of radio advertisements, rhyme is used to make the advertisement sound good on the ear. This is particularly important because the target market is dependent on sound for the message. Moreover, rhyme makes the advertisement easier to remember because listeners remember the message more easily.
- **Word Games.** This practice is employed to keep the targeted consumers' attention or to create humour. Word games use homophones, homonyms and polysemic words and are common in advertisements, according to Myers (1994: 65).

Due to space restrictions attention cannot be given here to an overview of all the relevant language-related characteristics needed to create authentic and credible radio-advertising. These include the use of, or reference to, shared knowledge, historical events, humour intertextuality, irony, auditory nature (background noise and music), controversy, the cyclic nature of time, stereotyping, etc. Authors like Goddard (1998) and Myers (1994) describe the importance of these characteristics of normal everyday communication in the creation of credible radio advertisements that echo word-of-mouth advertising.

Analysis of Radio Advertisements in Advertising Competitions (Entries for the Pendoring and Loerie Awards)

Because of constraints of space, only one example from each competition will be discussed here.

SABC radio sales (Pendoring Awards)

A text of the advertisement in its original Afrikaans (13.1) and a loose translation of the text (13.2).

Box 13.1: Pendoring Advertisement for a Radio Station: Original Text in Afrikaans

JOHAN:	Goeie môre, good morning.
TANNIE MARIET:	Hallo Johan, dit is Mariet van Pretoria wat hier praat. Ag Johan, jy weet toe ek nou die dag gebel het omtrent die plot vir die haweloses, ongelukkig het my selfoon gekonk, en hy't sy gesiggie verloor, en ek vra asseblief laat die mense my sal bel op my landlyn, dis 01…
JOHAN:	…Ek mag ongelukkig nie sulke telefoonnommers oor die lug gee nie.
TANNIE MARIET:	Nee Johan, …my selfoon werk nie…
JOHAN:	Ek glo en ek verstaan…
TANNIE MARIET:	…wag! Ek gee hom gou…01…
JOHAN:	Wag…(*lag*)…Tannie Mariet (*lag*)…ek kan dit nie doen nie…
TANNIE MARIET:	…dis 01…
JOHAN:	Tannie Mariet…(*lag*)…
TANNIE MARIET:	…01…
JOHAN:	Kyk, Tannie Mariet try nou daai ding lekker kry daarso… (*lag*)
AANKONDIGER:	Met meer as 24 miljoen mense wat elke dag luister, sal jy ook bitter graag op radio wil adverteer. Skakel 714 7000. *SABC*-radioverkope – praat met ons en jy praat met die nasie.

Linguistic Characteristics

The broadcaster is trying to be informal and, in order to do so, he mixes his codes when he says, "try nou daai ding lekker kry daarso". Tannie Mariet's voice is very credibly stereotypical of an older Afrikaans-speaking lady. It supports the perception of the voice of a typecast older Afrikaans-speaking person on a phone-in radio programme. The frustration she feels because she is not allowed to give her number is clear from her tone of voice. This plays an important role in the marketing message, in contrast to that of the conventional voice of the radio announcer. His voice is even more credible than hers because it is recognisable

Box 13.2: Loose Translation of Pendoring Advertisement in English	
JOHAN:	Goeie môre, good morning.
TANNIE MARIET:	Hallo Johan, this is Mariet van Pretoria. Ag Johan, you know that I phoned the other day about the plot for the homeless, unluckily my cell phone conked out and it lost its little old face and I want you to tell the people to phone me on my land line, it's 01…
JOHAN:	Unfortunately, I am not allowed to give such numbers over the air.
TANNIE MARIET:	No Johan, …my cell phone doesn't work…
JOHAN:	I believe you and I understand…
TANNIE MARIET:	…wait! Here it is …01…
JOHAN:	Wait!…(*laughs*)…Tannie Mariet (*laughs*)…I can't do it …
TANNIE MARIET:	…it's 01…
JOHAN:	Tannie Mariet…(*laughs*)
TANNIE MARIET:	…01…
JOHAN:	Listen, Tannie Mariet, now come on! You are trying a lekker thing there … (*laughs*)
ANNOUNCER:	With a daily audience of more than 24 million people, you will also be keen to advertise on radio. Telephone 714 7000. *SABC* radio sales – talk to us and you talk to the nation.

as that of one of the most well-known radio personalities on the radio station in question, RSG.

Typical of dialogue are the many examples of turn-taking and interruptions which make the conversation credible, and the use of these features in a phone-in programme makes the situation even more convincing. The uncertainty of the announcer (in terms of how to react to Tannie Mariet's repeated and insistent attempts to talk) contribute to the credibility of the advertisement. In addition, the way in which the two characters, Johan and Tannie Mariet, continuously interrupt each other and do not give each other a chance to speak is typical of everyday conversation. The names and forms of address of the characters also contribute to the credibility of the advertisement. Tannie Mariet's choice of words also supports the stereotypical image of an older Afrikaans-speaking radio guest: "gesiggie, ingekonk" ("conked out and it lost its little old face").

Language-related Characteristics

Humour definitely plays one of the most important roles in the success of this advertisement. It is amusing to hear how Tannie Mariet keeps insisting on giving her telephone number, despite being warned not to do so. Tannie Mariet's character is a stereotype of the older generation of Afrikaners who take part in phone-in radio programmes. Her determined character is apparent from her repeated efforts to supply her telephone number. Her choice of words, her use of language and her reason for calling support the perception that older people (women in Particular) are not very familiar with the latest technology.

The behaviour of the announcer and his courtesy towards the caller are also in accordance with the stereotype of Afrikaans radio announcers and one's expectations of them, particularly of those who work on a radio station such as RSG, which is the radio station concerned in this case and the station with which the voice of this particular announcer is associated.

Marketing Message

Radio is a popular medium for advertising and, according to the advertisement, people will do almost anything to get their product mentioned (i.e. advertised) on radio.

Lemon Twist – Twist Lemon (Buttercup guesthouse) (Loerie Awards)

Linguistic Characteristics

One of the linguistic characteristics is word play. In order to emphasise the trade name, "Lemon Twist", this name becomes part of the word play and changes to Twist Lemon (the necessary repetition of the product being advertised is also achieved) This word play is functional if one considers the emphasis that is currently being placed on change and transformation in South Africa. Repetition (and the repetition of the name in reverse) stresses the name of the product

The register of Evelyn Nel's language stays polite and professional, but, as soon as she is informed of the proposed change of the name of her guest house, the definite "No" makes one aware of her being thrown off balance, as does the repetition of "NO, NO, NO, NO, NO, NO!" ("NO" is written here in capital letters to indicates how passionate-sounding her response is). The register of the official, Tolerance Maseko, remains formal and courteous throughout the conversation; he is expected to behave in this fashion because he is at work. The dialogue has features of a telephonic conversation that are very convincing. The tone and pronunciation of both speakers contribute to making the advertisement

> Box 13.3: Loerie Advertisement for a Soft Drink, Lemon Twist
>
> SFX: Phone ringing.
>
> FVO: Hello.
> MVO: Good morning. Is this Evelyn Nel?
> FVO: Yes speaking.
> MVO: Yes ma'am. My name is Tolerance Maseko from the Department of Name Transformation, yes.
> FVO: Yes.
> MVO: Ma'am we are changing the names in line with our constitution and Africanisation. You are the owner of the Buttercup guesthouse?
> FVO: That's right.
> MVO: Well ma'am I must inform you, happily, that the Department of Name Transformation have decided to change it to Langalipalele.
> FVO: No.
> MVO: Ma'am sorry. Why are you upset? It means 'sunshine' ma'am.
> FVO: NO, NO, NO, NO, NO, NO!!!
>
> ANNOUNCER: It takes time getting used to a new name. Lemon Twist is now called Twist Lemon. Put a twist in it.

seem like a plausible situation. Evelyn Nel's voice can be pinpointed as typical of an English-speaking lady who remains courteous despite being upset. Nevertheless, the definitive "NO" expresses her feelings about the proposed renaming of her guesthouse. Tolerance Maseko's voice is also convincing as that of a speaker of an African language. The audience can deduce that he is not a first-language English speaker and that the nature of his job forces him to speak many languages. Important turn-taking also occurs between the speakers. (Both speaker's turns are short and are interrupted by the other speaker) Finally, the advertisement uses different forms of address very successfully. Tolerance, whose mother tongue is an African language, uses the formal form of address ("Ma'am"). This is correct for his particular context as a service provider. The other speaker, Evelyn Nel, does not address Tolerance directly but is laconic in her answers: "Yes", "That's right" and "No".

Language-related Characteristics

The humour in the advertisement is linked to the social commentary implicit in it. The whole idea of change in South Africa - and the fact that different cultures have to become reconciled with each other - is difficult. In this case, it is dealt with in a humorous manner, and many South Africans can identify with the situation being depicted. The intertextual references to transformation in South Africa help to create the context for the advertisement. The members of the target market have to know about the different forms of change happening currently, for example, the name changes of cities, towns, streets etc. If they do not, the advertisement will not be very successful.

The name of the African, Tolerance Maseko, has been chosen for its ironic value. The message that he delivers does not elicit tolerance from the person he phones. On an intertextual level, his name also refers to the government's appeal for tolerance so that transformation in the country may take place. The advertisement requires a certain amount of common shared knowledge of different feelings that South Africans experience in terms of the current changes of names and place names in this country. The advertisement offers a credible image of the multicultural character of South Africa and the transformation taking place.

Marketing message

Changing people's names and place names makes no difference to the nature or appearance of the city or place; in the same way, changing the name of the cold drink from Lemon Twist to Twist Lemon will not change the taste of the drink.

Conclusions

Radio advertisements communicate with real people via real characters or spokespeople and echo the credibility of word-of-mouth advertising. Dialogue is a genre of radio advertisement that can be applied extremely successfully if the characteristics of spoken language are taken into account. The tone of voice and pronunciation of the speakers are two of the most important aspects to consider in order to create a radio advertisement that is credible. Once again, one may refer to radio as a theatre of the mind in which the targeted audience creates the context in their own minds. The use of the same voice throughout a series of advertisements is an intertextual advantage. Rhyme, word games and metaphors can be used functionally in radio advertisements because of the fact that radio relies for the transmission of the message on sound only.

Because radio has the advantage of being generally available and mobile, people often listen to it quite by chance or unintentionally. This means that the copywriter must introduce an advertisement in such an effective way that an unsuspecting listener becomes part of the target audience without having intended to do so. Radio can focus on a highly specific target market, which means that the advertisement is deliberately written with one message for a specific group in mind and for whom it was originally intended in the first place.

Because radio has the quality of immediacy, this characteristic should be exploited to give specific instructions to the people in the target market. These instructions should tell them exactly what to do, so that they react to the advertisement spontaneously and follow the instructions impulsively.

A disadvantage of radio is its fleeting quality. This implies that messages cannot be recalled. The copywriter has to deal with this problem by writing the advertisement in simple language. The opening line of the advertisement is the audience's first contact with the product, and so it has to be catchy. Although there are different genres of radio advertisements, each copywriter has to strive to tell a story that the people in the target market can recall in such a way that they link it correctly to the product being advertised.

Situations change with circumstances, and the arrival and departure of political leaders or place names, for example, are linked to historical events that take place within a certain timeframe. If the copywriter wishes to refer to matters such as these, he or she should establish that the facts are correct.

Humour may be used very successfully in advertisements. It creates an atmosphere of good cheer and provides amusement. However, it is an element that should be used with circumspection because, if it fails, the whole advertisement will fail. Irony and controversy are also techniques that can contribute to the success of an advertisement. Nevertheless, the copywriter should establish whether the people in the target market will be able to identify the irony or the controversy. If they do not, the advertisement will not deliver its marketing message.

Music is used in radio advertisements to create atmosphere and to evoke certain emotions in the people targeted. Additionally, music may also have an intertextual function: background sounds create the context and provide plenty of textual information. The copywriter should use these elements to create the theatre of the mind for the people in the target market. The copywriter should create characters that act as realistic representatives (stereotypes) of a specific section of the community. Different language-related variables are used repeatedly in the dataset and help to set guidelines in writing credible dialogue in radio advertisements in order to echo word-of-mouth advertising.

References

Carstens, W.A.M. 1997. *Afrikaanse tekslinguistiek: 'n inleiding*. Pretoria: J.L. van Schaik.
Cloete, T.T. 1992. *Literêre terme & teorieë*. Pretoria: Haum-Literêr.
Crystal, D. 1987. *Cambridge Encyclopedia of Language*. Cambridge: Cambridge University Press.
Cutting, J. 2008. *Pragmatics and Discourse. A Resource Book for Students*. Second Ed. New York: Routledge.
De Beer, A.S. 1998. Mass Media. *The South African Handbook of Mass Communication*. Pretoria: J.L. van Schaik.
Felton, G. 1994. *Advertising Concept and Copy*. Englewood Cliffs, NJ: Prentice Hall.
Fourie, P.J. 2001. *Media Studies*. Cape Town: Juta.
Goddard, A. 1998. *The Language of Advertising: Written Texts*. London: Routledge.
Halliday, M.A.K. and R. Hasan. 1976. *Cohesion in English*. London: Longman.
Lewis, H.G. 2004. *On the Art of Writing Copy*. New York: Racom Communications.
Matthews, P.H. 1997. *Concise Dictionary of Linguistics*. New York: Oxford University Press.
Meeske, M.D. 2003. *Copywriting for the Electronic Media. A Practical Guide*. Fourth Ed. Belmont: Wadsworth.
Myers, G. 1994. *Words in Ads*. New York: Routledge.
O' Day, D. n.d.. *Certified Professional Commercial Copywriter Course*. New York: The Radio Advertising Bureau.
Oosthuizen, L.M. 1996. *Introduction to Communication. Course Book 5. Journalism, Press and Radio Studies*. Kenwyn: Juta.
Salkie, R. 1995. *Text and Discourse Analysis*. London: Routledge.
Stubbs, M. 1983. *Discourse Analysis: The Sociolinguistic Analysis of Natural Language*. Oxford: Basil Blackwell.
Van Jaarsveld, G.J. 1987. *Wat bedoel jy?* Bloemfontein: Serva Uitgewers.

III
INTEGRATED MARKETING COMMUNICATION

CHAPTER 14

COVERT ADVERTISING IN HOME VIDEOS: IMPLICATIONS FOR BRAND MANAGEMENT

OLALEKAN GANIYU AKASHORO & SHAIBU HUSSEINI

Introduction

The diminishing effectiveness of broadcast advertising has made firms turn increasingly to covert advertising to promote brands. Though experiencing a significant growth due to the difficulty of reaching consumers with traditional advertising, covert advertising is not new. It is as old as the invention of television broadcasting.

Covert advertising involves (though not in all cases) a fee manufacturers pay to have their products mentioned or included as background and used as props on television and in movies. Many of us will remember seeing Tom Cruise's character John Anderton in the movie *Minority Report* wearing a wrist watch engraved with the Bulgari logo and using a phone with the Nokia logo clearly visible in the top corner, or Audrey Hepburn in *Breakfast at Tiffany's* wearing Givenchy apparel. Another famous example is lead actor Will Smith's mention of Converse shoes several times in the movie *I, Robot*, where he repeatedly refers to the shoes as 'classics' because the film is set far in the future. These examples represent just a few of the array of branded products that appear in movies and television programmes. In fact, it is estimated that advertisers spend as much as US$50 million annually in product placements in the movie industry (Elliot 1997). This figure would most likely quadruple if television placements were included. In a survey of a cross-section of television viewers in Atlanta, Georgia, to ascertain the impact of covert advertising on consumer purchase intentions, Upshaw (1995) reports that, having seen various products in films, viewers find themselves unconsciously drawn to such products, especially if they are used by their favourite actors or actresses. The study revealed that, in most cases, viewers ultimately purchase the same products.

In its simplest form, covert advertising involves the subtle use of products as props. This is done in such a way that it complements the scene in question yet serves as indirect advertising. In extreme cases, scripts are tailor-made for the desired brand, and the brand may also be mentioned during the course of the movie as well as used as a prop. The strategy is widely used in established film industries such as Hollywood and Bollywood (the Mumbai-based Indian film industry) but remains underutilised in Nollywood (the burgeoning Nigerian film industry). This suggests that Nigerian producers are either not aware of how the concept works or have not yet understood its marketing power. This chapter discusses the concept of covert advertising as a way of providing a foundation for increased understanding of the concept and its effectiveness. It examines the scope of the practice in the first part, its many facets in the second and its theoretical context in the third section. The chapter concludes by suggesting ways that advertisers can leverage the concept to project realism into the minds of film buffs as a result of the display of products or brand names in scenes and situations.

The Concept and Scope of Covert Advertising

Advertisers throughout the world have realised the need to harness the power of covert advertising which, in one of its simplest forms, involves the practice of including a brand name, package, trademark or product usage within a motion picture or television programme. The motive is to increase the memorability of a brand and propel recall and recognition of the brand at the point of purchase. Covert advertising is a more powerful alternative to the earlier practice of inserting advertising in breaks in motion pictures. Tapan (2008) argues that covert advertising, which he calls "entertainment economics", arose when advertisers realised that audiences find inserted advertising messages distracting. He points out that contemporary broadcasting offers many programme choices and technological advances that make it convenient to switch between television and video programmes to avoid the distraction caused by advertising messages that are not engrained into the entertainment. Therefore, to keep such media audiences attentive, he suggests that advertisers have learnt to "embed" their advertising messages into the entertainment content. This is achieved by incorporating the desired brands into scripts in such a way that it appears fitting and natural when the product or brand name is used or mentioned in the programme.

While leveraging the entertainment value and psychological impact of films on viewers is a key reason behind the deployment of this advertising strategy, Zeime (2007) points out that another important objective is to reduce production costs. Covert advertising helps cover costs either in cash or kind. Some filmmakers receive cash from advertisers or their agents, but, more often, firms secure product placement at no cost when they supply their product to the movie company. Osinuga (2006) explains that companies rarely pay for their brands to be used in movies. Instead, they supply their products to be used as costumes or props at no cost to the movie producers. When firms pay for covert advertising, the monies raised are used to offset production costs. However, the bottom line, irrespective of whether the placement is done in cash or kind, is that an agreement is reached, and the script is revised to place the brand appropriately so that it looks like a natural part of the story line.

Examples abound of how brand appearance in movies has resulted in increased brand performance. Hollywood has still not forgotten how dramatically the use of a Sony Ericsson mobile phone in a James Bond movie in 1997 increased the market share of the Ericsson trademark. Here in Nigeria, persons interviewed (personal communication) believe that the marketing of Lucozade Boost got an upward boost in visibility and market share when actor and filmmaker Kunle Afolayan took the energy drink as a way of replenishing lost energy after an endurance exercise in the movie *The Figurine*.

Tapan (2008) identifies three basic ways in which covert advertising can occur. The first is when, without any type of formal contractual agreement, a particular product or brand is used by a member of the cast or crew of a movie to enhance the scene, even though the product itself may not be seen or presented in a positive light. The second type occurs when the placement is arranged and the product itself serves as compensation. The third type occurs when placement is arranged and there is financial compensation. It is this third form that appeals most to filmmakers who need to offset the costs of movie production.

I examine covert advertising strategies in a later section, but it needs stressing that covert advertising can be implicit or explicit depending on the advertiser's requirements. While the motive can sometimes be to launch a new product, others rely on the strategy to demonstrate the long tradition of a brand. There are some advertisers who use it to fight competition, but the majority rely on the strategy to reinforce the brand image or its positioning message. In any case, a number of different covert advertising strategies are used.

Covert Advertising Strategies

Bacher and Rossler (2008) identify three basic covert advertising strategies which are not mutually exclusive. The first is implicit product placement, where the brand's name or the name of the firm appears without a clear demonstration of the product benefits. The product is present within the movie or television programme without being explicitly named. It plays a merely passive or contextual role. The second strategy is integrated product placement. Here, the attributes or benefits of the product are explicitly demonstrated; it plays an active role, and the brand or product name is formally expressed in the programme. An example is when one of the lead characters in the film *The Figurine* suggest to another character that the best energy drink to take is Lucozade Boost. The third type of covert advertising is what Bacher and Rossler (2008: page) call "non-integrated explicit product placement". In this case, the brand or product is not integrated into the programme or movie, but the company or brand name may appear in the beginning of the programme or the brand or company name appears on the screen. Bacher and Rossler contend that there could be multiple types of product placement within a given programme or movie just as there are multiple motives behind covert advertising. Such motives include improving corporate reputation, as when the Grand Oak Hotel in Asaba is used for grand parties in Enugu (corporate placement); demonstrating the characteristics of a product without a particular brand name, as when analgesics are used in movies without any mention of a particular brand name (generic placement); presenting public or private institutions (service placement); including facts, opinions or statements in a plot (idea placement); illustrating a long tradition of a brand (historic placement); presenting a competitor's product in a negative context (negative placement); and introducing a new product (innovation placement).

Similarly, Kashyap (2005) suggests three ways in which product placement can occur: placement occurring without any type of contractual agreement, placement arranged with the products serving as compensation and placement arranged for some form of financial compensation. The last is the kind of placement that appeals most to filmmakers, but the point that needs to be underscored is that the motives for deploying covert advertising vary.

Theoretical Backdrop

Previous studies of covert advertising have mostly been limited to measuring brand recall (Kashyap 2005, Bacher and Rossler 2008). In addition, these studies dealt with only one form of placement, the visual appearance of the brand on the screen. However, Elliot (1997) had in a study dealt with all three dimensions of covert advertising, namely, visual and auditory as well as placement within plots, and indicated that viewers were able to recognise brands placed within films. Scholars have often relied on theories like source credibility theory (acceptance of the advertised message depending on the expertness and trustworthiness of the source), source attractiveness (the acceptance of the message depending on familiarity, likeability and similarity) and meaning transfer (a celebrity encoding a unique set of meanings that can be transferred to the endorsed product) as the basis on which the methodology of covert advertising can best be appreciated. The central premises of all these theories is that covert advertising, whether auditory or visual, gives a brand a touch of glamour, provides added appeal and name recognition in a crowded market and helps increase the recall value of a brand.

McCracken's theory best explores the complex aspect of the development and transfer of meaning (Petty and Cacioppo 1981). Indeed, the articulation of the theoretical framework for covert advertising is best summarised in terms similar to McCracken's meaning transfer model (1990). The central premise of the theory is that a celebrity (film star) encodes a unique set of meanings which, if well used, can be transferred to the endorsed product. Such a transfer, according to McCracken (1990), takes place in three stages: encoding meanings, meaning transfer and meaning capture. The stage of encoding meanings is the first stage. Here, each celebrity has a unique set of meanings, which can be listed by age, gender, race, wealth, personality or lifestyle. In this way, the celebrities encode a set of meanings in their image. The second is the stage of meaning transfer, whereby the meanings transferred by the film star are transferred to the product. McCracken (1990) argues that, when skilfully portrayed, celebrities can communicate this image more powerfully than lay endorsers. The third stage, meaning capture, assumes that consumers purchase products not merely for their functional value, but also for their cultural and symbolic value. The theory says that consumers buy the endorsed product with the intention of capturing some of the desirable meanings which celebrities have passed on to the product. This works both theoretically and practically because, as McCracken (1990) contends, the qualities associated with the endorser are associated with the brand, and the brand, therefore, remains at the top of the consumer's mind.

However, one needs to realise that the impact of an endorser cannot be sustainable in all product categories and in all the stages of brand life-cycles. It really depends upon the type of product. So far, studies have shown that only lifestyle products such as clothes, perfumes and cellphones eminently justify covert advertising. Moreover, if the product is a "functional brand", the product itself is the hero. In this situation, any celebrity association with the brand in a movie, without corresponding performance of the product, will not be sustainable. What works for such a brand in most cases is message consistency, which reinforces the brand values and helps position the brand as the ultimate choice.

Positive Impacts of Covert Advertising

The American blockbuster romantic comedy *Sex in the City* may be a movie about fun, fashion and relationships, but it was also an extended covert advertisement for the emerging Middle Eastern business hub, Abu Dhabi, the capital of the United Arab Emirates. Just as New Zealand was displayed to advantage in the Indian movie *Kaho Na Pyar Hai*. A large part of both films was devoted to showing off their locations. *Sex in the City*, starring four of Hollywood's top actors, filled its script with discussions of how and why Abu Dhabi has emerged as a city that everyone must visit, but movie goers may not realise they are watching a commercial camouflaged as a screenplay. To many, this well-managed product placement of an entire city may have appeared natural, because it was so thoroughly embedded in the script. The movie was watched by tens of millions, and such was the impact of the strategy that Abu Dhabi is now widely spoken of as a potential location by both filmmakers and tourists.

The 2006 production of the James Bond film *Casino Royale* is a more typical example of product placement, focusing on specific consumer products, though all from one brand. It features Sony product placements throughout. Most of the characters in the film used Vaio laptops and Sony Ericsson cellphones. Another example of advertising in film is the generous use of Cadillac vehicles in the movie *Matrix Reloaded*. Indeed, there are no end of examples (mainly foreign) of how products and brands can be effectively embedded in entertainment and media. Nollywood, in particular, and the rest of Africa urgently needs to catch up.

Nevertheless, it is difficult to determine the direct effect of covert advertising on sales or profits. Although most firms say sales improve tremendously following the deployment of covert advertising, they agree that the improvement may not be attributable solely to the technique. However they are unanimously agreed that:

- The strategy is cheaper than overt advertising or sponsorship.
- The advertiser is guaranteed a captive audience who have decided to see a film.
- The strategy has the potential of appealing to a wider audience if the programme or film is successful.

- The product becomes linked to the film or programme and the ideology inherent in that text.

To promote a brand to the status of a market leader in its segment, firms deploying covert advertising must carefully use and select films and television programmes that will effectively transmit the selling message. The personality of the brand and that of the movie personnel, including the cast, have to complement one another. Kashyap (2005) admits that approval of a brand by a star fosters a sense of trust for that brand in the target audience. Kashyap (2005) also explains that, when a company uses famous personalities for brand endorsements, consumers tend to relate to the character that he or she plays. For example, Smriti Irani, who plays Tulsi in a famous soap in India, is believed to have garnered a lot of support from middle-class housewives in India today (Kashyap 2005). If she stars in a movie where she endorses a brand, the brand would gain more visibility and credibility. The point that needs to be underscored is that there is a demographic and psychographic connection between movie stars and their fans. On the demographic side, different stars appeal to different demographic segments relating to age, gender, class, geography etc. Psychographically, stars are loved and adored by their fans. Some stars have a universal appeal and, therefore, prove to be a good bet to generate interest among the masses.

Cultural Impact of Covert Advertising

Much more attention is being paid to the overall cultural impact of advertising in recent times. This may be because there are still many people who feel personally exempted from its influence. In a study conducted by Owens (1999) to assess the socio-cultural impact of advertising among consumers of dairy products, most respondents claimed they did not pay attention to advertising because they felt that it is not something to take seriously. Owens also notes that some of the respondents rehashed the common criticism that advertising is wasteful and does not add value and economic utility to products. Many respondents simply said that advertising has no effect on them, while others said they simply tune off any time they are confronted with advertising messages because most advertising messages are deceitful. The fact remains, however, that consumers are demonstrably influenced by advertising. Indeed, advertising critics such as Sut Jhally have remarked that not to be influenced by advertising would mean living outside one's culture (Kilbourne 1999). And since no human being lives outside his or her culture, it follows that human beings are inevitably influenced by advertising either through its reflection of societal values or through its place as a pervasive medium of influence and persuasion. The degree of influence may vary according to individual differences and levels of media literacy, but there is little doubt that advertising creates wants for individuals and induces desire for things they would ordinarily not want. On the other hand, Onyenyili-Onourah (2005) argues that the pervasive, intrusive and often distracting nature of advertising, particularly subliminal advertising, has made it an object of aversion to some consumers of mass media, who express their feelings by switching off or turning away from advertisements.

Although advertising, by definition, is only interested in materialistic values, it is cumulative, often subtle and primarily unconscious. It is also believed to be both a creator and perpetuator of the dominant values of the culture, as well as of the social norms by which most people govern their behaviour. At the very least, as Kilbourne (1999) contends, advertising helps to create a climate in which certain values flourish and others are not reflected. According to Kilbourne, the major motivating force for social change throughout the world today is the belief that happiness comes from the market and that the way to be happy, to find satisfaction and even to gain political freedom is through the consumption of the material objects which advertising promotes.

Limitations of Covert Advertising

One of the main reasons some covert advertising strategies have failed is the inability of the advertiser to define the relationship between advertising and the culture of the society where it is practiced. There is a necessity, argues Onyenyili-Onourah (2005), for advertising to reflect the culture of its target environment by identifying with the lifestyles, aspirations and motivations of its target audience in order to make the audience identify with the advertised product. This position is premised on the assumption that, while advertising increasingly mirrors the culture of its environment, the culture ought to be affected positively or negatively by the advertising it is exposed to. Likewise, if an advertisement embodies completely alien concepts, it will be alienated from the audience, and they will make little or no meaning out of the advertisement. Similarly, covert advertising is inhibited by audience assumptions, critical acclaim and violent film content. In addition, placement modality, character association and blatancy significantly affect the placement's value. Scott and Craig-Lees (2003) submit that the success of the concept depends on the involvement of consumers in the movie as well as its popularity. For this reason, they advise that, to be effective, advertisers and the filmmakers must take variables such as religion, culture, age, sex, literacy levels, context of the plot, match of the product with the movie type, story and characters, access to technology and audience liking for an endorser into consideration. Moreover, an endorsement in a bad movie, or in a movie that is not well cast, they argue, can be counter-productive both for the advertiser and the filmmaker. Nevertheless, when all the right factors are in place, the technique has great potential to strengthen a brand (or enhance its equity) while, at the same time, sourcing additional funds for film productions, especially in the face of the inability of film producers to source enough funds for movie production. Having established the relevance of the concept, I now turn to recommendations on how advertisers and filmmakers can maximise the benefits of covert advertising.

Conclusion

In this chapter, an attempt has been made to examine the relevance and effectiveness of covert advertising as a promotional tool. The concept of covert advertising was discussed within the context of an adapted meaning transfer model, in which the product meaning associated with a popular television show or film is ultimately transferred to the individual viewer. However, it is worth restating that advertising occupies a central position in integrated marketing communication strategies. This is the reason advertisers or their agencies are constantly in search of innovative techniques that can grab attention, particularly at a low cost per exposure. One innovative technique which advertisers have adopted is covert advertising. It is a response to the advent of more choice for media consumers, which has invariably changed the well-established equilibrium in which advertisers and audiences operate. Covert advertising has emerged as a form of cooperation between advertisers and creators of entertainment products and allows trademarked goods to be embedded into popular entertainment products in order to encourage their consumption. Covert advertising, described by Schejter (2004) as a form of advertising without disclosing it to the receiving party, has proved resourceful in achieving visibility for a brand without the distraction of sitting through advertising inserts that can last for upwards of 10 to 20 minutes. Filmmakers have adopted the technique of covert advertising very widely in developed film entertainment centres such as Hollywood and Bollywood, but the practice is just catching on in developing film centres in Nigeria, Ghana and Kenya.

Covert advertising has emerged as a viable alternative to traditional forms of advertising, especially if the intention is to reach a specific target group, since movies in most cases are made with specific target audiences in mind. Aside from its benefits to filmmakers, it is worth restating that advertisers have and will continue to benefit from the adoption of this strategy, if well deployed. Okon (2006) argues that viewers, having seen various products in movies, find themselves being drawn to such products unconsciously, especially when used by popular lead actors. It is our submission that the covert advertising provides a rare opportunity for the involved audience to get exposure to brands and products during the natural process of narration of movies or television programmes. Every stakeholder benefits; the movie producers, the advertisers and the audience. By aggressively seeking branding opportunities and sponsorship through product placement in films, as demonstrated in Afolayan's *The Figurine,* filmmakers can, through covert advertising, raise funds that can offset certain cost of production.

However, care should be taken to ensure that the opportunities offered through covert advertising are in the larger interests of the society. In deciding on the adoption of the concept, advertisers must be careful not to use placements in badly themed movies or movies that are not appropriately cast, as the credibility of the source has a great role to play in the appreciation of the selling message. A pre-production audit is necessary for advertisers in order to be well informed about what attributes the film possess and what attitudes and interests of their audience impact on brands and how they are impacted by branded goods. This is in order to understand the individual's propensity to be influenced by messages embedded in covert advertising. Advertisers must be consistent in adopting the technique if they intend to effectively transfer and associate the right value to the product endorsed. In a world that is increasingly entertainment-centred, covert advertising offers many benefits, although it may be incapable of matching, either in glamour or impact, the benefits of advertising through traditional media.

References

Bacher, J. and P. Rossler. 2008. Transcultural effect of product placement in movies. http://hogrefe.de/design/standard/images/seitschriften/zmp/2002/zmp1403098.pdf (retrieved 3/4/2010)

Elliot, S. 1997. The Spot on the Cutting-Room Floor, *The New York Times,* 07/03.

Kashyap, A.K. 2005. Product Placement in Movies and TV serials. http://www.scribd.com/doc/4613254/Product-Placement-in-TV-Serials-and-Movie-INDIA (retrieved 25/3/2010).

Kilbourne, J. 1999. *Can't Buy My Love: How Advertising Changes the Way We Think and Feel.* New York. Touch Stone.

McCracken, G. 1990. *Culture and Consumption: New Approaches to The Symbolic Character of Consumers Good and Activities.* Bloomington, IN: Indiana University Press.

Okon, A. 2006. Product placement as income earner for Nollywood. www.newage-online.com/nollywood article/12 (retrieved 23/3/2010)

Onyenyili-Onourah, J.E. 2005. *Advertising and Society.* Lagos. Raindrops Limited.

Osinuga, A. 2006. Motion picture production and marketing. Unpublished lecture notes. Lagos State University School of Communication, Lagos, Nigeria.

Owens, O. 1999. The socio-cultural impact of advertising among consumers of dairy products in Enugu Metropolis. Unpublished MSC Thesis. University of Nigeria, Enugu Campus.

Petty, R.E. and J.T. Cacioppo. 1981. *Attitude and Persuasion: Classic and Contemporary Approaches*. Dubuque, IA: William C. Brown.

Schejter, Amit M. 2004. Product placement as an international practice: Moral, legal, regulatory and trade implication. Unpublished paper presented at the 32nd Research Conference on Communication, Information and Internet Policy, Pennsylvania State University. http://docs-google.com/view? (retrieved 22/3/2010).

Scott, J. and M. Craig-Lees. 2003. Audience characteristics and product placement effects. Paper presented at Australian and New Zealand Marketing Academy Conference, Adelaide. smib.vuw.ac.nz:8081/www/ANZMAC2003/papers/ADV10_SCOTTJ.pdf. (retrieved 6/4/2010).

Tapan, P.K. 2008. Effectiveness of product placement in Indian films and its effects on brand memory and attitude with special reference to Hindi films. http://www.r.lib.sfu.ind/4157/etd2572.pdf (retrieved 30/3/2010).

Upshaw, L.B. 1995. *Building Brand Identity: A Strategy for Success in a Hostile Market Place*. New York: Wiley.

Zeime, G. 2007. Bonds mission successful. www.ericson com/infocentre/publications/contact/Bond.htm (retrieved 22/3/2010)

CHAPTER 15

CULTURAL PARADOXES OF GLOBAL ADVERTISING IN SATELLITE TV BROADCASTING

CHINENYE NWABUEZE

Introduction

Advertising persuades the audience to appreciate, desire and seek to acquire goods of any kind. The goods can be in the form of physical products, services, positive attitudes towards a goal (e.g. environmentally friendly culture) and lifestyles, among others. The audience for such messages can be local or international. If the advert message targets audiences across national frontiers, the activity has moved into the sphere of global advertising. This entails sponsored forms of mass communication through a mass medium about goods and services to an international audience. It is advertising aimed at foreign markets (Arens and Bovee 1994: 10).

Satellite broadcasting expands the horizon of international or global advertising. Satellite broadcasting, whether radio or television, consists of distributing audio and/or video signals via a satellite network. Satellite television broadcasting (also known as direct broadcast satellite or DBS) is a service in which a broadcaster, instead of using an aerial on the earth's surface, uses one located on a satellite in space with a very powerful transmitter capable of sending messages directly to individual receiving sets on earth (Okoye 2004: 80). The advent of satellite technology popularised global broadcasting and, with it, global advertising. Products manufactured in specific countries are targeted at foreign markets via global media made possible through satellite broadcasting. Thus, broadcasts received in a country often feature advertisements of foreign products projected through advertisements produced in foreign environments by foreign casts. This is especially common in some foreign soap operas, but the focus of this discussion is on adverts aired by satellite television channels such as Cable News Network (CNN), British Broadcasting Corporation (BBC) World News, Fox News, SuperSport and so on. Put in an all-encompassing way, the global adverts referred to here consist of adverts aired by television channels through various satellite and cable television service providers such as DSTV, HiTV, MyTV, CTL, Daar Sat and so on, including free-to-air channels. These are the most common ways of gaining access to foreign television programmes these days by audiences in developing countries.

Adverts, whether targeted at local or international audiences, do not just project the products or services being overtly advertised, they also covertly or overtly market the culture of the originating nation. The casts, their dress, the language and the environment of the advert are among various means through which the cultural values of the originating countries are projected to international audiences. These cultural values can influence the audience's perceptions of life even more than the advertised products.

This chapter discusses the implications of the cultural contents of global advertising on African values. I argue that such advertising is a form of cultural marketing, that audiences in Africa are widely exposed to it, that there is a relationship between exposure to satellite television programmes and consumption of the global adverts embedded in these programmes, that these adverts have cultural content and that exposure to satellite programmes on television can influence African audiences and cause the erosion of local cultural values. I conclude by making some suggestions on how African companies and product manufacturers can engage in cultural counter-marketing via satellite television stations owned or run by Africans.

Global Advertising and Satellite TV Broadcasting

Global advertising has been popularised by the emergence of global media networks, that is, media networks that target international audiences. Global television channels, the focus of this discussion, are among the mass media that broadcast to or reach audiences across national frontiers. The mass media were made truly global by the advent of satellite broadcasting, at which point "signals could be distributed not only internationally, that is, between two specific countries, as had previously been the case, but all over the world" (Baran 2004: 505). Satellite television channels penetrate countries largely unchecked and, in most cases, uncensored. Thus, programmes produced mostly in Western nations, which have the technology and resources to dominate satellite broadcasting, find their way into homes across the world, especially in developing countries where there is little technological base to provide alternative quality programming for local audiences.

The fact that the West possesses the technological capacity to operate satellite television broadcasting has ensured a largely one-way traffic of satellite TV broadcasting from the Western world to developing countries. Rahman (1998) observes that Cairo's rooftops are now filled to overflowing with satellite dishes, as opposed to the situation in the early 1980s, when access to satellite television was for the privileged few. Okoye (2004: 80) writes that "today, satellite TV antennas vie with local TV antennas for space in many areas of Lagos". Zureikat (1999) observes that the popularity of MTV (a satellite TV channel) among Egyptian viewers is demonstrated by the doubling of subscription rate for CNN within six months after MTV was introduced as a package with CNN through Cable News Egypt. Similarly, Nwabueze (2010), after a study of satellite TV households in the southeast geo-political zone of Nigeria, observed that viewers in these households watch more satellite TV than local TV.

With the huge popularity of satellite television channels among viewers in Africa, it follows that these viewers will also be exposed to the adverts contained in these television channels. Various kinds of programmes are aired by satellite television stations. Most times, these programmes are accompanied by adverts from sponsors. Satellite broadcast technology widens the reach of such advert messages. For instance, the popularity of English Premier League (EPL) football in Nigeria and most African nations exposes viewers to the adverts on these broadcasts, although there is need for empirical evidence to determine whether the popularity of these advert messages translates to purchase. Even though some viewers of the EPL programmes do not pay attention to the accompanying adverts, the wider reach provided for such adverts via the global media outlets is not in doubt. The same applies to all programmes on satellite television channels which have gained popularity among a global audience.

Adverts for products that are forbidden in certain parts of the world and cannot be advertised there find their way into such countries via satellite channels. For instance, alcoholic drinks cannot be advertised or sold in some Muslim countries, but these products are widely advertised in satellite television programmes which audiences in Muslim countries have access to. Heineken is the official sponsor of the UEFA Champions League, and virtually every local and satellite television channel that broadcasts UEFA games carries the Heineken advert. This, strangely, includes the Aljazeera sports channels, which are English/Arabic channels based in the Middle East and basically targeted at English-speaking and Arabic-speaking audiences in that part of the world. This underscores the enormity of air space, reach, coverage and audience horizon that satellite television broadcasting provides for global adverts. The inability to censor, restrict or disrupt satellite television signals has widened the scope of global advertising, including the contents of these advert messages.

Theoretical Construct

This discussion is anchored on cultural imperialism theory. This theory, propounded by Herb Schiller in 1973, has the following basic tenets (Anaeto et al. 2008: 151):

- Western nations dominate the media around the world, and this has a powerful effect on Third World cultures, leading to imposition of Western values and destruction of native cultures.
- Humans react to what they are exposed to on television because they only compare what they are exposed to on television to their own lives, and their lives are often portrayed as less than what they should be
- Television programmes from the Western world communicate the same messages about the beliefs already held by people of the Third World and influence them in the same way.

Cultural imperialism theory posits Western dominance of the rest of the world via mass media contents, especially at the level of international communication. As McQuail (2005: 80) notes: "the media to a large extent serve to constitute our perceptions and definitions of social reality and normality for the purposes of a public, shared social life, and are a key source of standards, models and norms".

The technological superiority of developed countries over developing ones invariably leads to dominance of international broadcasting by the developed countries and a "one-way traffic" of programmes from developed countries to developing countries. As Anaeto et al. (2008: 152) observe: "[t]he media messages from the developed nations come to us with their cultural values. The Western culture now dominates our local cultures because we are consuming their mass media messages".

The tenets of this theory relate to the central theme of this chapter based on the fact that the programmes beamed by the Western media to the developing nations also have global advert contents. The global adverts, often for foreign products, reflect Western culture or the culture of countries that own the satellite broadcast stations (Middle Eastern countries in some cases). The cultural contents of the global adverts influence the audiences in the developing countries of Africa, thereby eroding African cultural values. It is on this theoretical postulation that the following discussion is based.

Global Advertising and Cultural Marketing

Global advertising is a concept that is often used synonymously with international advertising. While this may not be entirely wrong on face value, the concept of global advertising paints a stronger picture of worldwide advertising. An advert that targets more than one country is already international in nature. It becomes *global* when it has worldwide reach. Thus, global advertising is international advertising targeted at a worldwide audience.

Multinational companies are always grappling with how to reach a global audience more effectively through global advertising. These companies have direct investments in many countries and have to decide whether to have different country-specific adverts promoting a global product or a global brand and advert message for several countries. Kotler (2003: 571) captures the challenges faced by firms interested in global advertising and promotion in the following words:

> Multinational companies wrestle with a number of challenges in developing global communication programs: They must decide whether the product is appropriate for a country. They must make sure the market segment they address is both legal and customary. They must decide if the style of the ad is acceptable, and they must decide if ads should be created at headquarters or locally.

Whether the advert is created at headquarters or locally, once it is conveyed through satellite television channels, the audience becomes global, giving rise to the question of what other 'products' are being conveyed to the audience? In other words, what is being 'forced down the throats' of the audience through the casts, slogans, the product itself, the environment of the advert production and so on. This raises the issue of culture and advertising, that is, the marketing of a specific culture through adverts.

Culture has variously been defined as the manifestations of human intellectual achievement regarded collectively, that is, the customs, civilisation and achievements of a particular time or people (Sinclair, cited in Onyeisi 2007: 48); all the material and spiritual characteristics and products of human intelligence acquired from the remote past, in the advancement of humanity (Mbagwu 2007: 64); the patterns of behaviour and thinking that people living in a social group learn, create and share (*Encarta Encyclopedia*: 2006); and the entirety of norms, values, belief systems and life patterns that give a group of people an identity (Nwabueze 2007: 184). In any case, culture cannot be divorced from advertising. Advert messages have a cumulative effect on the culture of the audience, and this runs far deeper than the slogans and images of particular products. Solomon et al. (2010) observe that advertising is an integral part of culture and culture an integral part of advertising. Thus, they argue for the need to understand the norms, beliefs and practices of a culture in order to communicate with the people who inhabit it. They note that many advertising practices relate to a culture's myths and rituals and that, in some cases, advertising creates new myths and rituals. Advertising is intricately connected with the principles of consumption, and many consumers will buy anything that advertisements say is good for them, including culture and values. Consumers exposed to an advert are also exposed to the cultural content of the message, because the advert is embedded in a cultural vehicle. Cultural marketing invariably takes place alongside product marketing.

Cultural marketing consists of the adoption of marketing principles to cause a willingness to identify with a people's culture (Nwabueze 2007). The process is direct when lifestyles or norms are being promoted, as in adverts promoting Fulani clothes, which simply promote the lifestyle of Nigerians, or indirect when the lifestyle being promoted is embedded in a product advert (Nwabueze 2007). For instance, teenagers in India who watch Channel "O" or MTV end up asking their parents for more Westernised clothes and other symbols of American pop culture and values. If, for instance, a multi-national company such as Mercedes-Benz produces a global advert in the home country (Germany), what will be beamed to the world will be an advert waxed in German culture. In this way, German culture is inevitably marketed to the world along with German cars. The audience may not just love the product, but they may also learn to love Germany and desire to visit the country or to identify with German culture.

The United States dominates international broadcasting due to its technological power. As a result, many critics of globalisation argue, the world is gradually being Americanised (Kotler and Armstrong 2007). Such critics point out, for instance, that, in China, most people never drank coffee before Starbucks (an American firm) entered the market. Today Chinese consumers throng Starbucks because it is viewed as a symbol of a new kind of lifestyle. For Americans, this is a positive development; as they market their culture through satellite television advertising, the demand for American products increases.

However, for countries which lack the technological power to operate satellite television networks, global advertising can be considered a threat to their cultural integrity. This is true of the developing countries of Africa which are at the receiving end of these satellite TV channels. Although some African countries have started marking worthwhile inroads into the satellite TV world, the gap is still huge. In Nigeria, for instance, a number of TV channels now operate satellite networks. Among them are Africa Independent Television (AIT) and Nigeria Television Authority (NTA) International. A good number of the adverts aired through these channels are produced in Nigeria and reflect African culture in terms of dress, environment of production and the cultural background upon which the message is conveyed. The satellite TV service provider HiTV has gained popularity in Nigeria and some other African countries because it airs the English Premier League (EPL). A good number of the adverts aired during breaks in the EPL games aired by HiTV sports channels express African cultural values, even though the product might not be manufactured by firms owned by Africans. The point here is that the originator of the advert has the opportunity of marketing his country's culture, and a popular satellite TV service provider in a particular country could be relatively accessible to local firms in that country wishing to advertise their products.

Nevertheless, Western programmes and advertising still dominate satellite television in Africa sphere, and a great many adverts depicting Western lifestyles get beamed to African audiences, thereby eroding the culture of the receiving countries. As critics of globalisation have observed concerning American dominance of the media, "...exposure to American values and products erodes other cultures and Westernizes the world" (Kotler and Armstrong 2004: 604).

Global advertising via satellite TV channels often does not consider the cultural values of the receiving nations, and satellite broadcast channels get into many nations uncensored and undisrupted. The cultural underpinning of an advert message may not be acceptable in a receiving country, yet audiences there are exposed to the message. Product manufacturers only react if they discover that the demand for their product is not improving in a specific country because of the offensive overt or covert cultural content of the advert message. Bologna (2009) gives one such instance when she explains that, in 2003, Mattel Barbie dolls were outlawed in Saudi Arabia because the doll did not conform to the ideals of Islam. An alternative doll named Fulla was designed to be more acceptable to an Islamic market, although the doll was not made by Mattel. A similar scenario played out in Nigeria in 2005, when MTN, a multinational mobile telecommunication company, had to stop airing one of its adverts because of its perceived offensive cultural content. The advert, popularly referred to as "Mama na boy", depicted a man calling his mother in the village to tell her that his wife had just delivered of a baby boy. The entire village then celebrates. This advert met with series of protests, especially from women's interest organisations which argued that it was offensive in a society fighting against the preference for male children. MTN had to redo the advert with the same cast and village environment, but now showing the young man simply telling his mother, "Mama, she don born", and keeping silent on the sex on the child. The original MTN advert was created specifically for the Nigerian market, but, if MTN had made the advert for a global market, it would have been considered offensive in some other countries as well. This further underscores the need for companies engaged in global advertising to always monitor how the adverts they air via satellite channels are perceived in various countries in order not to risk having such adverts affect their products negatively due to offensive cultural content.

Satellite Television and Audience Exposure to Global Advertising

Advertisers prefer to advertise their products in media which have wide reach and large audiences. For a mass medium to enjoy a large audience size, its content should not just be of good quality but should be interesting enough to attract audience attention. People are exposed to global adverts aired on satellite TV channels because of the contents of these channels. They are either attracted to the programme quality or are not satisfied by the local media in their countries. After a study of satellite TV viewers in the southeast geopolitical zone of Nigeria, Nwabueze (2010) found that respondents watched more satellite TV than local TV basically because of the high-quality visual production and creativity of satellite TV programmes. After a study of audiences in Saudi Arabia, Marghalani et al. (1998) found that the 24-hour-per-day availability of a great variety of quality programming was the major motive for satellite TV viewing and that, as a result, audiences there also watched more satellite TV than local TV. After a uses and gratifications study of Egyptian viewers, Abdalla (cited in Zureikat 1999) found that the audience watched satellite TV due to the creativity and high-quality visual production of its programming. Quality programming, therefore, is the main reason people watch satellite TV in preference to local channels, but as the audience watches these programmes, they are also exposed to the adverts aired by these channels, especially those embedded in the programmes they watch.

Some countries have attempted to protect their cultures from being eroded by satellite television. For example, India enacted a law in 1997 forbidding direct transmissions by foreign broadcasters (Zureikat 1999). Other countries have tried to use punitive taxation of reception materials such as satellite dishes, decoders and cable TV subscriptions (Mboho and Nwabueze 2008). What these countries seek to protect their nation from is the cultural invasion by foreign programmes and accompanying adverts. The link between exposure to satellite television channels and the content of these channels is not in doubt. The quality of the channels and their programmes attract viewers to them. The implication for cultural marketing is that adverts originating from the home countries of multinational companies, including the cultural values contained in the adverts, are fed to the receiving nations exposed to the satellite TV channels. Developing countries basically end up at the receiving end of a one-way communication traffic and are constantly faced with the risk of having their cultural values eroded by the foreign culture contained in the satellite TV adverts.

Global Advert Contents: Implications for African Values

A blanket condemnation of global adverts aired on satellite TV would be unrealistic. These adverts, just like other satellite television programmes, also have positive effects which benefit audiences in developing countries. As several scholars have noted (Idemili 1985, cited in Ugande 2007, Okigbo 1996, Okoye 2004), despite the one-way traffic of satellite TV communication from developed to developing world, the developing world still benefits from some of the content of satellite-based media Some of the products advertised on satellite TV, despite their Western cultural context, are useful to African audiencess. These products introduce Africans to better or easier ways of life or better solution to their problems. The products of companies owned by Africans are also advertised by these satellite TV stations.

However, the fact remains that global adverts on satellite TV are contained in cultural packages which, in some cases, influence audiences more than the main product. The adverts often create new cultural perceptions. For example, many grandmothers in small villages in Italy no longer spend each morning visiting local meat, bread and produce markets to gather the ingredients for dinner but now shop at Walmart superstores, according to critics of globalization (Kotler and Armstrong 2004). This is largely due to exposure to programmes and adverts on satellite TV networks. With specific reference to Africa, the negative effect of the cultural contents of global adverts on Africa values is not in doubt. Agber (1994, cited in Ugande 2007) writes that the constant exposure of African peoples to cultural materials from other countries causes them to acquire or imbibe alien tastes and values which are gradually changing African political, economic, social and cultural systems. Similarly, Nzekwe and Mgbemena (1985) argue that the infiltration of a foreign image of life through the mass media can create an alien image that deforms traditional values and is detrimental to the development of national cultures in emerging societies.

Some global adverts openly devalue and ridicule African culture. A typical example is an advert by Land Rover which generated controversy in South Africa, following which a court in that country ruled that the company must issue a public apology in all the publications that carried the advert (Garrett 2001). The advert featured a semi-naked African woman in native dress whose elongated breasts were blown sideways by the tailwind of the vehicle being advertised. This image appeared next to the caption: "The new more powerful Freelander." The company admitted that the advert was a serious error in judgment and dropped the agency that produced it. South Africa's advertising watchdog, the Advertising Standards Authority (ASA), described the advert as irresponsible and exploitative and found that it constituted racial stereotyping, violated human dignity and was an insensitive portrayal of a woman that mocked African culture (Garrett 2001). Although this advert ran in magazines, the incident illustrates how some global adverts can be insensitive to African cultural values. At the same time, it also shows that product manufacturers can suffer harsh repercussions for such harmful adverts.

However, the Land Rover advert was an extreme negative case. Most global adverts aired on satellite TV may not seem harmful at face value, but a close look may reveal cultural contents capable of eroding African culture. Culture is expressed through dress, lifestyle, food and many other phenomena. Adverts on satellite TV, in most cases, do not reflect typical African culture. They reflect Western culture, especially in dress and the environment of the advert. Of course, Western dress codes (both casual and corporate) are gradually becoming dominant in Africa today. Although there are other reasons responsible for this trend, global adverts on satellite and local TV are capable of contributing. Thompson (2005) argues that values, folkways, mores, customs and the attitudes of family members and society must always be the basis for clothing choice. She further notes that most families and societies have values and beliefs that regulate the degree of body exposure that is permissible in public. When a female American pop star endorses a product for women, African women may not just be influenced by the product but other cultural inputs in the advert, including the pop star's style of dress.

Most often, Africans or Africa-themed images are featured on satellite TV channels only in public service advertising themes on issues such as polio eradication, the fight against malaria, poor water conditions, poverty eradication and so on. Admittedly, these adverts are in the interest of Africans, but more positive aspects of African life hardly find their way into these media. Some African countries, however, buy airtime on satellite TV channels to advertise the sights and sounds of their countries, and some HiTV channels feature adverts that reflect African culture in terms of dress, lifestyle and setting. This should be an eye-opener for other broadcasters in Africa, indicating that African ownership of more satellite

TV channels could be a means of countering the current one-way traffic of satellite TV communication.

Conclusion

The strong link between satellite broadcasting and exposure to global advertising among viewers in developing countries is clear. Various empirical studies also established a higher exposure to satellite television than local television by viewers in Africa. This means that audiences are highly exposed to the global adverts embedded in the satellite television programmes they watch. Satellite television channels owned by the West contain a great deal of Western-oriented adverts contained in cultural packages that are also Western oriented. A strong link also exists between advertising and culture. Advertising cannot be divorced from culture. Solomon et al. (2010) show that we cannot understand advertising unless we consider its cultural content. They further note that culture is the lens through which consumers make sense of marketing communications. Global advertising is a channel for marketing a people's culture. This could be a positive or negative development, depending on who is the initiator of the advert and who is at the receiving end. The initiator of the advert markets his country's culture, while the receivers of the message, particularly audiences in developing countries in Africa, are at risk of cultural erosion through exposure to global adverts on satellite television.

What can be done by nations at the receiving end who are at risk of this cultural erosion? The way forward must begin by challenging advertisers and advertising agencies in Africa, along with advertising regulatory bodies and governments in various African countries, to take steps towards counter-cultural marketing via satellite television advertising. Developing countries must strive to provide alternatives for audiences in their countries. Empirical evidence has established that quality programming and availability of 24-hour choice are behind the high exposure to satellite television by audiences in developing countries. If alternative African channels can provide programmes of such quality as the ones aired by Western satellite television channels, audiences will watch them. South Africa, Egypt, some Middle Eastern countries and India are following this path by operating home-grown satellite television channels which can compete with those of the West in terms of quality and variety. A good number of adverts aired by some of these television channels reflect the culture of the countries where the stations are based. Middle Eastern-based channels such as Aljazeera and Show Sports are typical examples. Egypt and Saudi Arabia also own satellite television channels. Nigeria has made an inroad in this area with television stations such as AIT, Channels, NTA International and others, including satellite television service providers such as Daar Sat and HiTV which are owned and managed by Nigerians. The advantage of this development is that it provides relatively cheaper access to home-made products and also encourages multi-national companies to adapt adverts to the cultural values of African audiences.

The strategy adopted by the South African advert watchdog ASA, which entails monitoring of adverts to ensure their content is not detrimental to local cultures, should be considered in Nigeria and other developing countries. This is in view of the fact that censoring or disrupting satellite television operations is no longer realistic in this technological age. Global adverts on satellite television channels should be monitored and, if found harmful to local culture, the company whose product is advertised should be sanctioned. Adapting global adverts to local cultures will help salvage the situation. This entails the creation of adverts to reflect the culture of specific countries or regions, as is done by Coca-Cola, MTN, Toyota and some other multinational companies. The Advertising Practitioners' Council of Nigeria (APCON), the advert watchdog in Nigeria, should organise workshops and seminars for advertising practitioners to raise the consciousness of these stakeholders on the implications of the cultural contents of global adverts for Nigerian cultural values. This will encourage the production of global adverts on local products which reflect African values or the adaptation of multinational companies' products to local adverts reflecting Nigerian culture, which can be aired on satellite television channels owned or run by Nigerians. This is because access to such channels will be cheaper than access to satellite television channels owned and dominated by Europe and North America networks.

Encouraging more local stations in Nigeria to run satellite networks could help in cultural marketing through local programming. Such encouragement will require the federal government to create the enabling environment for more broadcast media houses to commence satellite broadcasting, as was successfully done in India. The Indian government developed policies aimed at liberalising the broadcast sector and winning back the audiences the country was losing to foreign satellite television channels by ensuring unregulated cable television, the introduction of satellite television services such as STAR TV and Zee TV, the use of the legal and institutional power by the state to obtain the rights for programming capable of attracting large audiences and advertising, the easing of restrictions on the operations of private broadcasters by allowing them to own and operate commercial satellite systems, enabling them to uplink directly from India using Indian or foreign satellite (provided they meet certain criteria) and allowing foreign direct investment in the media sector, among others (Chadha and Kavoori 2005).

Encouraging home-grown satellite television channels could lead to international marketing of local cultures through programming while also providing relatively cheap access to global advertising of local products packaged in local cultures to an international audience. Researchers and scholars in developing nations should consider research studies to establish the extent to which exposure to global adverts on satellite television channels influences African cultural values. This will provide empirical data to put future discussions in a better prospective.

References

Anaeto, S. G., Onabajo, O. S., and J.B. Osifeso. 2008. *Models and Theories of Communication*. Maryland: African Renaissance Books.

Arens, W.F. and C.L. Bovee. 1994. *Contemporary Advertising*. Fifth Edition. Burr Ridge: Richard D. Irwin.

Baran, S. 2004. *Introduction to mass communication: Media literacy and culture*. Third Edition. Boston : McGraw-Hill

Bologna, S. 2009. Cross-cultural advertising. www.wintranslation.com/newsletters (retrieved 01/04/2010).

Chadha, K. and A. Kavoori. 2005. Globalization and national media systems: mapping interactions in policies, markets and formats. In J. Curran and M. Gurevitch, eds. *Mass Media and Society*. Fourth Ed. London: Hodder, pp. 84–103.

Garrett, J. 2001. Land Rover ordered to apologize for mocking African culture. *The Independent*, 11/04. www.independent .co.uk/news/media (retrieved 12-4-2010).

Kotler, P. 2003. *Marketing Management*. Eleventh Ed. New Delhi: Pearson.

Kolter, P. and G. Armstrong. 2004. *Principles of Marketing*. New Delhi: Pearson.

Marghalani, K., Palmgreen, P. and Boyd, D. 1998. The utilization of direct satellite broadcasting (DBS) in Saudi Arabia. *Journal of Broadcasting & Electronic Media* 42.

McQuail, D. 2005. *McQuail's Mass Communication Theory*. Fifth Edition. London: Sage.

Mbagwu, F.C. 2007. The relevance of traditional values and beliefs as components of culture. http://www/wsn.edu/gened/learn-modules (retrieved 25/10/09).

Mboho, M and C. Nwabueze. 2008. International media contents: Implications for the audience and the creative capacity of broadcast stations in developing nations. *Journal of Media and Communication* 1 (1) April: 70–78.

Nwabueze, C. 2007. Cultural marketing in a globalized society: Critical role of broadcasting. *Journal of Nigerian languages and Culture* 1: 184–91.

Nwabueze, C. 2010. Satellite TV broadcasting and local media use among viewers in the south east geopolitical zone. Unpublished PhD thesis. University of Uyo, Nigeria.

Nzekwu, O. and Mgbemena, N. 1985. Africa and the New Information Order: A Nigerian Perspective. In: Nwuneli, O.E. (Ed.), *Mass Communication in Nigeria: A Book of Reading*. Enugu: Fourth Dimension Publishers, pp. 60–72.

Okigbo C. 1996. International information flow and the challenge of the twenty-first century. In L.U. Uka, ed). *North-South Information Culture: Trends in Global Communications and Research Paradigms*. Ikeja: Longman, 284–300.

Okoye, I. 2004. Needs gratification versus knowledge gaps: A comparative study of the uses of satellite and local TV. *International Journal of Communication* 1: 70–100.

Onyeisi, E.M. 2007. Cultural mobilization through drama. *Journal of Nigerian Languages and Culture* 9 (1): 48–50.

Rahman, H. 1998. Uses and gratifications of satellite TV in Egypt. http://www.tbsjournal.com (retrieved 23/01/2008).

Solomon, M.R., Cornell, L.D. and A. Nizan. 2010. Culture globalization and advertising. www.flatworldknowledge.com. (retrieved 10/04/2010).

Thompson, D. 2005. The Contemporary Nigerian woman's dress: From aesthetics to survival. *Journal of Home Economics Research* 6 (1): 35–39.

Ugande, G. 2007. Direct broadcast satellite and developing nations: Threats and opportunities. In I.E. Nwosu and E.O. Soola, eds. *Communication in Global ICTs and Ecosystem Perspectives: Insights from Nigeria*. Enugu: African Council for Communication Education (Nigeria chapter) and Precision Publishers, 245–58.

Zureikat, D. 1999. Satellite broadcasting in the Middle East and North Africa: Regulations, access and impact. http://www.tbsjournal.com/article (retrieved 15/12/2007).

CHAPTER 16

INTERNET USAGE AND THE IMPERATIVE OF ONLINE ADVERTISING IN AFRICA

OLUSEYI SOREMEKUN

Introduction

Communication media have developed enormously through the ages, with significant changes in structure, architecture and uses, especially in the recent past. Emerging technologies have driven most of the changes, with the modern period communication age arguably traceable to the invention of printing from movable type by Johannes Gutenberg about 1448. This singular invention gave rise to posters, handbills, printed books and, ultimately, the newspaper as media of mass communication. After this came radio and film in the early years of the last century and television, which got going in the United States in the late 1920s but did not reach the African continent until 1959, when the Western Nigeria Television (WNTV) network was established in Ibadan. Until the 1990s, the major media of communication and, by implication, of advertising remained newspapers, radio, film and television, which came to be grouped together as the "mass media".

Since then, developments in the information and communication technology (ICT) sector have massively reshaped the media landscape. The advent of the internet and other computer mediated communication (CMC) systems has provided a huge new platform for advertising. The beginning of internet advertising has been traced to the invention of the World Wide Web by Tim Berners-Lee in 1989 while working with CERN, the European Particle Physics Laboratory. However, the first set of ads on the internet did not appear until October 1994, when the HotWired site launched with ads from Volvo, AT&T and Sprint, among others.

What Is Internet Advertising?

There have been many attempts to define internet advertising. However, not all the definitions have been definitions in the true sense of the word. Some are mere explanations or examples of what internet advertising entails. For instance, web1marketing.com sees internet advertising as various specific internet advertising methods such as banner ads, search engine advertising and email marketing. According to businessdictionary.com, internet advertising is the use of the internet as an advertising medium through promotional messages which appear on a computer screen. This definition limits internet advertising to the computer, whereas there has been an increasing convergence of platforms and technologies which now makes it possible for internet adverts to be delivered to mobile phones, tablets (such as the iPad) and other devices. Pcmag.com defines internet advertising more comprehensively as "[d]elivering ads to internet users via Web sites, e-mail, ad-supported software, text messaging and internet-enabled cellphones".

Thus, internet advertising, otherwise known as online advertising, is the delivery of marketing communication messages through the internet or the World Wide Web to a prospective customer who is online at the time of delivery. In other words, it is the dissemination of messages through the internet by enabling direct consumer interaction with the advertisement to trigger seller-buyer transactions. As this implies, one of the major attractions of internet advertising is the opportunity of online interactivity between prospective buyers and advertisers. For example, a prospective buyer can click on the ad for further information concerning the product or service and be led to purchase in the same online session.

Types of Internet Advertising

Sudharsan (2010) classifies internet advertising under two categories: target advertising and behavioural advertising. Target advertising (or static advertising consists of ads linked to the content or key words of a particular web page. Wikipedia (2011) refers to this form of online advertising as "semantic advertising" because it applies semantic analysis to web pages.

> The process is meant to accurately interpret and classify the meaning and/or main subject of the page and then populate it with targeted advertising spots. By closely linking content to advertising, it is assumed that the viewer will be more likely to show an interest in the advertised product or service.

For instance, a webpage concerned with travel and tours will have ads on selected destinations, accommodation and associated services. Such ads are called target advertising because the ad is seen by the target audience. To see this in practice, go to Google and enter any keywords or subject you like. Google will then give you its search engine results for your keywords, but, on the right-hand side of the page, there will be ads for products and services related to your search strong.

Behavioural advertising (or dynamic advertising) is a recent improvement by Google. This method is called 'dynamic' because the ads can change from user to user (Sudharsan 2010). According to Wikipedia, the method is also known as "behavioural targeting" because it is based on a user's online behaviour. For instance, if you are interested in gardening and you often search Google for tips on gardening, Google stores your interest and, whenever you browse the internet, ads on gardening will be delivered to you wherever you are on the internet. Your online behaviour (based on your interests) determines the advertisements you see rather than the keywords of the webpages you visit.

Other cross-cutting types of internet advertising include email advertising, which sends advertising messages through bulk email delivery. It is also known as opt-in email advertising to differentiate it from unsolicited email (known as spam or junk), which is not legitimate. Affiliate marketing is a type of online advertising in which advertising campaigns are run with a number of publishers, who get paid based on the traffic attracted. In most cases, payment is also based on the number of forms, sign-ups or, better still, online sales. Pop-up advertising uses a new window which opens in front of the current one, displaying an advertisement or an entire webpage. Pop-under advertising is similar, except that the new window is loaded or sent behind the current window, so that the user does not see it until they close one or more active windows. Video ads are similar to banner ads, except that, instead of a static or animated image, moving video clips are displayed. This is the kind of advertising most prominent on television, and many advertisers will use the clips for both television and online spots. Finally, mobile ads are SMS text or multi-media messages sent to a cell phone.

Advantages of Internet Advertising

Internet advertising, recent as it is, has some advantages over 'traditional' mass-media advertising which make it attractive to advertisers and advertising agencies. First, it enables a high degree of precision targeting. It provides an opportunity to target an audience very precisely with messages that are customised to their specific interests. This implies that only those who are meant to see the advertisement will see it, while users outside the primary target audience will not see the message. In most cases, such ads are run based on search engine results. internet advertising also has an advantage in terms of frequency. internet ads can be delivered at any time of the day, 24 hours a day, 7 days a week and 31 days a month. They are also highly flexible and interactive. For instance, a prospective customer can interact with the product, test it, buy it and leave a comment, all in a single online session. internet advertising also provides a platform to monitor the interactions of prospective customers with products online. From careful tracking of interactive consumer behaviour, information is gathered so that adjustments and improvement can be made in product message presentation and offerings. Similarly, internet advertising provides real-time statistics. By reviewing click-through data, advertisers can see, at any time, how many people have seen the ad and how many times the ad has been viewed by prospects.

Above all, internet advertising appears to be effective. For example, in a 2007 study, ehow.com found that consumers who browse online for products spend up to 41 percent more when they come to the store. In addition, 61 percent of the people who follow up on their online query offline actually make purchases.

At the same time, an internet ad campaign is less expensive than conventional media advertising. For instance, in pay-per-click internet advertising, an advertiser only pays when somebody clicks on the ad display. This means that one is not paying for TV commercial spots and press ad insertions which are not seen and radio spots which are not heard. According to IB Serve (2008), internet ad packages are offered for as little as US$10 for a period of one month, or by a set amount of 'hits', depending on the advertiser you go with. internet ads can also be updated more or less instantly, unlike TV, radio and print ads, and have the further advantage of immediacy of publishing (posting) information without limitations of time and geography.

Disadvantages of Internet Advertising

Difficulty in attracting customers is the main disadvantage of internet advertising. According to Lendor (2005), "[s]mall business may not have the resources to pay for paid directory inclusion [or] pay per click inclusions and often have to rely solely on search engine optimisation or word-of-mouth to drive traffic to their sites". Moreover, as promising as internet advertising is in so many ways, its scope, in terms of market, is still limited. That is, internet advertising cannot be relied upon to deliver the market. internet advertising, therefore, needs to be used as one part of the media mix in order to conquer the market.

Internet Usage and the Imperative of Online Advertising

Over the past decade, the internet has expanded so much in usage that it is now associated with a myriad of different activities by different people. While some people see it as just a way of browsing cyberspace for social interaction, others see it as a vital platform for business transactions. From whatever angle one looks at it, the fact remains that there are many media tools that are internet-driven. Known collectively as the new media, these tools include blogs, e-zines, online chats and forums, social networking sites (Facebook, Myspace etc.), podcasts, spiral e-mail, short messaging service (SMS), multi-media messaging service (MMS) and others. Soremekun (2011) captures this variety graphically in Figure 16.1, which shows that the internet is propelled by information and communication technology, while the internet itself drives the new media tools. The new

Figure 16.1: The New Media Concept and the Society

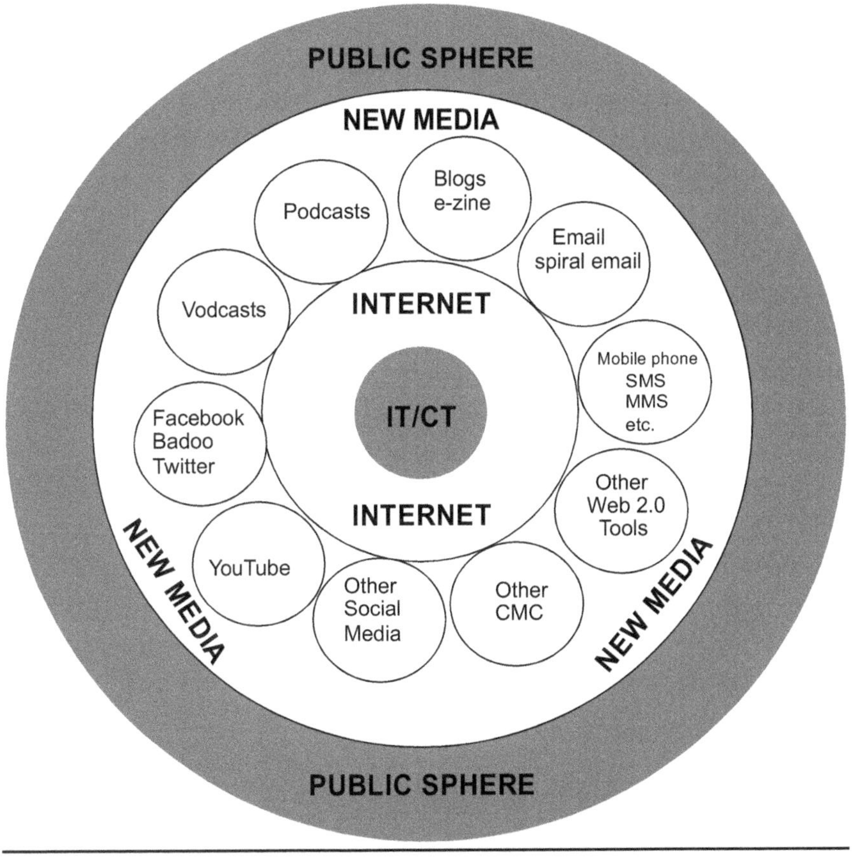

Source: Soremekun (2011)

media derive their existence from the internet and, therefore, cannot function without it. Accordingly, the internet is at the inner core of the new media tools:

> The new media tools have become more attractive in appeal, widespread in usage, vibrant in outlook and with great tendency to trigger addiction amongst users. The tools, especially the internet as exemplified by e-mails and social networking sites and the mobile phones are growing rapidly which emphasises their relevance in modern communication (Soremekun 2011: 2).

According to internetworldstats.com, as of September 30, 2009, approximately 1.7 billion people were internet users out of the 6.7 billion global population. From 2000 to 2009, internet usage in Africa grew by 1,392.4 percent compared to 297.8 percent in Europe, 134 percent in North America and 545.9 percent in Asia. Global average growth was 380.3 percent. Table 16.1 shows that, by June, 2010, over 1.9 billion people were internet users across the globe, a penetration of 28.7 percent of the global population. The global growth from 2000 (360,985,492 users) to 2010 (1,966,514,816 users) was a tremendous 444.8 percent.

A closer look at Table 16.1 also shows that Africa had the highest percentage of growth between 2000 and 2010. In December 2000, there were 4,514,400 internet users in Africa, and, in June 2010, there were 110,931,700 (10.9 percent of the population), a growth rate of 2,357.3 percent. These figures place Africa number five in total number of internet users after Asia (825,094,396), Europe (475,069,448), North America (266,224,500) and Latin America/Caribbean (204,689,836) and last in terms of internet penetration. As can be seen from Table 16.2 below, the 47 African countries have 74,368,500 users, representing 67% of the total users on the continent.

Table 16.2 also shows that Nigeria takes the lead in sub-Saharan Africa in internet usage. As of June 30, 2010, it had by far the highest number of internet users (43,982,200), representing 28.9 percent of her population (estimated at 152,217,341 in 2010). However, this penetration rate is only the sixth-highest in Africa, showing that Nigeria is a growing market for internet usage. internet users in Nigeria grew from a mere 200,000 users in 2000 to 43,982,200 users in 2010, a growth of 21,891.1 percent, the fourth fastest growth rate on the continent. Nearly forty percent of all internet users in sub-Saharan Africa are in Nigeria.

Table 16.1: World Internet Usage and Population Statistics

World Regions	Population (2010 Est.)	Internet Users Dec. 31, 2000	Internet Users Latest Data	Penetration (% Population)	Growth 2000-2010	Users % of Table
Africa	1,013,779,050	4,514,400	110,931,700	10.9 %	2,357.3 %	5.6 %
Asia	3,834,792,852	114,304,000	825,094,396	21.5 %	621.8 %	42.0 %
Europe	813,319,511	105,096,093	475,069,448	58.4 %	352.0 %	24.2 %
Middle East	212,336,924	3,284,800	63,240,946	29.8 %	1,825.3 %	3.2 %
North America	344,124,450	108,096,800	266,224,500	77.4 %	146.3 %	13.5 %
Latin America/Caribbean	592,556,972	18,068,919	204,689,836	34.5 %	1,032.8 %	10.4 %
Oceania / Australia	34,700,201	7,620,480	21,263,990	61.3 %	179.0 %	1.1 %
Total	6,845,609,960	360,985,492	1,966,514,816	28.7 %	444.8 %	100.0 %

Source: internetworldstats.com. Note: *Africa Internet Statistics* were updated for June 30, 2010.

Table 16.2: Internet Usage Statistics for Africa

Africa	Population (2010 Est.)	Internet Users Dec. 2000	Internet Users Latest Data '000	Penetration (% Population)	User Growth (2000–2010) %	% Users in Africa
Algeria	34,586,184	50,000	4,700,000	13.6	9,300.0	4.3
Angola	13,068,161	30,000	607,400	4.6	1,924.7	0.5
Benin	9,056,010	15,000	200,000	2.2	1,233.3	0.2
Botswana	2,029,307	15,000	120,000	5.9	700.0	0.1
Burkina Faso	16,241,811	10,000	178,200	1.1	1,682.0	0.2
Burundi	9,863,117	3,000	65,000	0.7	2,066.7	0.1
Cameroon	19,294,149	20,000	750,000	3.9	3,650.0	0.7
Cape Verde	508,659	8,000	150,000	29.5	1,775.0	0.1
Central African Rep.	4,844,927	1,500	22,600	0.5	1,406.7	0.0
Chad	10,543,464	1,000	187,800	1.8	18,680.0	0.2
Comoros	773,407	1,500	24,300	3.1	1,520.0	0.0
Congo	4,125,916	500	245,200	5.9	48,940.0	0.2
Congo, Dem. Rep.	70,916,439	500	365,000	0.5	72,900.0	0.3
Cote d'Ivoire	21,058,798	40,000	968,000	4.6	2,320.0	0.9
Djibouti	740,528	1,400	25,900	3.5	1,750.0	0.0
Egypt	80,471,869	450,000	17,060,000	21.2	3,691.1	15.4
Equatorial Guinea	650,702	500	14,400	2.2	2,780.0	0.0
Eritrea	5,792,984	5,000	250,000	4.3	4,900.0	0.2
Ethiopia	88,013,491	10,000	445,400	0.5	4,354.0	0.4
Gabon	1,545,255	15,000	98,800	6.4	558.7	0.1
Gambia	1,824,158	4,000	130,100	7.1	3,152.5	0.1

Table 16.2: Internet Usage Statistics for Africa

Africa	Population (2010 Est.)	Internet Users Dec. 2000	Internet Users Latest Data '000	Penetration (% Population)	User Growth (2000–2010) %	% Users in Africa
Ghana	24,339,838	30,000	1,297,000	5.3	4,223.3	1.2
Guinea	10,324,025	8,000	95,000	0.9	1,087.5	0.1
Guinea-Bissau	1,565,126	1,500	37,100	2.4	2,373.3	0.0
Kenya	40,046,566	200,000	3,995,500	10.0	1,897.8	3.6
Lesotho	1,919,552	4,000	76,800	4.0	1,820.0	0.1
Liberia	3,685,076	500	20,000	0.5	3,900.0	0.0
Libya	6,461,454	10,000	353,900	5.5	3,439.0	0.3
Madagascar	21,281,844	30,000	320,000	1.5	966.7	0.3
Malawi	15,447,500	15,000	716,400	4.6	4,676.0	0.6
Mali	13,796,354	18,800	250,000	1.8	1,229.8	0.2
Mauritania	3,205,060	5,000	75,000	2.3	1,400.0	0.1
Mauritius	1,294,104	87,000	290,000	22.4	233.3	0.3
Mayotte (FR)	231,139	---	---	---	---	0.0
Morocco	31,627,428	100,000	10,442,500	33.0	10,342.5	9.4
Mozambique	22,061,451	30,000	612,500	2.8	1,941.7	0.6
Namibia	2,128,471	30,000	127,500	6.0	325.0	0.1
Niger	15,878,271	5,000	115,900	0.7	2,218.0	0.1
Nigeria	152,217,341	200,000	43,982,200	28.9	21,891.1	39.6
Reunion (FR)	822,986	130,000	300,000	36.5	130.8	0.3
Rwanda	11,055,976	5,000	450,000	4.1	8,900.0	0.4
Saint Helena (UK)	7,670	n/a	800	10.4	n/a	0.0
Sao Tomé e Principe	175,808	6,500	26,700	15.2	310.8	0.0

Table 16.2: Internet Usage Statistics for Africa (Contd.)

Africa	Population (2010 Est.)	Internet Users Dec. 2000	Internet Users Latest Data '000	Penetration (% Population)	User Growth (2000–2010) (%)	% Users in Africa
Senegal	14,086,103	40,000	923,000	6.6	2,207.5	0.8
Seychelles	88,340	6,000	33,900	38.4	465.0	0.0
Sierra Leone	5,245,695	5,000	14,900	0.3	198.0	0.0
Somalia	10,112,453	200	106,000	1.0	52,900.0	0.1
South Africa	49,109,107	2,400,000	5,300,000	10.8	120.8	4.8
Sudan	41,980,182	30,000	4,200,000	10.0	13,900.0	3.8
Swaziland	1,354,051	10,000	90,000	6.6	800.0	0.1
Tanzania	41,892,895	115,000	676,000	1.6	487.8	0.6
Togo	6,199,841	100,000	356,300	5.7	256.3	0.3
Tunisia	10,589,025	100,000	3,600,000	34.0	3,500.0	3.2
Uganda	33,398,682	40,000	3,200,000	9.6	7,900.0	2.9
Western Sahara	491,519	---	---	---	---	0.0
Zambia	12,056,923	20,000	816,700	6.8	3,983.5	0.7
Zimbabwe	11,651,858	50,000	1,422,000	12.2	2,744.0	1.3
TOTAL AFRICA	1,013,779,050	4,514,400	110,931,700	10.9	2,357.3	100.0

Source:: internetworldstats.com

Note: Africa internet Statistics were updated for June 30, 2010.

Table 16.3: The Top Fifteen African Countries in Internet Usage

	Countries	Population (2010 Est.)	internet Users (Dec 2000)	internet Users (June 2010)
1	Nigeria	152,217,341	200,000	43,982,200
2	Egypt*	80,471,869	450,000	17,060,000
3	Morocco*	31,627,428	100,000	10,442,500
4	South Africa	49,109,107	2,400,000	5,300,000
5	Algeria*	34,586,184	50,000	4,700,000
6	Sudan	41,980,182	30,000	4,200,000
7	Kenya	40,046,566	200,000	3,995,500
8	Tunisia*	10,589,025	100,000	3,600,000
9	Uganda	33,398,682	40,000	3,200,000
10	Zimbabwe	11,651,858	50,000	1,422,000
11	Ghana	24,339,838	30,000	1,297,000
12	Cote d'Ivoire	21,058,798	40,000	968,000
13	Senegal	14,086,103	40,000	923,000
14	Zambia	12,056,923	20,000	816,700
15	Cameroon	19,294,149	20,000	750,000

* Not in sub-Saharan Africa

Table 16.3 shows that eleven countries in the sub-Saharan region are among the continent's top fifteen internet users. Eight are in the top ten. Of the fifteen countries above, the West African coast contributes five (Nigeria, Ghana, Cote d' Ivoire, Senegal and Cameroon). As regards internet penetration, sub-Saharan Africa performs averagely, with five countries in the top ten. The sub-region makes a particularly strong showing in the users' growth index, as shown in Table 16.4. However, of the eight sub-Saharan African countries in the top ten, only Nigeria belongs to West Africa. Central and eastern African countries are the top performers in the growth sector.

From the foregoing statistical presentation, it is obvious that the internet has not only come to stay in Africa but will become a dominant medium in the near future. This implies that, as a medium of mass communication, the internet cannot be overlooked in advertising campaign planning. Already the internet has displaced the magazine as an advertising medium in Nigeria. According to AMPS (2009) TV in Nigeria has a penetration of 79.9 percent of the adult population radio 82.6 percent, out-of-home 66.9 percent, newspapers 27.4 percent, the internet 22.1 precent and magazines only 21.0 percent. According to the International

Data Corporation (IDC): "Worldwide spending on internet advertising will total $65.2 billion in 2008, or nearly 10 percent of all ad spend across all media, and grow 15–20 percent a year to reach $106.6 billion in 2011, or 13.6 percent of total ad spend" (MC 2008).

Table 16.4: The Top Ten African Countries in Internet User Growth

	Countries	Internet Users (Dec/2000)	Internet Users (June 2010)	User Growth (2000–2010)
1	DRCongo	500	365,000	72,900%
2	Somalia	200	106,000	52,900.0
3	Congo	500	245,200	48,940.0%
4	Nigeria	200,000	43,982,200	21,891.1%
5	Chad	1,000	187,800	18,680%
6	Sudan	30,000	4,200,000	13,900.0%
7	Morocco*	100,000	10,442,500	10,342.5
8	Algeria*	50,000	4,700,000	9,300.0%
9	Rwanda	5,000	450,000	8,900.0%
10	Uganda	40,000	3,200,000	7,900.0%

* Not in sub-Saharan Africa

This forecast also predicts that the United States will lead the world in both total advertising spend and online ad spend throughout the forecast period, with expenditures in 2011of more than $265 billion and US$45 billion respectively. Thus, as Karsten Weide, programme director, Digital Media and Entertainment (cited in MC 2008), observes: "Marketers already recognize that online advertising must be incorporated into any comprehensive ad strategy. This will continue to drive growth in online ad spending well beyond the forecast period".

Quoting the Internet Advertising Bureau, Reuters reports that social media, video and mobile advertising pushed British online ad spending above 4 billion pounds ($6.4 billion) for the first time in 2010, an increase of 12.8 percent. Until recently, advertisers rarely used online advertising to build their brands, preferring television or poster campaigns, while the internet was considered best suited for paid search such as Google's sponsored results.

However, the rise of social media is helping to change that perception, as users spend more time on single sites like Facebook and less time searching.

Tim Weber (2010), the Business editor, BBC News website, reports that the Canadian folk singer, Dave Carroll's "United Breaks Guitars" video has been watched 9.23 million times. According to the report, United Airlines baggage handlers damaged his US$3,500 guitar, but the airline refused to pay compensation, and its customer service agents were less than courteous. After nine months of complaining, he had had enough and made a music video about the experience. On July 6, 2009, Carroll posted the video on YouTube. Within three days, it had been watched half a million times. By mid-August it had reached five million views, and United had a massive public relations crisis on its hands, not least because thousands of other unhappy customers were now coming forward to vent their own frustrations. The episode dramatically showed the new power of the internet.

As rapid as it has been, the growth of internet users in Nigeria still falls below that of mobile phones subscribers. The Nigerian Communications Commission (NCC) reports that the country continues to be one of the fastest growing markets in Africa, with triple-digit growth rates almost every single year since 2001. Nigeria overtook Egypt and Morocco in 2004 to become Africa's second largest mobile market after South Africa. Statistics from NCC show that, in 2007, mobile phone subscribers in Nigeria already totalled 40,395,611, but, by April 2010, the figure increased to 77,395,332, a 91.5 percent increase in only three years. In view of this huge subscribers' base in Nigeria, many platforms with convergent technologies (i.e. internet and telecommunication) have been set up to attract and engage users. Interface between mobile phones and the internet has been strengthened to quicken activities across media and tools. This has been found attractive by advertisers and advertising agencies. It was, therefore, not surprising when, in April 2011, political campaigns in Nigeria were taken to internet and mobile platforms. The internet, especially through new media tools such as Facebook, enjoyed lots of political online advertising.

Pavlik (2001) observes that an increasing number of political candidates and other individuals and organisations with political objectives are using the internet increasingly effectively to reach the public, without the filter of a traditional news media gatekeeper. Nigeria's 'Thisday' newspaper (September 15, 2010) reports that a Presidential aspirant of the Nigerian ruling party, former Vice President Alhaji Abubakar Atiku attracted over 2000 hits in less than 24 hours when he launched his campaign website (www.atiku.org) on September 13, 2010. Former military ruler Ibrahim Babangida has a website providing links to his Facebook and Twitter accounts and allowing BlackBerry users to scan a barcode for updates on his campaign progress. His Facebook page has just over 10,000 fans, compared to more than 195,000 for President Jonathan (Reuters September 2010). After the party primaries in Nigeria, the romance with online political advertising continued. All six visible presidential candidates for the April 2011 elections were on Facebook advertising their programmes and persons. As of April 4, 2011, President Jonathan's (PDP) Facebook page had 521,236 followers/likes.

Mallam Nuhu Ribadu (ACN) had 172,640 likes, Prof Pat Utomi (SDMP) recorded 148,585 followers/likes, General Muhammadu Buhari (CPC) had 14,803 likes, Mallam Ibrahim Shekarau (ANPP) recorded 868 likes and Dele Momodu (NCP) had 454 likes. Goodluck Jonathan followed up on his new media strategy with a bulk SMS to mobile phone subscribers in Nigeria saying "We are on the road to rebuild our nation. Stand with me, Stand for transformation".

Online Ads in Selected African Newspapers[1]

The foregoing discussion has established the fact that sub-Saharan Africa is abreast of the usage and growth of internet in the world. It is, therefore, germane at this point to examine selected online newspapers in several countries in the region with a viewing to determining if they run online ads. Where they do, the ads are analysed based on creativity and layout.

Uganda : Uganda's The Independent, in its online edition of May 22, 2011, has an ad for "Radio Flash 89.2 FM" (Figure 16.2a) on its home page. The ad is a classic example of contrast as a layout principle. A processed blue and red on a solid black background cannot be missed by anybody. The ad is strong and impactful. The layout, the choice of fonts and the arrangement of copy allow for easy reading. The payoff, "The best mix of music" is creatively simple and crisp.

Senegal: Senegal's online *Kepaar News* carries an ad for Kepaar Radio on its home page. The ad (shown in Figure 16.2b) is outstanding in layout and creativity. The creative treatment of the brand logo and the payoff woven around the base of the microphone stand is refreshing, especially as the elements creatively float in space against a gradual background fade in magenta.

South Africa: The Independent Online (IOL) newspaper has quite a number of online ads on its homepage under its business directory section. Two are particularly interesting, the Laptop City and Excalibur ads reproduced in Figures 16.2c and 16.2d. The Laptop City ad is very weak in terms of visibility, impact and contrast. A grey and light blue over a white background cannot attract attention. There is just no contrast at all. However, it makes up for this deficiency with highly legible fonts. In addition, the creative treatment of the graphics is above average. The dot on the "I" of "city" is a globe held by the leg of the first "P" in "Laptop" and the "I" in "city". Besides, the message is straightforward. The second ad, "Excalibur", is good in terms of layout and copy. It employs the method of arranging the elements of the design around the mathematical centre of the page to achieve balance, as against the optical centre method. There is also good contrast in the ad. The sword and the copy are in harmony. The position

Figure 16.2: Selected Online Advertisements

Figure 16.2a

Figure 16.2b

Figure 16.2c

Figure 16.2d

of the sword also serves to underline the brand name "Excalibur". The copy is short and sharp.

Nigeria: Figure 16.2e is an ad on the Facebook page of one of Nigeria's Telecom Operators, Glo. The ad, headlined, 'Biiig Five Promo: Get Five times credit on every recharge instantly' looks attractive with two-third of the space occupied by a human element. The facial expression of the female model conveys the

Figure 16.2: Selected Online Advertisements (Contd.)

Figure 16.2e

Figure 16.2f

Figure 16.2g

expected excitement seemingly derivable from getting five times credit on every recharge. However, her demonstration of the 'five times' claim is at variance with her gesticulation (spreading ten fingers instead of five). The body language of the model contradicts the message. Her overt display of ten fingers seems confusing, perhaps deceitful.

Ghana: *The Mail* is one of the leading newspapers in Ghana. On its May 22, 2011 homepage is an ad for Rocket Mobile Broadband, a product of Multilinks Telkom.

The ad (see Figure 16.2f) is a good example of an informal layout method. That is, the elements are seemingly arranged on the page without any particular pattern. There is nothing wrong with this method as long as it is reader friendly.

The use of the product pack shot to support the copy induces audience interest and enhances understanding of the message. The key proposition of the ad is the fast speed of the product. In other words, the product benefit on offer, according to the ad, is speed. This benefit is creatively illustrated through creation of speed effects around the letter "O" in "Rocket". In all, the ad is above average.

Liberia: 'The Informer Online', an online newspaper features a banner ad of 'Comium' in its July 7, 2013 edition (See Figure 16.2g). The ad which takes a vantage position above the masthead, is headlined, 'When you smile the whole world smiles'. This copy is illustrated by seven persons, full of infectious smiles and in a 'happy-go-happy' mood. However, the ad says nothing about what 'Comium' stands for in terms of its services and products. The ad could pass for a toothpaste ad. A quick check of the world's top 45 most recognised logos or brand names reveals the absence of 'Comium'. Therefore, there is no reason why they should assume that everybody would know what the company sells. The pay off, 'We're better together' says little.

Conclusion

From the foregoing, it is clear that the importance of internet advertising in today's advertising campaign planning cannot be disputed. Although it is not advisable to use the internet as the only media vehicle for a campaign, it is also not wise, given the growth and level of acceptability of the internet today, to concentrate on the conventional mass media and neglect internet advertising. internet advertising, though still at the infancy stage in Nigeria, has a bright future. The rapid increase in its patronage in sub-Saharan Africa makes the platform an important component of the media mix for advertising.

Businesses should, therefore, leverage on the wide acceptability and rapid user growth of the internet by investing more in online advertising to complement the conventional media. Furthermore, agencies involved in media research should channel resources into online advertising research, especially as related to campaign budgets and spend comparative to the conventional mass media.

Note

For samples of the adverts in their original colours, see various websites or http://www.amalion.net/images/uploads/figures-chap16.pdf

References

AMPS. 2009. *Media Facts Book 2009: Nigeria, West and Central Africa*. Lagos: MediaReach OMD.

IB Serve. 2008. Advantages and disadvantages of internet advertising. http://www.articlealley.com/article_690918_81.html (retrieved 15/05/2011).

Lendor, C. 2005. Internet promotion: Advantages and disadvantages. http://ezinearticles.com/?internet-Promotion---Advantages-and-Disadvantages&id=53561"=53561 (retrieved 17/05/2011).

MC. 2008. Worldwide internet advertising spending to surpass $106 billion in 2011 http://www.marketingcharts.com/television/worldwide-internet-advertising-spending-to-surpass-106-billion-in-2011-5068/ (retrieved 15/05/2010).

Pavlik, J. V. 2001. *Journalism and New Media*. New York: Columbia University Press.

Soremekun, S. 2011. The uses of new media among Nigerian youths. Unpublished MA thesis. Olabisi Onabanjo University, Ago-Iwoye, Nigeria.

Sudharsan, N. 2010. Different types of internet advertising. http://www.technoskillonline.com/2010/09/different-types-of-internet-or-online-advertising/ (retrieved 14/05/2011).

Weber, T. 2010. Why companies watch your every Facebook, YouTube, Twitter move. http://www.bbc.co.uk/news/business-11450923 (retrieved 11/10/2010).

Wikipedia. 2011. Online advertising. http://en.wikipedia.org/wiki/Online_advertising (retrieved 15/05/2011).

INDEX

A

Abacha, Sani 91
Advertisers' Association of Nigeria (ADVAN) 62, 77
advertising
 definitions 30, 37
 history 3, 5
advertising (ad) agencies xviii, 8, 57–60, 68, 101–6, 225, 231, 241
Advertising and Marketing Services 102
Advertising Code of Ethics, Nigeria 77
advertising ethics 61, 75, 106–8
advertising messages xix, xxi, 3, 5, 9, 28, 48, 53, 55–9, 62, 65, 68, 74, 105, 123–4, 127, 137–9, 205, 210, 231
Advertising Practitioners Council of Nigeria (APCON) xvii, 30–1, 61–2, 73, 77, 108, 226
advertising revenue 113–5, 131
press freedom 118
Advertising Standards Authority of South Africa (ASA) 126, 224
Advertising Standards Panel (ASP) 61–3
affiliate marketing 231
Afolayan, Kunle 206
Africa Independent Television (AIT) 221
African Christian Democratic Party (ACDP) 170, 174–8
African National Congress (ANC) 164, 170, 174–8
Aga Khan 112
agenda-setting 53–4, 129
Aljazeera 217, 225
All Media Products Survey (AMPS) 155

ambience 190
American Marketing Association 37
apartheid xx, 138, 142–4, 149
Arens, W.E. 2, 41, 53, 69–76, 106, 107–8, 215
assertion 87, 93
association 24, 42, 46, 48, 60, 87, 107, 164, 185, 192, 209, 211
Association of Advertising Agencies of Nigeria (AAAN) 62, 77
Atiku, Abubakar 241
audience xvii–xxi, 5, 9, 10, 17–9, 23–32, 45, 52–61, 73, 76, 82, 84, 91–227, 231, 245

B

Babangida, Ibrahim 103, 241
'bad' propaganda 79
bandwagon 91, 94
banner ads 230–2
Bantu Education Act (No. 47) of 1953 142
Barbie 221
Barletta, M. 127
Barthes, Roland 13, 45
Beckham, David 134
behavioural targeting 231
Beijing Platform of Action 130
Bernays, Edward 80, 85
Berners-Lee, Tim 229
billboards 7, 18, 47, 162, 179
black propaganda 85, 93
blogs 233
body images 131, 134
Bogart, L. 162, 177
Bollywood 205, 212

Borchers, T. 162, 177
Boston Newsletter 8, 100
Botha, P.W. 143
Bouwman, H. 145–7
Bovee, C.L. 2, 41, 53, 215
brand xvii, xxi, 18, 26, 32, 33, 36–50, 53, 59, 71, 104–6, 118, 205–12, 219, 242–3
brand characters 41
brand communication 41, 45–8
brand equity 39–41, 45–6
branding 37, 39, 41, 48, 71, 213
family branding 41
individual branding 41
brand loyalty 26, 53
brand management
xvii, xxi, 36–41, 45–8
brand reflection 40
brand strategy 41–2, 46
Breakfast at Tiffany's 204
brevity 32
broadcast xvi, 8, 61, 143, 147, 153, 173, 185, 204, 215–18, 221, 226
Buhari, Muhammadu 242
Bukeko, Charles 126
Burke, Edmund 167
Business Week 39
'buying mood' 117
buying power 127, 172

C

Cable News Network (CNN) 216–7
cable TV 222
Cameroon 236, 239, 245
capitalism 3, 8, 69
card-stacking 94
Carroll, Dave 240–1
Carstens, W.A.M. 183–4, 193–4
Casino Royale 209
Catholicism 166
Caxton, William 8
censorship xx, 31, 42, 90, 93, 116, 120–1, 141, 147–56, 239

Central Bank of Nigeria 62, 77, 108
Channel "O" 220
character appeals 178–9
children and advertising
20, 23, 59, 63, 65, 70–3, 77, 115, 129, 134, 177, 179, 187, 221
China 220
Chishango 18–9
Chomsky, Noam , 111, 116–7
civic educator xx
co-branding 41
Coca-Cola 69, 113, 226
code mixing 195
Code of Advertising Practice xvii, 73
code-shifting 194
code switching 182–3, 194–5
coding 151–2, 171
Cold War 93
colonial era 4, 7, 8, 102–3, 111–2
Comium 245
commercials 10, 27, 58–9, 64–5, 72–3
communication xv–xxi, 2–6, 9, 26, 28, 30, 36–55, 61–2, 70, 79–85, 90, 93, 96, 105, 128, 129, 136, 145–76, 182–4, 188, 193, 195, 206, 212, 215, 218–9, 223, 225, 229–34, 239
community relations 83
competitive advertising 36
computer mediated communication 229
Congress of the People (Cope) 170, 174–8
constructionist approach 22–3, 28
consumer culture 36
Consumer Protection Council 62, 77, 108
content xix–xxii, xix, 14, 23, 44, 51–2, 65, 75–6, 87, 106, 111–19, 123, 139–57, 160–4, 167, 170–77, 179, 184, 205, 211, 216, 220–6, 230
content analysis xvii, xvi-ii, 119, 123, 141, 146–7, 150–55, 160, 163–4, 170–74

controversy 52, 70, 73, 192, 195, 201, 223
copywriting 9, 30, 182–3, 186–92, 191, 201
covert advertising xxi, 204–13
creative brief 188
creative strategies xviii, 104, 106
creativity 187
credibility 57, 85, 188, 190, 193, 197, 200, 208, 210, 213
Cross, M. 53, 59, 60
cultivation analysis 141, 147–8, 153
cultural content xix, xxii, 216, 218, 220–26
cultural imperialism 218
cultural indicators 2, 141, 145–8
cultural marketing xxi, 216, 219–20, 222, 225–6
cultural norms theory 2, 54–5
cultural values 2, 71, 216–19, 221–27
culture xv–xxii, 2, 3, 13, 18–9, 23, 40–55, 62, 65, 71, 74, 77, 84, 100, 104, 106, 116, 125, 130, 142, 145–9, 156, 163, 166, 193, 210–26
culture and advertising 2
Cunningham, F. 165–8
customer loyalty 46
customer relations 83

D

Daar Sat 216, 226
Daily Nation 112–3, 119–20
dance-drama 4, 7, 102
Davidson, Basil xv
deception xvii, 51–67, 77, 97, 167
decoders 222
default beliefs 89
de Klerk, F.W. 144, 155
deliberation 162, 167–9
deliberative democracy 160, 165–9, 179
de Lille, Patricia 177–8

democracy 86, 94, 97–8, 113, 117, 120–21, 142, 156, 159–79
deliberative democracy 160, 165–9, 179
'digital' democracy 165
liberal democracy 160
Democratic Alliance (DA) 170, 174–8
de Saussure, Ferdinand 42
development xv, xviii, xxii, 4, 5, 9, 37, 42, 74, 76, 79, 86, 96, 97, 100, 103, 105, 108, 112–5, 120, 144, 146, 161, 166, 175, 184, 208, 2 20,
223–6
Dewey, John 167
dialogue xix, xx, 4, 5, 53, 87, 90, 116, 182–3, 189, 193–201
characteristics 193
'digital' democracy 165
direct broadcast satellite 215
direct marketing xxii, 10, 38
direct selling 10
discourse analysis 183
Dominick, J.R. 53, 55, 150–2, 170
drama 4, 7, 10, 102, 151
Dryzek, S.J. 165–8
DSTV 216
dynamic advertising 231

E

early history of advertising 100
East African Standard 111–2
'economy brand' 41
Eco, Umberto 13, 37, 42–4
Egypt 4, 217, 225, 236, 239, 241
election campaign 159, 161, 163
electronic media xix, 9, 84, 112–18
email advertising 231
Employment Equity Act xx, 141–56
endorsements 95, 210
English Premier League (EPL) 217, 221
"entertainment economics" 205
ethical issues xvii, 59–61, 68, 70, 75–7, 80, 106–7, 127

ethics 61, 76, 105–8, 115
e.TV 149, 153, 172
Europe 3–5, 8, 20, 234–5
extensional fallacy 44
e-zines 233

F

Facebook 233, 240–1
factuality 14–5
family branding 41
Federal Trade Commission, US (FTC) 56–7, 108
feminism 124, 129–31, 136–7
'fighting brand' 41
film xxi, 93, 187, 204–13, 229
Film and Allied Workers Organisation (FAWO) 144
First World War 90, 93
Food and Drug Administration (FDA) 77, 108
Foundation for Public Relations Research and Education 80
France 4, 91, 166
Freedom Front Plus (FF+) 170, 174–8
free speech xv, xviii

G

gender xix, 27, 70, 73, 77, 123–149, 153, 169, 173, 208, 210
gender discrimination 141, 221–2
Gerbner, George 145, 147, 148, 152
Germany 90, 91, 220
Ghana 6, 212, 237, 239, 244
glittering generalities 94, 95
Glo 33, 243
global brands 104, 106
globalisation xv–xxii, 2, 9, 48, 99–110, 114, 220–1
glocalisation xvi–vii, 48, 104–6
Goebbels, Joseph 89, 91
Goffman, Erving 27
good governance 115
Google 231, 240

Graham & Gills (G&G) 102
Grant Advertising 102
Graphological Devices 33
gray propaganda 84–5, 93
Guinness Nigeria 10, 42
Gutenberg, Johannes 8, 229

H

Habermas, Jurgen 169
Halliday, MAK 31, 194
Haupt, Paul 144
hawking 6, 8, 102
Heilbroner, Robert 80
Hepburn, Audrey 204
Herman, Edward , 111, 116, 117
'hired guns' 97
Hitler, Adolf 87, 90
HiTV 216, 221, 224, 226
HIV/AIDS 47, 74, 126, 129, 173–6
Hollywood 205, 206, 209, 212
Holtz-Bacha, C. 159–61, 174
home video xxi
homographs xvii
human rights xvii, 174
humour xx, 33, 59, 128, 182, 183, 190, 195, 200, 201
hype 59, 97
hyperbole 89–90

I

ideophones 5
image xx, 25–6, 37, 39, 40, 45, 58, 69, 92, 104–5, 116, 123–7, 135, 144, 147, 148, 160, 162–4, 177–8, 188, 191, 197, 200, 206, 208, 223–4, 231
image vs text 162
image vs political reality 161
Independent Democrats (ID) 170, 174, 176–8
"independent" media xix
India 210, 220, 222, 225, 226
indigenous advertising 5

indigenous media xv, xvi, 2–11, 103, 112
indigenous press 112
individual branding 41
indoctrination 31, 167
informational content 176
Information Communication Technologies (ICTs) 9, 165, 229
Institute of Practitioners in Advertising 37
institutional process analysis (IPA) 147
Integrated Marketing Communication 10
intentional approach 14, 15, 18, 19
interactivity xxii, 230
Interbrand 39
internet advertising xxii, 10, 17, 61, 229–32, 240, 245
intertextuality xx, 182–4, 195, 201
Irani, Smriti 210
I, Robot 204
irony 201

J

Jannini, Michael 39
Jeevanjee, Alibhai Mulla 111
Jhally, Sut 26–8, 210
jingle 186
Jonathan, Goodluck 241–2
journalism 23, 70, 111–21

K

Kaid, L. 159–61, 174
Kaufman, Theodore 91
Kenya xix, 111–21, 212, 237, 239
Kenya Broadcasting Corporation 112
Kenya Broadcasting Service 112–3
Kepaar News 242
Kikuyu Central Association 112
Kilbourne, J. 210, 211
Klapper, Joseph 54, 55

L

labelling 92, 95, 152
labour market xx, 141–8, 153, 155

Laffer curves 88
Lagos State Signage and Advertisements Agency (LASAA) 77
language and culture 23
language of advertising xvi, 13, 15, 18–32, 58, 60
Le Bon, Gustave 87
liberal democracy 160, 165–7
liberalisation xvii, 111–5
liberalism 103, 165, 167
Liberia 237, 245
linguistic strategies xvi, 30, 183
LINTAS 9, 102
living standard measurement 172
Loerie Awards xx, 182, 195–9
logo 45, 46, 104–5, 204, 242
Lonrho Ltd 112

M

magazine advertising 125, 131–7
Magazine Publishers of America 131
magazines xix, 55, 123–5, 130–6, 224, 239
Malawi 15, 17–20, 237
Malawi Censorship Board 19
"Man-in-the-street" 186
manipulation 93, 114, 167, 177
marginalisation 138
Marie Claire 125, 132–3
Mariet, Tannie 196–8
marketers 39, 240
marketing communication xvi-ii, xxii, 2, 5, 36–9, 212, 230
market segmentation 26, 115, 185
Maseko, Tolerance 198–200
mass media 3, 9–10, 54–5, 68, 70, 74, 86, 96, 98, 116–7, 125–6, 130–1, 139, 146–7, 160–1, 184, 211, 216, 218, 223, 229, 245
materialism 70, 72, 77
Mbeki, Thabo 176

McCracken, G. 46, 208
McKinsey and Company 39
McLuhan, Marshall 51
McNair, B. 159–61, 165, 174, 177
meaning xvi, 13–5, 17–31, 35, 37, 42–7, 56, 116, 148, 152, 161, 185, 208, 211–2, 230
Meaning-Making xvi, 30
meaning transfer 208, 212
media advocacy 120
media and behaviour 54
media censorship xx, 31, 90, 93, 114–6, 120–1, 156
media content xix, 113, 117, 147, 150–1, 153
media culture xv, 3
media freedom 120
media liberalisation xix, 111–21
media literacy 63
media orientation 161
media ownership 96, 112, 115
media pluralism 164
Meeske, M.D. 185–7, 190
Men's Health 125, 132–5
"mentions" theory 44
Mercedes-Benz 220
message 5, 7, 9, 46
message system analysis (MSA) 147–8, 152
Middle Ages 4
Middle East 209, 218, 225
Mill, John Stuart 167
minorities 138
Minority Report 204
misrepresentation 23, 61
M-Net 143–4, 156
Momodu, Dele 242
mood 117, 121, 190, 194
Morocco 237, 239–41
moves 15–8, 60
move-joining 15, 17, 18
move-splitting 15, 17
movie 204–13

MTN 32–4, 149, 221–2, 226
MTV 217, 220
Muiguithania 112
multi-media messages 231, 233
Myspace 233

N

name-calling 95
National Agency for Food and Drug Administration and Control (NAFDAC) 62, 77, 108
Nation Media Group 118
Nazi Germany 89, 90, 93
'negative space' 192
Nel, Evelyn 198–9
neoliberalism xviii, 104
new media xvi, 9, 74, 108, 233–4, 241–2
newspapers 8, 55, 85, 112–3, 119, 146, 162, 164, 179, 229, 239, 242, 244
Nigeria xv, xvi, xix, 6–10, 17, 30–3, 42, 52, 61–3, 68–8, 91, 102–4, 108–9, 206–17, 220–26, 229, 234, 237, 239–45
Nigeria Copyrights Commission 108
Nigerian Civil War 91
Nigerian Communications Commission (NCC) 108, 241
Nigeria Television Authority (NTA) 221
Njoka, Mwenda 114
Nollywood xxi, 205, 209
nudity 124, 132

O

Obasanjo, Olusegun 103
objectification 132–3, 138
Ogilvy, Benson and Mather (OB&M) 102
Ojukwu, Odumegwu 91
Omnicom 101–2
online advertising xxii, 233
Onyenyili-Onourah, J.E. 211
oral media xxii, 3, 4, 9

oral narratives 4
Outdoor Advertising Association of Nigeria 62, 77
outdoor media 10, 47, 61, 162
Owens, O. 210

P

Patent and Trademark Office 108
payoffs xiv, 33
peddling 7
Peirce, Charles Sanders 42
Pendoring Awards xx, 182, 195–7
persuasion xvi-ii, 35, 37, 59, 63, 72, 79–90, 96, 167, 211
phonographological devices xiv, 32
'plain folks' 92, 95
PlusNews 126
podcasts 233
political advertising xviii, 159–64, 170–9, 241–2
political liberalisation xvii
political parties 160–3, 170, 175–6, 179
Political Warfare Executive, UK
pop culture 220
Population Services International (PSI) 18, 19
pop-under advertising 231
pop-up 231
Portfolio Committee on Communications 144–5
positioning 40, 105–6, 153, 206
Potter, David 22, 63
pre-colonial 4, 7, 102, 103
press freedom 35, 46, 72, 74, 91–4, 112–3, 120, 164–6, 174–5, 211
press relations 82, 84
printing technology 4, 8
print media xvi, xix, 8, 9, 18, 30, 35, 61, 100, 112–3, 173, 183, 232
privatisation xix, 113
product packaging 37, 45

product placement xvii, xxi, 45, 48, 206–9, 211, 213
profitability 39
promotional campaigns 105
propaganda xviii, 31, 79, 81–98, 111, 116, 167, 176–8
  techniques 90, 93
  transfer 96
Propagandaministerium
"prototype" strategy xviii, 104
public health communication 17–9, 126, 224
public opinion 79, 80, 85, 86, 97, 116, 129, 163, 169
public relations xviii, 6, 10, 36, 38, 79–86, 96–8, 105, 114, 241
Public Relations Associations 80
public sphere 68, 116, 118, 121, 160, 168–70, 179
puffery xvii, 51, 56–60, 63, 65
pun 33, 59
purpose 70

Q

qualitative research 160, 170, 172, 174

R

race 2, 73, 115, 138, 142, 144–9, 153, 163, 173–5, 178, 194, 208
racial integration 143, 144, 155
radio xx, 10, 42, 93, 112–3, 143, 179, 182–201, 215, 229, 232, 239, 242
radio advertising xx, 186–7, 192, 195
rationalisation 92
Reagan, Ronald 88
reality 15, 19–28, 54, 63, 64, 90, 106, 128, 143–4, 148–9, 164, 176, 178, 179, 218
referential fallacy 44
referent system 25
reflective approach 19–23

regulation xvii–xxi, 51, 56–9, 62–77, 108, 137, 156, 166, 184, 225
regulatory bodies xxi, 51, 59, 65, 137, 225
regulatory frameworks xvii, xviii
Reijnders, N. 145–7
religion and media 152
Renaissance 166
representation xvi, xx, 6, 13–28, 56, 58, 129, 130, 137, 141–56
constructionist approach 22, 23, 28
Intentional Approach 14
reflective approach 19
religion 20
resonance theory 26
"resonant thesis" 148
rhyme 182, 184, 195
Ribadu, Nuhu 242
rock art 3, 5
Royal Niger Company (RNC) 8
Rwanda 125, 138, 237, 240

S

Safaricom 113–4
sales promotion 10, 36, 38, 63
satellite television xxi, 108, 215–27
scapegoating 92
Schiller, Herb 218
Schulz-Herzenburg, C. 163
Scott, A. 43–5, 211
Second World War 89, 91, 93
selective omission 94
self-censorship xx, 121, 156
self-deception approach 89
self-persuasion 89, 90
semiology 42
semiotics xvi, xvii, 23–5, 36–50, 149, 153–5
sensationalism 31, 97, 115, 118, 121
sequel 187
sexual health advertising 18–9, 47, 138
sexuality 18, 53, 115

Shekarau, Ibrahim 242
short messaging service (SMS) 231, 233, 242
Show Sports 225
Sign 42–3
signboards 3
signification 43, 44
sign-production 44
slang 193, 194
slogans 17–20, 32–4, 89, 93, 161, 175–8, 186–7, 192, 219–20
social choice theory 167
"socialist realism"
socially responsible advertising 74
social networking 233–4
social reality 27, 218
social responsibility 62, 107–8, 121
Solomon, M.R. 220, 225
South Africa xx, 13–29, 47, 121–202, 223–5, 238–42
South African Advertising Research Foundation (SAARF) 144–5, 156
South African Broadcasting Corporation (SABC) 21, 149, 153, 170, 172
Soviet Union 93
Spain 166
spin 97
standard 111–2, 118–20
standardisation xviii, 104–5
Standard Media Group 118
Starbucks 220
stereotypes xix, 70–3, 77, 123–30, 137–9, 143, 149, 155–6, 201
stereotyping 28, 92, 93, 128, 130, 144, 173, 195, 224
street callers 3
structural adjustment xviii, 103, 104
Stubbs, M. 183
Sudharsan, N. 230–1, 246
SuperSport 216
Sweden 125, 145–6
symbolography 6
systemic functional grammar (SFG) 31

T

tablet 230
Taifa Jumapili 112
Taifa Leo 112
talking drums 6, 7
Tanaka, K. 25, 26
target market 41, 45, 183–95, 200–1
Telekom Networks Malawi 20
telemarketing 10
television advertising xx, 42, 126, 141–55, 220, 225
testimonials 62, 65, 83, 95
text 14, 15, 18, 19, 25, 45, 46, 48, 153, 162, 172, 177, 179, 183–4, 189, 196, 210, 230
textual communication 184
theatre 4, 8, 93, 185, 200, 201
The Figurine 206, 213
"The Mexican Statement" 80
Thompson, J. Walter 100–2
town criers 3–5, 102
Toyota 34, 226
trademark 40, 77, 190, 194, 205–6
traffic 189, 217–8, 223, 225, 231–2
transfer of signs 24
turn-taking 193
Twitter 241

U

UEFA Champions League 217
Unilever 102
Union of Soviet Writers
United African Company (UAC) 9
United Arab Emirates 209
United Kingdom 9, 100, 102
United States 3, 5, 8, 90, 93, 97, 100, 108, 131, 159, 220, 229, 234–5, 240
usage patterns 26
Utomi, Pat 242

V

values xx, 2, 40, 45, 52, 55, 59, 64–5, 69, 71–4, 86–9, 105, 108, 117, 138, 145, 163, 168, 174–5, 209–11, 216, 218–27
Van Jaarsveld, G.J. 184
visibility 17, 18, 153, 163, 182, 206, 210, 212, 242
Vodacom 20, 125–6, 138
voice 5, 16, 24, 83, 174, 190–200
Voice of Kenya 112
Volney B. Palmer 8, 37
Vorster, B.J. 143

W

watchdogs xix, 116
Weber, Tim 240
Weide, Karsten 240
West African Milk Company (WAMCO) 41
West Africa Publicity Limited (WAP) 9, 102
Western advertising traditions xv, 3, 8, 10
Western Nigeria Television 229
white noise 186
white propaganda 79, 84, 96
Wimmer, D. 150–2, 170
witnesses 186
women and advertising xix, xx, 27, 73, 83, 123–46, 169, 172, 177, 198, 221, 224
word games 60, 182, 195, 200
word-of-mouth xix, xxii, 4, 10, 102, 182, 185, 195, 200–1, 232
WPP 101, 102

X

xenophobia 138

Y

Young and Rubicam (Y&R) 101, 102

YouTube 241
Yuppie New Age 185

Z

Zuma, Jacob 176